DATE DUE

SE 10 '02		
NO 04 '02		
FE 03 '04		
FE 16 '04		
AP 28 '0		
MR 07 '05		
JE 21 '05		
OC 03 '05		
MR 2 6 '07		
JA 1 1 '08		
MY 1 5 '13		

DEMCO 38-297

knitter's stash

 INTERWEAVE PRESS

Interweave Press
201 East Fourth Street
Loveland, Colorado 80537
www.interweave.com

Printed in Singapore

Library of Congress Cataloging-in-Publication Data

Albright, Barbara.
    Knitter's stash : favorite patterns from America's yarn shops / edited by Barbara Albright.
        p.   cm.
    ISBN 1-883010-89-6
        1. Knitting—Patterns.   I. Title.

TT825 .A42 2001
746.43'2041—dc21   2001039265

First printing: IWP:10M:701:TWP
Second printing: IWP:5M:1101:TWP

acknowledgements

Special thanks: To Linda Skolnik, for the seed of an idea, and Melanie Falick, for helping it to grow. To the editor's supportive family (Ted Westray, and Samantha and Stone), and friends Anna Harvey, Ellen Harvey, Julie Johnson, Diane Reinert, Holli Williamson, and Meg Wittman. To models Anna Cordiner, Kira Fish, Amy Lamb, Sharon Merkel, Grace Nunnelee, and Lauren and Grace Sluss. And to Carol Anderson and Linda Carlson of Colorado State University for special photo props.

Editor: Barbara Albright
Managing editor: Marilyn Murphy
Assistant editor: Elaine Lipson
Technical editors: Jean Lampe and Ann Budd
Photography (except for shop shots): Joe Coca
Photo styling: Linda Ligon and Ann Swanson
Design: Bren Frisch
Production: Dean Howes
Print management: Nancy Arndt and Don Schmidt
Tracking: Bonnie Hoover, Carol Leonard, and Laurie Ramirez
Prop handling: Rod Baum

foreword

Because I am editor of *Interweave Knits*, yarn companies tend to be very generous with me, sending me a sample skein—if not more—of nearly every yarn they carry. Book publishers do the same. Most of them make sure I receive their knitting titles immediately after they come off press, often before they reach the stores. The truth is that I could do my job—as well as my personal knitting projects—without ever setting foot in a yarn shop.

But I enjoy going to yarn shops. Like most knitters, when I visit a new city, one of the first things I do is investigate the yarn sources—shops, farms, galleries—and decide which ones I absolutely must see. When I am home, I treasure any time I can spend at my local yarn shop. Like most every other knitter, I love to fondle the fibers, to savor the colors, to sit with other customers and work on my projects. We talk about what we are knitting. We talk about life. Through yarn, we find support, we find friendship, we find acceptance—none of which come to my office door just because I am the editor of a knitting magazine.

When I walk into a great yarn shop and see imaginative yarn displays and sample garments, I almost always feel a bit ravenous. On the one hand, I can't look around fast enough, as I want to consume it all at once; on the other, I want to experience everything slowly so I can savor it. These urges are about yarn and knitting, but they're also about something deeper: my desire, my need, to be creative. They're also about fantasy. I hold the yarn and my inner voice imagines, "If I make this sweater or those socks, I will wear them hiking, or entertaining, or traveling. It will be grand, it will be romantic, I will be happy."

I've been to some of the shops featured in this book; I am eager to visit others. What strikes me as I read about them is the diversity of the people that run them. They have come to the yarn business from many different avenues and they manage their businesses in many different ways. What they share is a passion for knitting. And their shops are successful, in large part, because their passion is contagious.

While it's true that technology is taking over vast portions of our lives, while it's true that we could probably buy all the yarn we need over the worldwide web, who really wants that kind of reality—or virtual reality? While it can be exciting—and convenient—to purchase patterns, yarns, tools, and books with a few clicks of a button, if I had to choose between that possibility and a wonderful local yarn shop, I would choose the latter. Because at the latter I do more than buy my materials, I do more than learn how to make my way through a tricky technique. At a yarn shop I am part of something real. At a yarn shop I make connections and friends. At a yarn shop I am at the heart of the knitting community I love so much.

Melanie Falick
Editor, *Interweave Knits*
June, 2001

editor's introduction
by Barbara Albright

Who knows best what knitters want? Yarn shop owners. Their shops are where knitters go: to find yarn, to touch and feel, to look for patterns, to plan projects, to find other knitters. Their shops are a major source of knitting inspiration. This book is meant to take you on an intimate armchair tour of thirty-three of America's premier stores.

In the summer of 2000, we sent letters out to all the knitting shops in the United States asking for their most popular original patterns—those patterns that make their customers want to drop everything, pick up their needles, and start knitting. The response was amazing; it was like Christmas opening up the piles of boxes. And it wasn't just their handknit items—it was snapshots of their shops and customers, it was hints and tips and a generous dose of life wisdom.

As we sifted through the material, we were impressed by the shops' variety, ranging from chic and trendy to comfy and rural. Most of all, we were impressed with the wonderfully eclectic assortment of knitted items. Making final selections was not easy.

We tried to cover a lot of bases, from major garments to small accessories. Some patterns are easy enough for the brand new knitter. Some are especially appealing because of a clever yet simple design feature or an interesting use of yarn. Others are more intricate, providing fun and challenge for the more experienced knitter.

We learned that knitters come from all walks of life and have many different tastes, styles, and sensibilities. Yet the goal of a good shop is the same, no matter where it is or who its customers are. Janet Scanlon, one of the owners of My Yarn Shop in Coos Bay, Oregon, summed up her observation of the traits that knitters share: "Knitters . . . delight in color and form and have heightened tactile senses. They love containers and tools and have an almost endless amount of patience and ability for self-entertainment." Yarn shops are a reflection of those traits.

As you leaf through this book we hope that you will be delighted to be part of this very special community of knitters as we celebrate the yarn shops that bring us all together.

"As we sifted through the material, we were impressed by the shops' variety, ranging from chic and trendy to comfy and rural. Most of all, we were impressed with the wonderfully eclectic assortment of knitted items. Making final selections was not easy."

Imagine seeing, all at once, the best knitting that eighty-five yarn shops have to offer. Imagine having to choose only thirty projects. (Imagine cheating and slipping in a couple of extra ones.) We cannot overemphasize either the privilege and excitement or the difficulty. We did our best, but there's an amazing amount that you simply don't get to see. So go to your local yarn shop. Go to the yarn shops in your region. Take a road trip—use this list and the directory of shops that begins on page xxx. See for yourself.

yarn shop honor roll

Acorn Street Yarn Shop, Seattle, Washington
* **Amazing Threads,** Lake Katrine, New York
* **Amazing Yarns,** Redwood City, California
Ana-Cross Stitch, Anacortes, Washington
And The Beadz Go On, Wickford, Rhode Island
Ball & Skein & More, Cambria, California
Bare Hill Studios & Fiber Loft, Harvard, Massachusetts
* **Bette Bornside Company,** New Orleans, Louisiana
* **Big Sky Studio & Gallery,** Lafayette, California
Bonnie Knits, Monroeville, Pennsylvania
Cascade Yarns Distributor of Fine Yarns, Tukwila, Washington
Cass Street Depot, Fort Wayne, Indiana
* **Countrywool,** Hudson, New York
Crafty Lady, Macomb, Michigan
Dharma Trading Company, San Rafael, California
Earth Guild, Asheville, North Carolina
Edgewood Arts, Waupaca, Wisconsin
* **Elegant Ewe, The,** Concord, New Hampshire
Embraceable Ewe, Hamburg, New York
* **Eva's Needlework,** Thousand Oaks, California
* **Ewe-Nique Knits,** Royal Oak, Michigan
* **Fiber Space,** Sterling, Colorado
Fiberspace, Inc., Durham, North Carolina
Fifth Stitch, The, Defiance, Ohio
* **Fine Points, Inc.,** Cleveland, Ohio
Florence's Attic, Pocatello, Idaho
General Bailey Homestead Farm, Greenfield Center, New York
Genuine Purl, Chattanooga, Tennessee
Great Yarns, Raleigh, North Carolina
* **Green Mountain Spinnery,** Putney, Vermont
Handknitters, Ltd., Louisville, Kentucky
* **Haneke Wool Fashions,** Meridian, Idaho
Heindeselman's Yarn Needlework & Gift Shops, Provo, Utah
Heritage Arts, Cleburne, Texas
* **Idle Hours Needle Art,** Fort Myers, Florida
* **Kathy's Kreations,** Ligonier, Pennsylvania
Knitting Basket, The, Oakland, California
* **Knitting Tree, The,** Madison, Wisconsin
Knits & Pieces, Newton, Massachusetts
* **Knitting By the Sea,** Carmel, California
Knitting Room, Birmingham, Michigan
* **L'Atelier,** Redondo Beach, California
* **La Lana Wools,** Taos, New Mexico
Lambspun of Colorado, Fort Collins, Colorado
* **Marji's Yarncrafts,** Granby, Connecticut
Mind's Eye Yarns, Cambridge, Massachusetts

Molehill Farm, Lake Oswego, Oregon
Mosaic Yarn Studio, Ltd., Des Plaines, Illinois
* **My Yarn Shop,** Coos Bay, Oregon
Needles 'n Pins Yarn Shoppe, Delavan, Wisconsin
* **Northampton Wools,** Northampton, Massachusetts
* **Over the Moon,** Longmont, Colorado
* **Patternworks,** Poughkeepsie, New York
* **Pine Tree Yarns,** Damariscotta, Maine
Red Needle West, The, Colorado Springs, Colorado
Rochelle Imber's Knit Knit Knit, West Bloomfield, Michigan
* **Rumpelstiltskin,** Sacramento, California
* **S.W.A.K. Knits-Fine Yarn Fun Knits,** Guthrie, Oklahoma
Shuttles, Spindles & Skeins, Inc., Boulder, Colorado
Sip & Knit, Winter Park, Florida
Sisu Designs, Ely, Minnesota
Skeins Minnetonka, Minnesota
* **Sophie's Yarns,** Philadelphia, Pennsylvania
Spin-A-Yarn, Edmonds, Washington
Stitching Mantis, The, Cape Elizabeth, Maine
Susan's Fiber Shop, Columbus, Wisconsin
Sutter's Gold 'n Fleece, St. Germain, Wisconsin
Tawas Bay Yarn Co, Tawas City, Michigan
Textile Fiber Arts Studio, Glocester, Rhode Island
Threadbender Yarn Shop, Wyoming, Michigan
* **Tricoter,** Seattle, Washington
Weaving Southwest, Taos, New Mexico
Wild and Woolly Yarn Company, The, Poulsbo, Washington
Wool Cabin, The, Salt Lake City, Utah
Wool Co., Bandon, Oregon
Wool Connection, The, Avon, Connecticut
Yarn Barn, The, Dillwyn, Virginia
Yarn Co., The, New York, New York
* **Yarnery, The,** St. Paul, Minnesota
* **Yarn Heaven,** Arlington, Texas
Yarn House, The, Elm Grove, Wisconsin
Yarns International, Washington, D.C.
* **Yarns International,** Bethesda, Maryland
Yarn Shop, The, Glen Arbor, Michigan
Yarn Shop, The, Bozeman, Montana
Yarnworks, Gainesville, Florida

*Projects from these shops are featured in this book.

table of contents

introduction

Your local yarn shop. Maybe it's just down the street, maybe it's only in your mind. It's a magical, colorful home away from home where you can go to touch, to scheme, to dream. There you find friends who share your obsession, who speak the secret language of K1 P2, who understand your need to stash. There you find yarn and more yarn, patterns to make your fingers itch, possibilities that make your pocketbook cry uncle.

When we began thinking of a book that would be like comfort food for the knitter's soul, we naturally turned to local yarn shops. Who would better understand what knitters want? Who would be a better resource for those tried and true patterns that we love to knit first one way, then the other? Patterns to whip out in a weekend, or to pack along for a long car trip, or to conjure with over a whole long winter?

Local yarn shops, embodied in their dedicated owners and staff, are a rich repository for knitting knowledge, invention, and ingenuity. These people understand yarn, technique, shortcuts, and even the mental discipline that's required to finish one project and move on to the next (or juggle ten at once). So when we reached out to yarn shops across the country with a call for their customers' favorite patterns, they responded. They responded with notes, sketches, swatches, and boxes and boxes of knitted . . . things. Sweaters, jackets, ponchos, afghans, rugs, tea cozies, socks, booties, and . . . fish. Truly. You'll see them right here and we dare you to resist.

So here you are. Patterns for yourself, your kids, your friends, your spouse, your floor, your couch. Some have a contemporary flair, others are timeless. All lend themselves to invention and variation and using up, or at least diminishing, that bottomless stash.

GREAT YARNS, INC. • A big display window featuring hand-knitted items beckons customers into Great Yarns, Inc. As they enter the store, they're faced with a wall of vivid color created by columns of shelves filled with yarn. Several boutique areas highlight specialty yarns and buttons and provide visual stimulation galore.

Encouraging knitters to think outside the box has been a mission of Great Yarns since it opened in 1986. Founder Jane Weir, a knitter, weaver, and fiber artist, created this wonderful haven for fiber fanatics of all types, and only recently sold it in order to travel. Its new owner, Linda Pratt, says the store's goal is to create inspiration for knitters and help them achieve their goals. Besides managing two yarn shops, Linda worked for many years as the director of sales for Classic Elite Yarns and as marketing manager for JCA, Inc.—the parent company of Reynolds, Unger, and Adrienne Vittadini yarns—so knowing what knitters want is second nature.

Great Yarns is located in a shopping center filled with independent merchants, including an award-winning book shop, a garden shop, a gallery, and a wine shop. The store gets a lot of college-related traffic from area schools, as well as people shopping for projects to knit while watching sporting events. Even though the climate in Raleigh is on the warm side, area knitters are not deterred. As soon as the doors open at 10 A.M., insatiable customers arrive, sometimes buying yarn right out of the delivery boxes. Great Yarns offers a full schedule of classes throughout the year as well as special workshops and retreats featuring some of the big names in the handknitting field.

Linda says that her greatest satisfaction comes from helping customers, "whether they are totally new to knitting and in angst over their first few rows, or seasoned knitters wondering what to do with the latest designer yarn."

GREAT YARNS, INC.

1208 RIDGE ROAD
RALEIGH, NC 27607
PHONE: (919) 832-3599
ORDERS ONLY: (800) 810-0045
WEBSITE: WWW.GREAT-YARNS.COM
E-MAIL: GREATYRN@GTE.NET

OUTER BANKS THROW

Every knitter knows to make a swatch before starting a project. Designer Linda Pratt describes the Outer Banks Throw as a swatch that has been expanded into a marvelous piece of home decor. The luxury fibers create a subtle flow of colors as the afghan changes from greens to peaches and then to off-whites. Knitted on big needles, this throw can be completed in a remarkably short amount of time.

OUTER BANKS THROW
Linda Pratt

Pattern Stitch:
Row 1: (RS) Knit.
Row 2: (WS) K10, purl to last 10 sts, k10.
Repeat Rows 1 and 2 for pattern.

Yarn Color Sequence:
Row 1: 1 strand Mohair and 1 strand Zanziba.
Row 2: 1 strand Isis.
Row 3: 1 strand Skye.
Repeat Rows 1–3 for pattern.

With Mohair and Zanziba held tog, CO 116 sts. Following the yarn color sequence, work garter st (knit every row) until piece measures 6" (15 cm) from beg, ending with a WS row. Cont yarn colors as established, beg with Row 1 and work swatch pattern st until piece measures 42" (106.5 cm) from beg. Work garter st for 6" (15 cm), ending with a WS row—piece should measure about 48" (122 cm) from beg. BO all sts loosely. Weave in loose ends.

FINISHED SIZE
About 58" (147.5 cm) wide and 48" (122 cm) long.

YARN
Colinette Mohair (78% mohair, 13% wool, 9% nylon; 191 yd [175 m]/100 g]): #95 Twilight, 2 skeins. Colinette Zanziba (51% wool, 48% viscose, 1% nylon; 102 yd [94 m]/100 g): #102 pierro, 3 skeins. Colinette Isis (100% viscose; 109 yd [100 m]/100 g): #124 celadon, 3 skeins. Colinette Skye (100% wool; 163 yd [150 m]/100 g): #102 pierro, 2 skeins.

NEEDLES
Size 17 (12 mm). Adjust needle size if necessary to obtain the correct gauge.

NOTIONS
Tapestry needle.

GAUGE
8 sts and 12 rows = 4" (10 cm) in pattern stitch.

tips

GAUGE SWATCHING

When knitting anything to fit, the gauge is the most important component for successful results. Take the time to make a large swatch, and "dress" the swatch— wash and block the swatch as you intend for the completed sweater, then measure. If a pattern stitch is being used, make a gauge swatch in pattern. Continue to measure your gauge as you work; gauge can change as you relax into the rhythm of the stitchwork.

Kathy's Kreations

Knit the first three rows of your gauge swatch in garter stitch, as well as the first three stitches on either side. It keeps the knitting from rolling and makes it easier to measure your swatch for a true gauge.

Yarn Heaven

You can't usually rely on a flat swatch for a piece that's going to be worked in the round. I suggest starting with a sleeve in the round to act as your gauge, giving you a head start on the project. If you find you're not knitting to gauge, you only have to rip out a small amount of sleeve.

Knitting by the Sea

Students often have a hard time with measuring gauge in handspun or thick-and-thin yarns, and in rayon tapes or yarns that 'droop.' For handspun or thick-and-thin yarns, knit a slightly larger swatch of 6″ by 6″ (15-cm square). Check the stitch gauge in several areas of the fabric, taking an average, or simply divide the number of stitches you've been knitting by the width of the swatch. For rayon tapes and droopy yarns, pin the swatch to a hanger and leave it for a day or two, then check gauge and adjust needle size as needed.

The Elegant Ewe

KNITTING BY THE SEA •

Walking into Knitting By the Sea is like walking into a cozy one-room home—a knitter's dream home, that is. A vivid rainbow of yarns is arranged in tall cabinets around the walls. One front window alcove is a special children's corner and the other is home to books, magazines, and patterns. A large skylight washes the shop in natural light, and a fireplace takes the nip out of the air on chilly days. In the center of the room customers gather around a large oak table to chat or get help with projects.

Outside the shop, the quaint community of Carmel sits amid tall stands of pine and eucalyptus, overlooking famous white sandy beaches and the Pacific Ocean.

Maurya McBride, the present owner of Knitting By the Sea, has a diverse background in fashion design and mechanical engineering—not as different as you might think. "With both fashion design and engineering, you have the goal of making your materials conform to form and function," she explains. People frequently ask how someone so young knows so much about knitting and her answer is, "I have an unfair advantage, I'm an engineer." But looking around the shop, you see that there is a soft knitting side to this engineer.

KNITTING BY THE SEA

FIFTH AVENUE NEAR JUNIPERO
PO BOX Y-1
CARMEL, CA 93921
PHONE: (831) 624-3189
ORDERS ONLY: (800) 823-3189

GRADUATED RIBBED TOP

You'll find ingenious engineering in this understated ribbed sweater. It's knitted in the round from the bottom up and is cleverly shaped with increases and decreases. The I-cord cast-off at the neckline provides a clean, elegant finish.

GRADUATED RIBBED TOP

Maurya McBride

FINISHED SIZE
32 (34, 36)" (81.5 [86.5, 91.5] cm) chest/bust circumference. Sweater shown measures 34" (86.5 cm).

YARN
Euro Yarns Clip (100% cotton; 180 yd [165 m]/100 g): #119 green, 6 (6, 7) skeins.

NEEDLES
Size 6 (4 mm): 29" (80-cm) circular (cir) and set of 4 double-pointed (dpn). Adjust needle size if necessary to obtain the correct gauge.

NOTIONS
Stitch holders; markers (m); tapestry needle.

GAUGE
24 sts and 28 rnds = 4" (10 cm) in k4, p2 rib worked in the rnd.

Body
With cir needle, CO 192 (204, 216) sts. Place marker (pm) and join, being careful not to twist sts. Work k4, p2 rib, establishing 32 (34, 36) rib repeats. Work even in patt until piece measures 11" (28 cm) from beg, or desired length to underarm. Place sts on holder. Do not cut yarn.

Sleeves
Note: Use M1 increases (see Glossary) for sleeve increases. Both knit and purl methods are worked to maintain overall patt.

With dpn, CO 42 sts. Join, being careful not to twist sts. Work k4, p2 rib, establishing 7 rib repeats, and pm bet last 2 purl sts to mark center of underarm. Sl m every rnd. Work even until piece measures 2" (5 cm) from beg. Beg with Row 1, work Sleeve Increase chart, inc 2 sts every 4 rnds (the first 2 incs pairs are purl incs; the following 4 pairs are knit incs) 18 (21, 24) times—78 (84, 90) sts; 13 (14, 15) ribs. Place 1 m each side of center-most inc'd sts as foll: Pm, [k4, p2] 1 (2, 3) times, k4, pm, work to end. Cont even in patt until piece measures 16" (40.5 cm) from beg. Place sts on holders with markers in place. Do not cut yarn.

Join Body and Sleeves
Place sts on needles as foll: *Using the sleeve center-most sts bet markers as guides, align and match the underarm rib patts of sleeves and body. Place markers at beg and end of matching patts sts on body as foll: Pm, [k4, p2] 1 (2, 3) times, k4, pm. Work across sleeve underarm sts bet markers, work to first m on body sts (but do not work the corresponding body sts), place RS of sleeve and body tog, with the sleeve yarn and using the three-needle bind-off (see Glossary) BO 10 (16, 22) underarm sts tog, turn work to RS, using the body yarn, pick up and knit 1 st at join of sleeve and body (this st is centered bet the 2 purl sts of sleeve and body and will form the raised raglan "seam"), work sleeve sts as established, pick up and knit 1 st at join of sleeve and body (this st is also centered bet

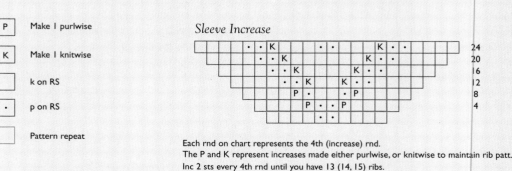

P	Make 1 purlwise
K	Make 1 knitwise
	k on RS
·	p on RS
	Pattern repeat

Sleeve Increase

Each rnd on chart represents the 4th (increase) rnd.
The P and K represent increases made either purlwise, or knitwise to maintain rib patt.
Inc 2 sts every 4th rnd until you have 13 (14, 15) ribs.

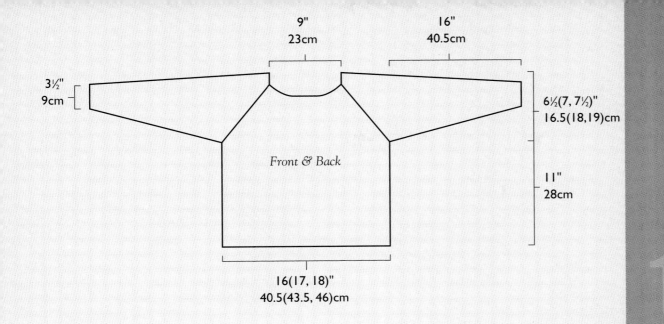

9"
23cm

16"
40.5cm

3½"
9cm

6½(7, 7½)"
16.5(18,19)cm

Front & Back

11"
28cm

16(17, 18)"
40.5(43.5, 46)cm

2 purl sts), work across body sts until there are 14 ribs plus 2 purl sts from join; rep from *—4 sts inc'd; 312 sts. Cont in rib patt (knitting each of the 4 inc'd sts) across all sts for 1" (2.5 cm). *Shape raglan:* Work centered double dec (sl 2 tog kwise, k1, p2sso) every other row (the slipped sts are the st before the picked-up st and the picked-up st) 23 times—128 sts rem.

Finishing
I-Cord BO: (see Glossary) Sl 1 st from right needle to left needle, CO 3 sts. *K2, ssk (using last CO st and 1 neckline st), sl 3 sts back to left needle tip; rep from * until no neckline sts rem. Work duplicate sts (see Glossary) to join end of edging as seamlessly as possible. Weave in loose ends. Steam block lightly, if desired.

KATHY'S KREATIONS ● The setting for

Kathy's Kreations is right out of a Norman Rockwell painting of Main Street, U.S.A. Located in an old building with tin ceilings and lots of character, the bright, inviting shop is part of a family business in the scenic Laurel Highlands of western Pennsylvania. Large windows loaded with displays of bright, colorful, and "do-able" projects function as a big welcome sign to passersby, beckoning them to come in.

The shop began in 1980 as a custom handknitting business, and it evolved into a well-stocked yarn shop as Kathy Zimmerman began to keep the supplies she needed for her own projects. Today, the shop is a gathering place for knitters, who find it filled with a large selection of natural fiber yarns and premium synthetics and lots of needles and knitting gadgets. There's also a large bookcase filled with resource material.

Kathy's Kreations is a full-service knitting shop, and even more: A woodshop on the premises makes custom storage boxes for knitting needles and accessories, even cedar chests for those precious handknitted sweaters. As such, the shop really lives up to its motto: "You supply the creativity, we'll supply everything else."

KATHY'S KREATIONS

141 EAST MAIN STREET
LIGONIER, PA 15658
PHONE: (724) 238-9320
WEBSITE: WWW.KATHYS-KREATIONS.COM
E-MAIL: KATHY@KATHYS-KREATIONS.COM

AGE OF AQUARIUS TRIO

If you've spent much time flipping through the pages of knitting magazines, you've probably seen one of Kathy Zimmerman's lovely designs. This handsome sweater, with its intricate cablework, reflects the popular patterns she features in her store. Look closely and you'll see motifs that recall 1970s "Age of Aquarius" themes: The cabled hearts symbolize love and the mirrored rope cables represent balance, peace, and harmony. Kathy and Lisa Carnahan worked together to design the inside-out socks which sensibly put reverse stockinette on the outside to blend with the cable stitch background and leave smooth stockinette on the inside for cozy comfort.

FINISHED SIZE

Sweater: 40 (44, 47, 51)" (101.5 [112, 119.5, 129.5] cm) bust/chest circumference. Socks: 8" (20 cm) around foot and 9½" (24 cm) long. Cap: 22" (56 cm) circumference. Sweater shown measures 44" (112 cm).

YARN

Classic Elite Montera (50% llama, 50% wool; 127 yd [115 m]/100 g): #3803 falcon gray. Sweater: 11 (12, 13, 15) skeins; Socks: 2 skeins; Cap: 2 skeins.

NEEDLES

Sweater Body—Size 9 (5.5 mm). Sweater Sleeves—Size 7 (4.5mm). Sweater Neckband—Size 7 (4.5 mm): 16" (40-cm) circular (cir). Socks—Size 7 (4.5 mm): Set of 4 double-pointed (dpn). Cap—Size 9 (5.5 mm) and 7 (4.5mm): Set of 4 dpn. Adjust needle sizes if necessary to obtain the correct gauge.

NOTIONS

Cable needle (cn); markers (m); stitch holders; tapestry needle.

GAUGE

18 sts and 23 rows = 4" (10 cm) in reverse stockinette stitch on larger needles, after blocking; 9 st mirrored rope cable panel = 1½" (3.8 cm); 27-st windblown hearts cable panel = 4" (10 cm); 24 rows = 4" (10 cm) in cable panels.

AGE OF AQUARIUS TRIO
Kathy Zimmerman and Lisa Carnahan

SWEATER

Back

With larger needles, CO 127 (141, 151, 165) sts. With WS facing and beg and end as indicated for your size, set-up for Body chart, placing markers (pm) bet patt reps as follows: [k1, p4] 1 (0, 1, 0) time; [k3, p4, k1, p4] 1, (2, 2, 3) time(s), pm, work 25 sts in Patt 2 as follows, *K3, p2, k3,* p4, k1, p4; rep between ** once, pm, work 9 sts in Patt 1 as follows: P4, k1, p4, pm, rep 25 sts in Patt 2, pm, work 9 sts in Patt 1, pm, then work 25 sts in Patt 2, pm, [p4, k1, p4, k3] 1, (2, 2, 3) time(s), [p4, k1] 1, (0, 1, 0) time. Sl markers every row. Cont as charted, inc 6 sts on Row 10 as shown—133 (147, 157, 171) sts. Rep Rows 11–18 until piece measures 15¾ (16, 16, 17½)" (40 [40.5, 40.5, 44.5] cm) from beg, ending with a WS row. *Shape armholes:* At beg of next 2 rows, BO 12 (13, 12, 13) sts—109 (121, 133, 145) sts rem. Cont even in patt until armholes measure about 8¼ (9, 9, 9½)" (21 [23, 23, 24] cm), ending with Row 18 of patt. *Shape neck:* Cont in patt, work 36 (40, 46, 50) sts, join new yarn, work center 37 (41, 41, 45) sts and place on holder for neck, work to end—36 (40, 46, 50) sts each side. Working each side separately, BO 3 sts at neck edge 2 times—30 (34, 40, 44) sts rem each side. Work 2 rows even. Place all sts on holders.

Front

Work as for back until armholes measure about 6¼ (6½, 6½, 7¾)" (16 [16.5, 16.5. 20] cm), ending with Row 18 of chart. *Shape front neck:* (RS) Keeping in patt, work 40 (42, 48, 52) sts, join new yarn, work center 29 (37, 37, 41) sts and place on holder for neck, work to end—40 (42, 48, 52) sts

each side. Working each side separately, dec 2 sts at neck edge every RS row 4 (0, 0, 3) times as foll: Sl 2 sts as if to p2tog tbl (insert right needle through back loops of sts from left to right), p1, p2sso. Then dec 1 st at neck edge every 2 rows 2 (8, 8, 2) times as foll: Work first st, ssk, work to last 3 sts, k2tog, work last st—30 (34, 40, 44) sts rem each side. Cont in patt until piece measures same as back to shoulder. Place all sts on holders.

Sleeves

With smaller needles, CO 53 (59, 63, 67) sts. Beg with Set-up row (WS), work Sleeve chart, beg and ending as indicated for your size and placing markers bet patts. Work Rows 1–18, inc 2 sts on Row 10 as shown on chart, and changing to larger needles on Row 10. Rep Rows 11–18 for main patt, and *at the same time,* inc 1 st each end of needle every 2 rows 5 (4, 2, 2) times, then every 4 rows 13 (11, 8, 7) times, then every 6 rows 4 (7, 10, 11) times—99 (105, 105, 109) sts, working new sts in patt. Work even in patt until piece measures 17 (18, 18½, 19)" (43 [46, 47, 48.5] cm) from beg. Mark edge for underarm placement. Work even for 2" (5 cm) more. BO all sts loosely in patt.

Finishing

Neckband: Using the three-needle bind-off (see Glossary) join front to back at shoulders. With cir needle, RS facing, and beg at left shoulder seam, pick up and knit 11 (17, 17, 12) sts along left front neck, place marker (pm), work 29 (37, 37, 41) held front neck sts in patt, pm, pick up and knit 11 (17, 17, 12) sts along right front neck and 7 (7, 7, 8) sts along right back

Body

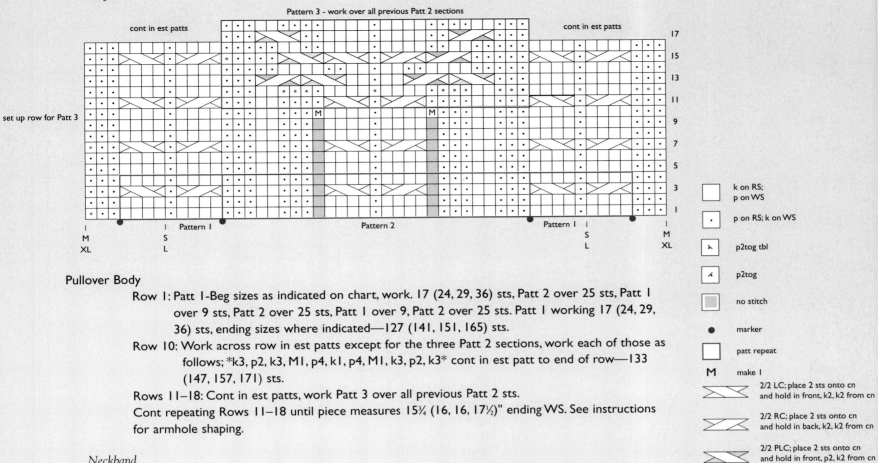

Pattern 3 - work over all previous Patt 2 sections

cont in est patts

cont in est patts

set up row for Patt 3

17
15
13
11
9
7
5
3
1

M
XL

S
L

Pattern 1

Pattern 2

Pattern 1

S
L

M
XL

	k on RS; p on WS
·	p on RS; k on WS
↘	p2tog tbl
↙	p2tog
▨	no stitch
●	marker
	patt repeat
M	make 1
	2/2 LC; place 2 sts onto cn and hold in front, k2, k2 from cn
	2/2 RC; place 2 sts onto cn and hold in back, k2, k2 from cn
	2/2 PLC; place 2 sts onto cn and hold in front, p2, k2 from cn
	2/2 PRC; place 2 sts onto cn and hold in back, k2, p2 from cn

Pullover Body

Row 1: Patt 1-Beg sizes as indicated on chart, work. 17 (24, 29, 36) sts, Patt 2 over 25 sts, Patt 1 over 9 sts, Patt 2 over 25 sts, Patt 1 over 9 sts, Patt 2 over 25 sts. Patt 1 working 17 (24, 29, 36) sts, ending sizes where indicated—127 (141, 151, 165) sts.

Row 10: Work across row in est patts except for the three Patt 2 sections, work each of those as follows; *k3, p2, k3, M1, p4, k1, p4, M1, k3, p2, k3* cont in est patt to end of row—133 (147, 157, 171) sts.

Rows 11–18: Cont in est patts, work Patt 3 over all previous Patt 2 sts.

Cont repeating Rows 11–18 until piece measures 15¾ (16, 16, 17½)" ending WS. See instructions for armhole shaping.

Neckband

3

1

Sleeve

17
15
13
11
9
7
5
3
1

(WS) set-up row

XL L M S

S M L XL

Starting with set up row (WS), follow chart, beg as indicated for your size. Place markers between patts. Work Rows 1-10, inc 2 sts on Row 10 as shown—55 (61, 65, 69) sts
Rep Rows 11-18 for sleeve. Refer to instructions for sleeve shaping.

neck and 7 (7, 7, 8) sts along right back neck, pm, work 37 (41, 41, 45) held back neck sts in patt, pm, pick up and knit 7 (7, 7, 8) sts along left back neck, pm, and join—102 (126, 126, 126) sts total. *Set-up rnd:* P0 (3, 3, 0), [k2, p3] 3 (2, 2, 2) times, [work 9 sts according to Rnd 1 of Neckband chart, p3] 0 (1, 1, 1) time, k2, p2, p2tog tbl, work 9 sts in cable patt as before, p2tog, p2, [k2, p3] 4 (1, 1, 1) time(s), work 9 sts in cable patt, [p3, k2] 1 (3, 3, 3) times, [p3, work 9 sts in cable patt, p3, k2] 0 (1, 1, 1) time, p2, p2tog tbl, work 9 sts in cable patt, p2tog, p2, k2, p3, work 9 sts in cable patt, p3, p0 (0, 0, 3), k0

(2, 2, 2)—98 (122, 122, 122) sts rem. *Next rnd:* P0 (3, 3, 0), [k2, p3] 4 (2, 2, 2) times, [work 9 sts according to Rnd 2 of Neckband chart, p3] 0 (1, 1, 1) time, [k2, p3] 0 (1, 1, 1) time, work 9 sts in cable patt, p3, [k2, p3] 4 (1, 1, 1) time(s), work 9 sts in cable patt, [p3, k2] 1 (3, 3, 3) times, [p3, work 9 sts in cable patt, p3, k2] 0 (1, 1, 1) time, p3, work 9 sts in cable patt, p3, k2, p3, work 9 sts in cable patt, p3, p0 (0, 0, 3), k0 (2, 2, 2). Rep this rnd 9 more times, and *at the same time*, work through Rnd 4 of Neckband chart 2 times, then work Rnds 1–3 (11 rnds total). Loosely BO all sts on next rnd (Rnd 4 of

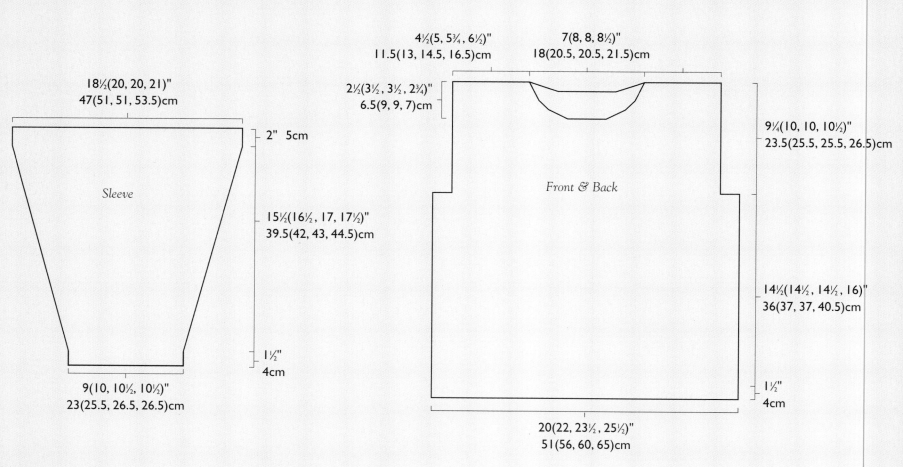

Sleeve

18½(20, 20, 21)"
47(51, 51, 53.5)cm

2" 5cm

15½(16½, 17, 17½)"
39.5(42, 43, 44.5)cm

1½"
4cm

9(10, 10½, 10½)"
23(25.5, 26.5, 26.5)cm

4½(5, 5¾, 6½)"
11.5(13, 14.5, 16.5)cm

7(8, 8, 8½)"
18(20.5, 20.5, 21.5)cm

2½(3½, 3½, 2¾)"
6.5(9, 9, 7)cm

Front & Back

9¼(10, 10, 10½)"
23.5(25.5, 25.5, 26.5)cm

14½(14½, 14½, 16)"
36(37, 37, 40.5)cm

1½"
4cm

20(22, 23½, 25½)"
51(56, 60, 65)cm

Sock and Hat

```
. . .      . . .    ⟋⟍ ⟍ . ⟋   ⟍     3
. . . .    . . . .            .
. . .      . . .    . . .     .
. . . .    . . . .        .   .  ⟍     1
```

Cap Crown

```
. . .      . . .    ⟍ . ⟋   ⟍   .  ⟍   4
. . . .    . . . .         .   .        3
. . .      . . .    . . .       .       2
. . . .    . . . .        .     .       1
```

PREPARING TO KNIT

Always wind a ball of yarn so it pulls from the center. To do so, with one hand, hold your first and second fingers together and drape a 12–18" (31–46 cm) tail end of the skein over them. With the other hand, wind the yarn several times around your fingers loosely. Take the yarn off your fingers, turn the "winding" 180 degrees, letting the tail hang free. Continue to wind more yarn loosely around your fingers, repeating turning and winding until the whole ball is wound. Pull the tail from the center and cast on! The space created by initially winding around your fingers should allow the yarn to pull out effortlessly.

Green Mountain Spinnery

as foll: Sl 2 sts as if to p2tog tbl, p1, p2sso. With yarn threaded on tapestry needle, sew sleeves into armholes. Sew side and sleeve seams. Weave in loose ends. Block lightly to measurements.

SOCKS

Note: Socks are photographed inside out.
Leg
With smaller dpn, loosely CO 51 sts. Divide sts evenly on 3 dpn. Place m, and join, being careful not to twist sts. Beg with Rnd 1, work Sock and Hat chart a total of 53 rnds, ending with Rnd 1 of chart. *Dec rnd:* Purl, dec 7 sts evenly spaced—44 sts rem.

Heel
Heel flap: P11, sl rem sts to next needle (this needle will hold the instep sts), turn, with empty needle, k11, then k11 from next needle, sl rem sts to instep needle—22 sts on each of 2 needles. Work back and forth on 22 heel sts for 24 rows as foll: *Sl 1, k1; rep from *, turn. End with a WS row.
Turn heel: Work short rows as foll:

Row 1: P13, p2tog, p1.
Row 2: Sl 1, k5, k2tog, k1.
Row 3: Sl 1, p6, p2tog, p1.
Row 4: Sl 1, k7, k2tog, k1.
Row 5: Sl 1, p8, p2tog, p1.
Row 6: Sl 1, k9, k2tog, k1.
Row 7: Sl 1, p10, p2tog, p1.
Row 8: Sl 1, k11, k2tog, k1—14 heel sts.
Gusset: P7, with empty dpn (needle 1) p7 more sts and then pick up and knit 14 sts along edge of heel flap; with needle 2 p22 instep sts; with needle 3 pick up and knit 14 sts along other edge of heel flap and p7 rem sts—64 sts total; 21 sts each on needles 1 and 3, 22 sts on needle 2; rnd begs at center of heel.
Rnd 1: Purl.
Rnd 2: Purl to last 3 sts of needle 1, p2tog tbl, p1; p22 sts of needle 2; p1, p2tog, purl to end of needle 3.
Repeat Rnds 1 and 2 until 44 sts rem.

Foot
Work even in rev St st until foot measures 8" (20.5 cm) from back of heel or about 1½" (3.8 cm) less than desired total length.

Arrange sts so that there are 11 sts each on needles 1 and 3, and 22 sts on needle 2.

Shape toe:
Rnd 1: Purl.

Rnd 2: Purl to last 3 sts of needle 1, p2tog tbl, p1; p1, p2tog, purl to last 3 sts of needle 2, p2tog tbl, p1; p1, p2tog, purl to end of needle 3.

Rep Rnds 1 and 2 until 20 sts rem. P5 sts from needle 1 onto needle 3—10 sts each on 2 dpn. Use the Kitchener st (see Glossary) to graft rem sts tog.

CAP

With smaller dpn, loosely CO 119 sts. Divide sts evenly onto 3 dpn. Join, being careful not to twist sts. Follow Sock and Hat chart for a total of 13 rnds—piece should measure about 2¼" (5.5 cm) from beg. Purl 1 rnd for turning ridge, and *at the same time,* dec 1 st at end of rnd—118 sts rem. Work k1, p1 ribbing for 12 rnds. *Next rnd:* M1, turn work inside out so that WS faces out—119 sts. Change to larger dpn

and work Cap Crown chart for a total of 29 rounds—piece should measure about 5" (12.5 cm) above rib. **Shape top:**

Rnd 1: *P1, P2tog tbl, k2, p2tog, p1, k4, p1, k4; rep from *—105 sts rem.

Rnd 2: *P2tog tbl, k2, p2tog, k4, p1, k4; rep from *—91 sts rem.

Rnd 3: *P1, k2, p1, 2/2RC, p1, 2/2LC; rep from *.

Rnd 4: *K2tog, ssk, k4, p1, k4; rep from *—77 sts rem.

Rnd 5: *K2tog, k4, p1, k4; rep from *—70 sts rem.

Rnd 6: *K2tog, k3, p1, k2, ssk; rep from *—56 sts rem.

Rnd 7: *K2tog, k2, p1, k1, ssk; rep from *—42 sts rem

Rnd 8: *K2tog, k1, p1, ssk; rep from *—28 sts rem.

Rnd 9: *K2tog, ssk; rep from *—14 sts rem.

Rnd 10: *K2tog; rep from *—7 sts rem.
Cut yarn, pull tail through rem sts, pull up tightly, and fasten off. Weave in loose ends.

PICKING UP STITCHES

When picking up stitches at the heel of a sock, we've found that if you just pick up the stitches that you are naturally able to, even if the number of stitches differs from the pattern, the heel seems to fit better. To eliminate holes, slip the first stitch on a knit row of the heel and knit the last stitch through the back loop.

Yarn Heaven

BETTE BORNSIDE COMPANY •

Any yarn shop with well over one hundred different lines of yarn should expect its customers to stay a while. That's why shoppers at Bette Bornside Company find a couch and comfortable chairs in which to while away their time studying the extensive library of patterns and books here; patient spouses can also sit, read, and snooze.

Located in the historic Faubourg-Marigny district near the French Quarter in New Orleans, Bette Bornside Company began as a typical mom-and-pop operation, opened by Bette and her husband in 1986 after she retired from a thirty-year career in microbiology. They began the company as a mail-order business supplying medium-priced yarns and accessories to knitters and crocheters, but soon realized they needed more stock room and a place to serve local customers. The resulting shop occupies the site of an old corner pharmacy in a neighborhood that feels like a step back into the nineteenth century.

Today Bette Bornside Company's business is about half mail order and half walk-in retail, and it offers a combination of old-time personal service and an up-to-date computerized inventory. Visitors include local customers, folks from out of state, and phone friends who send photos of their finished pieces for the store's bulletin board. The shop displays a skein or sample of every yarn it carries—an impressive display. Individual instruction helps customers achieve success at their own pace.

BETTE BORNSIDE COMPANY

2733 Dauphine Street
New Orleans, LA 70117
Phone: (504) 945-4069
(800) 221-9276
Website: bornsideyarns.com

Bette creates about four designs a year—versatile patterns that work well with more than one yarn. "We consider our customers to be designers, and we focus on helping them match yarns with their ideas and patterns," she says.

BETTE'S PONCHO

Designer Bette Bornside knows that when designing knitwear, "fabric is everything." That's especially true for a simple, classic design, such as this stylish poncho whose success depends on comfort and drape. Lace-weight mohair and an alpaca bouclé are used together for a soft, luscious, warm fabric. The square shape can be worn either with the ends pointed at center front and back, or straight across. Folded in half, it works as a shawl.

BETTE'S PONCHO
Bette Bornside

FINISHED SIZE
About 48" (122 cm) wide and 50" (127 cm) long.

YARN
Plymouth Yarns Indiecita Alpaca Bouclé (87% Alpaca, 13% nylon; 115 yd [105 m]/ 50 g): #104 cobblestone (MC), 9 balls. JCA/Reynolds Grignasco VIP (80% mohair, 20% nylon; 259 yd [237 m]/25 g): #417 beige (A), 5 balls; #472 gray (B), 3 balls.

NEEDLES
Body—Size 13 (9 mm). Neckband—Size 11 (8 mm): 16" or 24" (40- or 60-cm) circular (cir). Adjust needle sizes if necessary to obtain the correct gauge.

NOTIONS
Tapestry needle; marker (m); size K/10½ (6.5-mm) crochet hook.

GAUGE
10 sts and 14 rows = 4" (10 cm) in stockinette stitch on larger needles.

Stripe Pattern:
(Worked in St st)
Note: 1 strand of the alpaca bouclé (MC) and 2 strands of one color of the lace-weight mohair are used together throughout. The subtle stripes are made by switching the color of the mohair:
24 rows A; 20 rows B; 16 rows A; 12 rows B; 8 rows A; 4 rows B; 2 rows A; 2 rows B; 2 rows A; 2 rows B; 2 rows A; 4 rows B; 8 rows A; 12 rows B; 16 rows A; 20 rows B; 24 rows A.

Poncho
With larger needles and 1 strand MC and 2 strands A held tog, loosely CO 120 sts. Work St st, following stripe patt, for 74 rows, ending with a WS row—you will have worked 2 rows of an 8-row stripe of A.
Neck opening: Keeping in stripe patt, k57, join new yarn and BO 6 sts, work to end—57 sts each side. Working each side separately in established stripe patt, BO 1 st at neck edge on next row, BO 2 sts at neck edge on foll row, then BO 1 st at neck edge on the next 3 rows—51 sts rem each side. [Work 1 row even. BO 1 st at neck edge on next row] 2 times—49 sts rem each side. Work 10 rows even. [Inc 1 st at neck edge on next row. Work 1 row even] 2 times—51 sts each side. Inc 1 st at neck edge on each of the foll 4 rows, then inc 2 sts at neck edge on foll row—57 sts each side. On next row (WS), p57, use the backward loop method (see Glossary) to CO 6 sts and join both sides, purl to end—120 sts. Work to end of stripe patt. BO all sts loosely.

Finishing
Neckband: With cir needle, 1 strand MC, and 2 strands A, pick up and knit 52 sts evenly spaced around neck opening. Place m and join. Work k1, p1 ribbing for 3 rnds. Loosely BO all sts. *Edging:* With crochet hook, 1 strand MC, and 2 strands A, work 2 rows of single crochet (see Glossary) around outer edge of poncho. Weave in loose ends. *Tassels:* (Make 4) Cut 24 lengths of A and 8 lengths of MC, each 10" (25.5 cm) long. Hold all ends tog and fold group in half. Use crochet hook to pull fold through corner of poncho, then pull loose ends through fold.

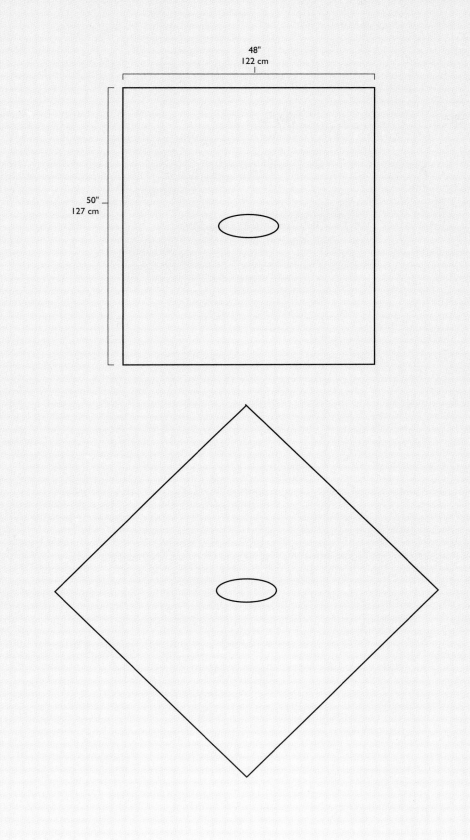

48"
122 cm

50"
127 cm

tips

WORKING WITH SPECIALTY YARNS

When knitting with bouclé or heavily textured yarn, there is sometimes little visual difference between the knit side and purl side of basic stockinette stitch fabric. Pin a stitch holder or brightly colored marking pin on the right side of your work to remind you that when the pin is facing you, you're on a knit row; when the pin is on the back of the work, you're on a purl row.

Kathy's Kreations

If your pattern calls for yarn that knits at 3.25 stitches to 1 inch and you can't find a suitable yarn that knits to that gauge, try combining two or more smaller yarns and knitting as one. Don't be afraid to combine two or more variegated yarns or a textured yarn with a variegated yarn.

Tricoter

THE ELEGANT EWE • The shop has a Celtic flair, with traditional music playing quietly in the background and even a bagpiper out in front on special occasions. It feels like a fine gallery, too, with its subtle lighting, careful attention to display, and sophisticated color arrangement. But the logo is a giveaway: a line drawing of a rare Lincoln Longwool with long, curly ringlets. The Elegant Ewe specializes in "knitting, spinning, rug hooking, and gifts."

Marci Richardson, a former emergency-room nurse, and her then-six-year-old daughter Marlee drew the logo to celebrate the opening of the shop in 1998. In the ensuing years, the shop has become known throughout New England for its commitment to quality and service. Customers come from as far north as Montreal and as far south as Connecticut, welcomed by the generous bay windows and held in thrall by an extensive assortment of designer yarns, including hard-to-find laceweights, and spinning and rughooking supplies. Tapestry bags are a specialty, too.

Before opening the shop, Marci spent a couple of years doing market research and taking classes at the Women's Business Center of New Hampshire. She selected Concord because it is an area known for its history and the arts, and, she selected a storefront that is close to the highway, easy to find, and has plenty of free parking. But it's more than location that draws visitors. A Tuesday night knitting clinic attracts those who can't commit to one of the six or more classes each week. Special events including "knitter of the month," and an annual fiber art show feature student works. Noted designers come often for lectures and book signings—there's always something happening at The Elegant Ewe.

THE ELEGANT EWE

71 SOUTH MAIN STREET
CONCORD, NH 03301
PHONE: (603) 226-0066
E-MAIL: ELEGANTU@WORLDPATH.NET

MEADOW FLOWERS SHAWL

Donna Kay's simply elegant shawl pattern, Meadow Flowers, was first used in a class she taught last year at The Elegant Ewe. Students used many different fibers—Shetland jumper weight, alpaca, homespun—each different, each stunning. You can knit the shawl as small or large as you like, and because of the garter-stitch structure, it is reversible. The version featured here uses a hand-dyed, lace-weight mohair. The shawl makes a great gift when you aren't sure of the size. The top edge can be folded back like a collar.

FINISHED SIZE

60" (153.5 cm) wide and 34" (86.5 cm) from the middle point to base, excluding border.

YARN

Lorna's Laces Heaven (90% kid mohair, 10% nylon; 975 yd [900 m]/200 g): #64 gold hill. Sample shown used about ⅔ of a skein.

NEEDLES

Body—Size 8 (5 mm): 24" (60-40cm) circular (cir). Border—Size 8 (5 mm): Set of 2 double-pointed (dpn). Adjust needle size if necessary to obtain correct gauge.

NOTIONS

Tapestry needle.

GAUGE

14 sts = 4" (10 cm), blocked. Note: The blocked size is about 30 percent larger than the unblocked size.

MEADOW FLOWERS SHAWL
Donna Kay

Body

CO 3 sts. Knit 1 row. Work Shawl chart as foll:

Row 1: [K1, yo] 2 times, k1—5 sts.

Row 2 and all even-numbered rows: Knit.

Row 3: K1, yo, k3, yo, k1—7 sts.

Row 5: K1, yo, k5, yo, k1—9 sts.

Row 7: K1, yo, k7, yo, k1—11sts.

Row 9: K1, yo, k9, yo, k1—13 sts.

Row 11: K1, yo, k5, yo, ssk, k4, k1—15 sts.

Row 13: K1, yo, k4, k2tog, yo, k1, yo, ssk, k4, yo, k1—17 sts.

Row 15: K1, yo, k7, yo, ssk, k6, yo, k1—19 sts.

Row 17: K1, yo, knit to last st, yo, k1—21 sts.

Row 19: K1, yo, k5, yo, ssk, k6, yo, ssk, k4, yo, k1—23 sts.

Row 21: K1, yo, k4, k2tog, yo, k1, yo, ssk, k3, k2tog, yo, k1, yo, ssk, k4, yo, k1—25 sts.

Row 23: K1, yo, k7, yo, ssk, k6, yo, ssk, k6, yo, k1—27 sts.

Row 25: Repeat Row 17—29 sts.

Row 27: K1, yo, k5, *yo, ssk, k6; rep from * to last 7 sts, yo, ssk, k4, yo, k1—31 sts.

Row 29: K1, yo, k4, *k2tog, yo, k1, yo, ssk, k3; rep from * to last 10 sts, k2tog, yo, k1, yo, ssk, k4, yo, k1—33 sts.

Row 31: K1, yo, k7, *yo, ssk, k6; rep from * to last 9 sts, yo, ssk, k6, yo, k1—35 sts.

Row 32: Knit.

Rep Rows 25–32 until piece measures desired length, ending with Row 26—8 sts inc'd per 8-row rep. *Next row:* K1, *yo, k2tog; rep from *. *Next row:* Knit, dec 1 st—180 sts. (*Note:* The final stitch number and the number of yarnovers along side edges should each be divisible by 6 in order to attach border sts.) Do not break yarn.

	k on RS and WS
/	k2tog
\	ssk
o	yarn over
	pattern repeat

Border

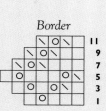

Shawl

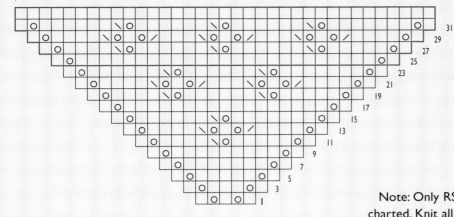

Note: Only RS rows are charted. Knit all WS rows.

Border

With dpn, CO 4 sts. Knit 1 row. From here on, you will work perpendicular to the shawl body. Follow Border chart, working odd-numbered rows in patt away from the body and even-numbered rows toward the body. Join border as foll:

Row 1 and all odd-numbered rows: Follow Border chart.

Row 2 and all even-numbered rows: Knit to last st, ssk (last border st and first body stitch).

Rep Rows 1 and 2 across shawl top until no live sts rem. Do not break yarn. Turn corner, and with cir needle pick up each yo along shawl side edge to next corner (90 yos in size shown). Work as before, foll chart for odd-numbered rows and attaching border to shawl sides on even-numbered rows. Turn corner at bottom of shawl and pick up each yo along rem side edge. Work as before until no live sts rem—4 border sts rem.

Finishing

With yarn threaded on a tapestry needle, use the Kitchener st (see Glossary) to graft rem live border sts to CO edge. Weave in loose ends. Steam block lightly to measurements.

YARN HEAVEN • Tarie Williams would

have you believe that her customers make Yarn Heaven what some have called "the 'Cheers' of yarn shops." In truth, it is probably her own indefatigable spirit that brings energy and attracts a lively and enthusiastic clientele. Even though Yarn Heaven is a friendly shop where everyone seems to know each other, things haven't always been so cheery in Tarie's life. It was a friend's effort to shake her out of a long bout of depression, in fact, that brought her to knitting. Out on a drive together, they saw a billboard for a yarn shop. Tarie was immediately intrigued. She had never heard of a yarn shop, let alone been in one. Her friend took her to the shop and, as Tarie says, "The rest is history. When I walked through the door, I felt reborn. I knew instantly what I would be doing with the rest of my life."

Even so, the path has not been easy. After a bad fire and a failed partnership, friends and customers helped her rebuild, and Yarn Heaven was the result. What began as a 500-square-foot shop has more than tripled, and inventory has evolved from basic acrylics and baby yarns to a varied rainbow, with hand-painted skeins being a particular customer favorite.

Yarn Heaven offers more than yarn, though. There's yarn in the making in the form of live Angora bunnies, for instance. And there's camaraderie. A favorite event is the annual Pajama Party Charity Knit-In, held the last Saturday in October. The doors are locked at midnight, and the group knits the night away making countless hats and booties for the local community hospital. A picnic-cum-craft fair takes place in the field across from the store in late spring, and a Craft Camp the last week of July teaches kids from seven to sixteen to knit, crochet, spin, weave, dye, and use their imaginations.

Conveniently situated between Dallas and Fort Worth, Yarn Heaven has more than survived its rugged start—it has created a lively community of knitters and doers.

YARN HEAVEN

1292 W. ARKANSAS LANE
ARLINGTON, TX 76013
PHONE: (817) 226-9276
WEBSITE: WWW.YARNHEAVEN.COM
E-MAIL: YARNHEAVEN@EARTHLINK.NET

MARIE LOUISE'S LACE SWEATER

Marie Louise Vallin, a teacher and designer at Yarn Heaven, came to Texas from her native Sweden and has adapted her skills to new yarns for what had been the unfamiliar climate. This lacy, feminine sweater combines the crispness of linen and the sheen of rayon, a perfect combination for mild Texas winters or for cool springs and summers anywhere.

FINISHED SIZE

39 (44, 49, 54)" (99 [112, 124.5, 137] cm) chest circumference. To fit sizes Small (Medium, Large, Extra Large). Sweater shown measures 39" [99 cm].

YARN

Berroco Linet (38% acrylic, 23% rayon, 23% nylon, 16% linen; 110 yd [101 m]/ 50 g): #3106 Wild Mushroom, 13 (13, 14, 15) skeins.

NEEDLES

Size 6 (4 mm) straight or circular (cir). Adjust needle size if necessary to obtain the correct gauge.

NOTIONS

Size D/3 (3.25 mm) crochet hook; tapestry needle.

GAUGE

24 sts and 32 rows = 4" (10 cm) in lace pattern; 24 sc = 4" (10 cm).

MARIE LOUISE'S LACE SWEATER
Marie Louise Vallin

Lace Pattern:

Row 1: (RS) K1 (selvedge st), k1, *yo, k2, sl 1, k2tog, psso, k2, yo, k1; rep from * to last st, k1 (selvedge st).

Rows 2, 4, and 6: Purl.

Row 3: K1, k2, *yo, k1, sl 1, k2tog, psso, k1, yo, k3; rep from * to last 8 sts, yo, k1, sl 1, k2tog, psso, k1, yo, k2, k1.

Row 5: K1, k3, *yo, sl 1, k2tog, psso, yo, k5; rep from * to last 7 sts, yo, sl 1, k2tog, psso, yo, k3, k1.

Rep Rows 1–6 for pattern.

Back

CO 115 (131, 147, 163) sts. Knit 1 (WS) row. Beg with Row 1, work through Row 6 of lace patt 15 (16, 17, 18) times, then rep Rows 5 and 6 only, and *at the same time*, when piece measures 13½ (14½, 15½, 17)" (34.5 [37, 39.5, 43] cm) from CO edge, **Shape armholes:** BO 4 (5, 5, 5) sts at beg of next 2 rows, then BO 2 (3, 3, 3) sts beg of next 4 (2, 2, 2) rows, then BO 0 (0, 2, 2) sts at beg of next 0 (0, 2, 2) rows. Dec

1 st each end of needle every other row 3 (5, 5, 6) times—93 (101, 117, 131) sts rem. Work even in patt until armholes measure 7½ (9, 9½, 10)" (19 [23, 24, 25.5] cm), ending with a WS row. **Shape neck:** Cont in patt, work 29 (31, 38, 43) sts, join new yarn and BO center 35 (39, 41, 45) sts, work to end—29 (31, 38, 43) sts each side. Working each side separately, BO 2 sts at neck edge once. Dec 0 (0, 1, 1) st at neck edge 0 (0, 1, 2) time(s)—27 (29, 35, 39) sts rem each side. Work even until armholes measure 8½ (10, 11, 12)" (21.5 [25.5, 28, 30.5] cm). BO all sts.

Front

Work as for back until piece measures 19½ (22, 23½, 25½)" (49.5 [56, 59.5, 65] cm) from beg. **Shape neck:** Keeping in patt, work 38 (41, 48, 53) sts, join new yarn and BO 17 (19, 21, 25) sts, work to end—38 (41, 48, 53) sts each side. Working each side separately, at neck edge BO 4 sts once for all sizes, then BO 2 (3, 3, 3) sts once,

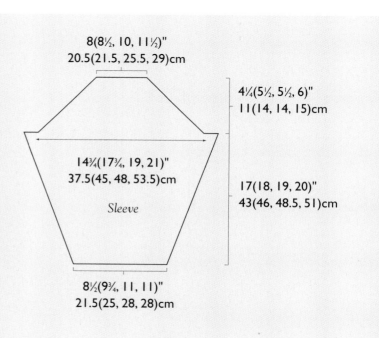

8(8½, 10, 11½)"
20.5(21.5, 25.5, 29)cm

4¼(5½, 5½, 6)"
11(14, 14, 15)cm

14¾(17¾, 19, 21)"
37.5(45, 48, 53.5)cm

Sleeve

17(18, 19, 20)"
43(46, 48.5, 51)cm

8½(9¾, 11, 11)"
21.5(25, 28, 28)cm

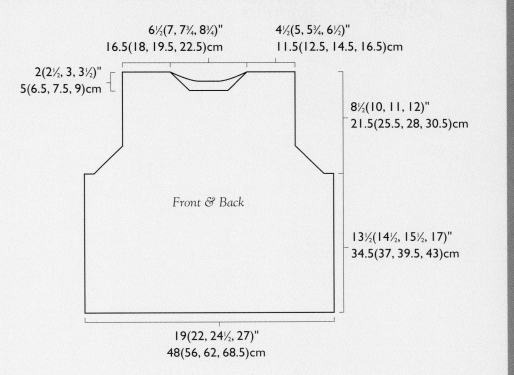

6½(7, 7¾, 8¾)"
16.5(18, 19.5, 22.5)cm

4½(5, 5¾, 6½)"
11.5(12.5, 14.5, 16.5)cm

2(2½, 3, 3½)"
5(6.5, 7.5, 9)cm

8½(10, 11, 12)"
21.5(25.5, 28, 30.5)cm

Front & Back

13½(14½, 15½, 17)"
34.5(37, 39.5, 43)cm

19(22, 24½, 27)"
48(56, 62, 68.5)cm

then BO 2 sts once, then BO 1(1, 2, 2,) st(s) once—29 (31, 37, 42) sts rem each side. Dec 1 st at neck edge every other row 2 (2, 2, 3) times—27 (29, 35, 39) sts rem each side. Work even in patt until piece measures same as back. BO all sts.

Sleeves

CO 51 (59, 67, 67) sts. Knit 1 (WS) row. Work Rows 1–6 of lace patt 6 (6, 7, 8) times—piece should measure about 4½ (4½, 5¼, 6)" (11.5 [11.5, 13.5, 15] cm) from beg. Rep Rows 5 and 6 only, and *at the same time*, inc 1 st inside each selvedge st every 4 (4, 4, 2) rows 10 (24, 24, 4) times, then every 6 (0, 0, 4) rows 9 (0, 0, 26) times, working new sts into patt as they become available—89 (107, 115, 127) sts. Work even in patt until piece measures 17 (18, 19, 20)" (43 [46, 48.5, 51] cm) from beg, ending with a WS row. **Shape cap:** BO 4 (5, 5, 6) sts at beg of next 2 rows, then BO 2 (3, 3, 3) sts at beg of next 8 (2, 2, 2) rows, then BO 0 (2, 2, 2) sts at beg of next 0 (10, 10, 8) rows. Dec 1 st each end of needle every 3 rows 8 (10, 10,

12) times—49 (51, 59, 69) sts rem. Loosely BO all sts.

Finishing

Steam block lightly, if desired. With yarn threaded on a tapestry needle, sew shoulder and side seams. Sew sleeve seams and ease sleeve caps to fit armhole as you attach sleeve to body. Weave in loose ends.

Neckband:

Rnd 1: With crochet hook, RS facing, and beg at left shoulder, work 102 (108, 114, 120) single crochet (sc; see Glossary), adjusting hook size if necessary to maintain a smooth, even neckline.

Rnd 2: *Working into 5 sc from previous row, work 1 sc in first st; 1 half double crochet (see Glossary) in the next st; work 3 double crochet in next st; work 1 half double crochet in next st; work 1 sc in 5th st, skip 1 sc on row below; rep from * to end of rnd—there will be about 17 (18, 19, 20) scallops around neckline.

tips

HANDKNITTERS LTD. • When Eileen Boyle

Young founded Handknitters Ltd. in 1999, it was the realization of a lifelong dream. Having knitted for over forty years, she shopped for yarn in shops, by mail order, and even at farms where the sheep lived, Eileen knew what she wanted in her own shop. And having made a career as a professor of education at Spalding University, she knew more than a little bit about teaching. So when she took a sabbatical from her position at Spalding, it was to study learning theory using knitting classes as her focus. In the process, she also became a Knitting Guild of America master handknitter.

Running Handknitters is a family affair. Eileen is assisted by her high-school age daughter, Britty; her oldest daughter, Jami, a practicing attorney; and her daughter-in-law, Jamie Leigh, all of whom were taught by Eileen.

Eileen has found many enthusiastic knitters who are grateful to be able to come into the shop to touch and feel the yarns that they had previously only been able to see in magazines or books. Only a year after opening, Eileen expanded into a bigger space complete with a classroom and a lot more room for great yarns to meet the growing demand. A monthly newsletter, "Random Thoughts and Mingled Threads," keeps customers looking forward to classes, new yarns, and fresh ideas. Daughter Jami writes many of Handknitter's in-shop patterns, designed to suit a variety of fibers and budgets from a once-in-a-lifetime splurge on angora or cashmere to a great everyday wool or cotton.

"I love to see my customers share their own love of knitting, teaching their friends and neighbors to knit, and I enjoy the energy and enthusiasm they bring to their projects. It's a privilege to share my love of knitting," Eileen says, in the spirit that has made Handknitters Ltd. such a success.

HANDKNITTERS LTD.

11726 MAIN STREET
LOUISVILLE, KY 40243
PHONE: (502) 254-9276 (YARN)
ORDERS ONLY: (866) GOT-YARN
WEBSITE: WWW.HANDKNITTERSLTD.COM
E-MAIL: HANDKNIT@BELLSOUTH.NET

WEEKEND TANK TOP

Jami Young designed this easy, stylish tank of 100%-cotton knitted ribbon. It works well under a suit jacket or dressed down with shorts.

WEEKEND TANK TOP

Jami Young

FINISHED SIZE

36 (42)" (91.5 [112] cm) bust/chest circumference. Sweater shown measures 36" (91.5cm).

YARN

Muench Yarns Free Spirit (100% cotton; 77 yd [70 m]/50 g): #708 purple, 5 (6) balls.

NEEDLES

Size 10 (6 mm). Adjust needle size if necessary to obtain the correct gauge.

NOTIONS

Tapestry needle; size G/6 (4.25-mm) crochet hook.

GAUGE

16 sts and 20 rows = 4" (10 cm) in stockinette stitch.

Back

CO 72 (84) sts. Work 4 rows garter st (knit every row). Work even in St st until piece measures 10 (12)" (25.5 [30.5] cm) from beg, ending with a WS row. **Shape armholes:** (RS) BO 2 sts at beg of next 10 (14) rows—52 (56) sts rem. Dec 1 st each end of needle every row 9 times—34 (38) sts rem. Work even until piece measures 15 (18)" (38 [46] cm) from beg, ending with a WS row. **Shape neck:** K11 (12), join new yarn and BO center 12 (14) sts, work to end—11 (12) sts each side. Working each side separately, BO 4 sts at neck edge once, then dec 1 st at neck edge every other row 4 times—3 (4) sts rem each side. Work even until piece measures 18 (20)" (46 [51] cm) from beg. BO all sts.

Front

Work as for back until piece measures 12 (14)" (30.5 [35.5] cm) from beg—34 (38) sts. **Shape neck:** K11 (12), join new yarn and BO center 12 (14) sts, work to end— 11 (12) sts each side. Working each side separately, BO 4 sts at neck edge once, then dec 1 st at neck edge every other row 4 times—3 (4) sts rem. Work even until piece measures 18 (20)" (46 [51] cm) from beg. BO all sts.

Finishing

With yarn threaded on a tapestry needle, sew shoulder and side seams. Work 1 rnd of single crochet (see Glossary) around neck, armhole, and lower edges. **Note:** Use a contrasting color yarn for the crocheted edging if desired.

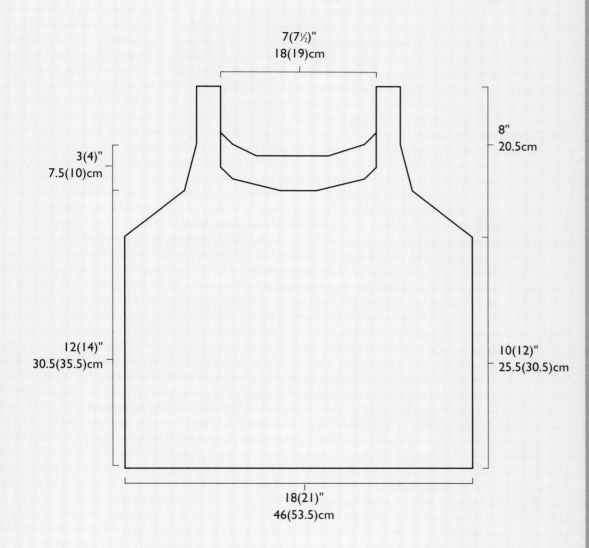

7(7½)"
18(19)cm

8"
20.5cm

3(4)"
7.5(10)cm

12(14)"
30.5(35.5)cm

10(12)"
25.5(30.5)cm

18(21)"
46(53.5)cm

tips

GETTING PROFESSIONAL RESULTS

Concentrate on the details of simple knitting. Knitters often relax, even get a little lazy, when a project seems easy for their skill level. Instead, do all the details of the knitting precisely. That includes the decreasing, the increasing, and any other shaping that is repeated throughout the work. Don't try different methods—do exactly the same thing, row-in and row-out. This alone will dramatically affect the quality of the finished piece. Remember, good-quality edges and shaping and properly finished ends will raise the finished piece from "home-made" to elegantly "hand-knit."

Big Sky Studio

YARNS INTERNATIONAL • Bonnie

Hassler and Betty Lindsay have followed a natural path from clinical therapy to consulting on color and image to the "perfect retirement job," Yarns International in Bethesda, Maryland. The culmination of many years of collaboration, Yarns International is dedicated to creating a "close-knit" community and keeping the tradition of knitting alive. The shop's team of expert knitters teach, design, and help customers problem-solve in an environment filled with high-quality yarns and classic sweater styles.

The owners' point of view that knitting is more than just a fashionable hobby predates Betty's first trip to the Shetland Islands. There she immersed herself in the ancient traditions of the native crofters, who raised Shetland sheep with coats in a rich and subtle range of natural colors. Convinced that there was a U. S. market for undyed and untreated Shetland yarn, she and Bonnie launched a joint venture, Shetland 2000, with a local wool mill, Jamieson and Smith Woolbrokers, who provide both naturals and a seemingly endless palette of dyed yarns.

A former customer-turned-designer, Ron Schweitzer, is so enthusiastic about the nine shades of natural wool yarn—spun only from the soft undercoat of the small, sturdy Shetland sheep—that he has authored three collections of Fair Isle sweater patterns which have been published by the shop.

Creating a line of traditional yarns, publishing design books, creating a rich and stimulating environment for their customers—all this is hardly what most people would call retirement. Yet it's a seamless and satisfying extension of Bonnie's and Betty's early work, helping people achieve creative fulfillment and keeping the craft of knitting alive.

YARNS INTERNATIONAL

WESTWOOD CENTER II
5110 RIDGEFIELD ROAD, SUITE 200
BETHESDA, MD 20816
PHONE: (301) 913-2980
ORDERS ONLY: (800) 927-6728
WEBSITE: WWW.YARNSINTERNATIONAL.COM
E-MAIL: INFO@YARNSINTERNATIONAL.COM

RIVER RUN PULLOVER

Ron Schweitzer's particular genius for using the minimally processed yarns of Shetland 2000 is evident in this popular unisex sweater, River Run Pullover, so named because the pattern reminds him of a wandering stream sculpting the mountain as it flows. The sweater uses nine shades of undyed yarn in an intricate vertical pattern reminiscent of brocade. The colors are named for the breeds of sheep that produce the yarn and range from white to brownish-black.

FINISHED SIZE

42 (45½, 49)" (106.5 [115.5, 124.5] cm) chest circumference.

YARN

Yarns International Shetland 2000 (100% wool, 190 yd [174 m]/50 g): Shetland black, 2 (3, 3) skeins, shaela (medium gray), 2 (2, 3) skeins, Shetland white, mooskit (light brown), moorit (dark brown), katmollet (light gray), yuglet (dark gray), 1 (2, 2) skeins each, gaulmgot (light tan) and sholmit (medium brown), 1 (1, 1) skein each.

NEEDLES

Ribbing—Size 3 (3.25 mm): 24" (60-cm) circular (cir) and set of 4 double-pointed (dpn). Body and Sleeves—Size 4 (3.5 mm): 32" (80-cm) cir and set of 4 dpn. Adjust needle sizes if necessary to obtain the correct gauge.

NOTIONS

Stitch holders; markers (m); tapestry needle.

GAUGE

32 sts and 32 rows = 4" (10 cm) in body patt on larger needles.

RIVER RUN PULLOVER

Ron Schweitzer

Body

With smaller cir needle and yuglet, CO 280 (310, 340) sts. Place marker (pm) and join, being careful not to twist sts. Work Rnds 1–21 of Ribbing chart, purling sts as indicated. *Next rnd:* Work with yuglet inc as foll: *Size small only:* K3, [M1, k5] 55 times, M1, k2—336 sts. *Size medium only:* K8, M1, k8, [M1, k5, M1, k6] 26 times, M1, k8—364 sts. *Size large only:* K5, M1, k5, [M1, k6, M1, k7] 25 times, M1, k5—392 sts. *All sizes:* Change to larger needle and beg and end as indicated for your size, work Rnd 1 of Body chart as foll: Work 168 (182, 196) sts in patt for front, pm, work 168 (182, 196) sts in patt for back. Work through Rnd 28, then rep Rnds 1–28 until piece measures 15½ (16, 16½)" (39.5 [40.5, 42] cm) from beg. ***Set up armhole steeks:*** Place last st of back and first st of front on holder, set left armhole steek as described in box on page 37, work in patt to last st of front, place last st of front and first st of back on holder, set right armhole steek as before, work in patt to end of rnd. Cont in patt as established until piece measures 22 (22½, 23½)" (56 [57, 59.5] cm) from beg. ***Set up front neck steek:*** Work 68 (73, 78) sts in patt, place next 30 (34, 38) sts on holder for front neck, set front neck steek, work in patt to end of rnd. Dec 1 st each side of front neck steek on next 5 (6, 7) rnds. *Work 1 rnd even. Dec 1 st each side of front neck steek on next rnd. Rep from * 6 (7, 8) more times—56 (59, 62) sts rem each shoulder. Cont in patt until piece measures 24 (25, 26)" (61 [63.5, 66] cm) from beg. ***Set up back neck steek:*** Cont in patt, work across all front sts, work 59 (62, 65) back sts, place next 48 (56, 64) sts on holder, set back neck steek, work to end of rnd. On the next rnd and foll alternate rnds, dec 1 st at each side of back neck steek 3 times—56 (59, 62) sts rem each shoulder. Cont in patt until piece measures 25 (26, 27)" (63.5 [66, 68.5] cm)

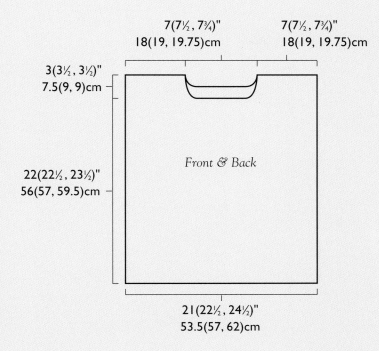

7(7½, 7¾)"
18(19, 19.75)cm

7(7½, 7¾)"
18(19, 19.75)cm

3(3½, 3½)"
7.5(9, 9)cm

22(22½, 23½)"
56(57, 59.5)cm

Front & Back

21(22½, 24½)"
53.5(57, 62)cm

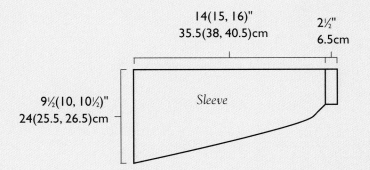

14(15, 16)"
35.5(38, 40.5)cm

2½"
6.5cm

9½(10, 10½)"
24(25.5, 26.5)cm

Sleeve

WORKING STEEKS

To maintain knitting in the round, set steeks at armholes and neck "openings" by casting on 10 extra stitches (using the backward loop method; see Glossary), alternating the two colors used in that row. Keeping first and last of these 10 stitches (the edge stitches) in the background color, alternate colors on the center 8 stitches to form checkerboard pattern. After knitting is complete, cut between 5th and 6th steek stitches (there is no need to baste before cutting because Shetland wools designed for Fair Isle knitting cling to each other and will not ravel). Pick up and knit stitches for sleeves or neckband from edge steek stitches (the ones worked in background color every round). To finish, trim steeks to 3 stitches in width and, with yarn threaded on a tapestry needle, use a cross-stitch as shown below to tack in place.

Ribbing

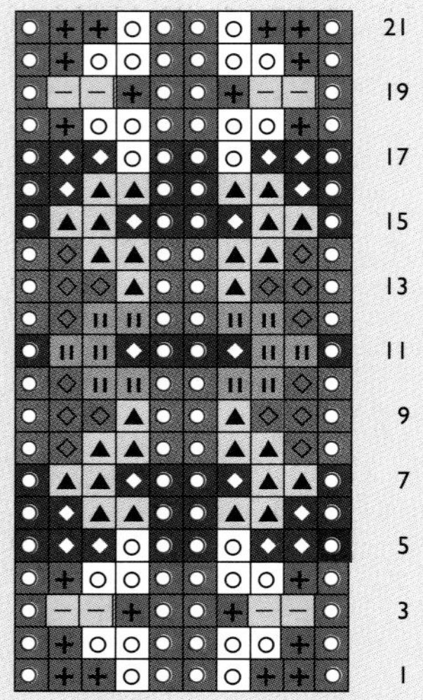

21
19
17
15
13
11
9
7
5
3
1

Legend:

- ○ Shetland White
- ▲ Gaulmgot (light tan)
- ‖ Mooskit (light brown)
- ✖ Sholmic (medium brown)
- ◆ Moorit (dark brown)
- — Katmollet (light gray)
- ● Shaela (medium gray)
- ✚ Yuglet (dark gray)
- ◆ Shetland Black
- ○ purl with appropriate color

beg L sleeve   beg M sleeve   beg S sleeve

Body

— beg S sleeve

27
25
23
21
19
17 beg L sleeve
15
13
11
9 beg M sleeve
7
5
3
1

end
S & L

beg
M

end
M

beg
S & L

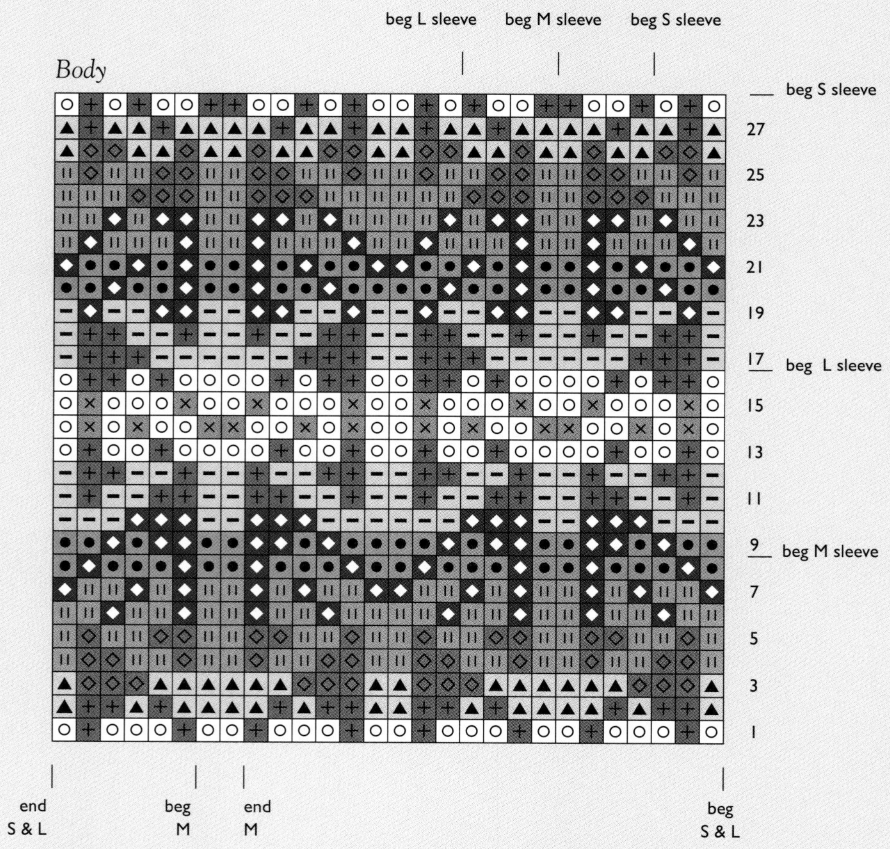

Work sleeve from top to bottom, reading chart from left to right.

38

from beg. On next rnd, BO all steek sts. Using the three-needle bind-off (see Glossary), join front to back at shoulders.

Sleeves

Cut armhole steek between center sts. With larger dpn, yuglet (Shetland black, yuglet), and beg at underarm, pick up and knit 73 (77, 81) sts to shoulder join and 73 (77, 81) sts back to underarm—146 (154, 162) sts, place 2 held sts on needle and knit them tog. This underarm st marks the "seam" line and is *not* included in the sleeve patt st count; it will be eliminated in the dec rnd before the sleeve ribbing. Place m and join into a rnd. *First patt rnd:* Work Body chart in the opposite direction (from top to bottom) and read from left to right. Beg with Rnd 28 (8, 16) starting at the st as indicated for your size, work to right edge of chart, work 28-st rep 5 times, work rem 3 (7, 11) sts. Work 2 (3, 2) rnds even. On next rnd (Rnd 25 [4, 13] of chart), and every foll 3 (4, 4) rnds, dec 1 st each side of underarm "seam" st 33 (6, 18) times, then every 2 (3, 3) rnds 5 (31, 18) times—

70 (80, 90) patt sts rem. Work 2 rnds even, ending with Rnd 1 of chart (all sizes). Change to smaller dpn and dec with yuglet as foll: *Size small only:* K1, k2tog, k2, [k2tog, k5] 9 times, k2tog, k1—60 sts rem. *Size medium only:* K1, k2tog, k2, [k2tog, k6] 9 times, k2tog, k2—70 sts rem. *Size large only:* K2, k2tog, k2, [k2tog, k7] 9 times, k2tog, k2—80 sts rem. **Cuff:** Work Ribbing chart in the opposite direction (from top to bottom) from Rnd 21 through Rnd 1. With yuglet, BO all sts knitwise.

Finishing

Neckband: Cut front and back neck steek sts between center sts. With smaller dpn and Shetland black, k48 (56, 64) held back neck sts, pick up and knit 21 (25, 24) sts to front neck, k30 (34, 38) held front neck sts, pick up and knit 21 (25, 24) sts to back neck—120 (140, 150) sts. Place m and join. Work Rnds 11 through 21 of Ribbing chart. With yuglet, BO all sts kwise. Trim all steeks and use cross st to sew in place as shown at right. Weave in loose ends. Wash and block to finished measurements.

CASTING ON

When casting on for double-pointed or circular needles, cast on all stitches on a straight needle, turn, and knit the first pattern row straight. On the second row, using the double-pointed or circular needles, join, making sure not to twist. After completing the piece, use the short cast-on tail to weave the first row together. This method makes it easier to ensure that the work isn't twisted, and the join is practically invisible.

Kathy's Kreations

S.W.A.K. KNITS • Guthrie, Oklahoma, is one of the quaintest and best-preserved frontier towns in the West, and S.W.A.K. Knits fits right into the historic character of the community. Antiques abound: an old armoire, a French-lily daybed, and a clawfoot bathtub are all used to display handknitting supplies . Owner Keely Stuever and her mother and partner, Sherry Stuever, like to rearrange and refurbish the store several times a year.

Keely grew up spending summers hanging around her mother's needlework shop, and she began designing sweaters and selling knitting patterns there under the label "Sealed With a Kiss, Sweater Art Designs by Keely" more than ten years ago. When the two opened S.W.A.K. in 1997, she understood what she was getting into. "I knew I wouldn't be able to sit around all day and socialize with knitters," she says. "As my customers do, I cherish the moments in the evening when I have time to knit." Sherry, on the other hand, has the dream job—she *does* sit and knit all day.

The two have developed a famous expertise in intarsia knitting and have co-authored a book, *Intarsia: A Workshop for Hand & Machine Knitting.* With a background in business, Keely loves running her own shop and keeping area knitters happy with great yarns, trunk shows, workshops, and original patterns.

S.W.A.K. KNITS

109 EAST OKLAHOMA
GUTHRIE, OK 73044
PHONE: (405) 282-8649
FAX: (520) 563-7408
WEBSITE: WWW.SWAKKNIT.COM
E-MAIL: SWAK@SWAKKNIT.COM

FARMHOUSE RUG

The Farmhouse Rug is a good introduction to intarsia knitting. Inspired by traditional folk art, its country scene reflects the fertile fields of the great plains of Oklahoma which designer Keely Stuever knows so well. Knitted on size 17 needles, it's a quick project.

QUICK KNIT RUG

The Quick-Knit Rug goes even faster. Both rugs wear well and can be machine-washed using the hand-wash cycle and cold water.

FINISHED SIZE

18½" (47 cm) wide and 29½" (75 cm) long.

YARN

Cascade Yarns Cascade 220 (100% wool; 220 yd [202 m]/100 g): #2414 rust (B), #8555 black (dk gray), #8010 cream (E), and #9325 cornflower (F), 2 skeins each. #4010 gold (C), #8234 lichen (A), #8267 forest (D), #8884 claret (G), and #8234 lichen and #8267 forest (H), 1 skein each. Yarn is used double throughout.

NEEDLES

Size 10½ (6.5 mm). Adjust needle size if necessary to obtain the correct gauge.

NOTIONS

Tapestry needle.

GAUGE

14 sts and 21 rows = 4" (10 cm) in stockinette stitch with yarn doubled.

FINISHED SIZE

22" (56 cm) wide and 32" (81.5 cm) long.

YARN

Classic Elite Waterspun Weekend (100% wool; 57 yd [53 m]/100 g): #7297 moss, 4 skeins. Yarn is used double throughout.

NEEDLES

Size 17 (12 mm). Adjust needle size if necessary to obtain the correct gauge.

NOTIONS

Tapestry needle.

GAUGE

7½ sts and 12 rows = 4" (10 cm) in stockinette stitch with yarn doubled.

FARMHOUSE RUG
Keely Stuever

With rust doubled, CO 108 sts. Beg with Row 1, work Farmhouse chart, working with all yarn doubled. BO all sts.

Finishing
Weave in loose ends. Steam block lightly, if desired.

QUICK KNIT RUG
Keely Stuever

Stitches
Seed Stitch:
(multiple of 2 sts; + 1)
All rows: *K1, p1; rep from * to last st, k1.

Seed Borders and St st Pattern:
Row 1: (RS) K1, p1, knit to last 2 sts, p1, k1.
Row 2: K1, p1, k1, purl to last 3 sts, k1, p1, k1.
With yarn doubled, CO 41 sts. Work seed st until piece measures 6" (15 cm) from beg, ending with a WS row. Change to seed borders and St st patt and work even until piece measures 26" (66 cm) from beg. Work seed st for 6" (15 cm)—piece should measure 32" (81.5 cm) from beg. BO all sts in seed st.

Finishing
Weave in loose ends. Steam block lightly, if desired.

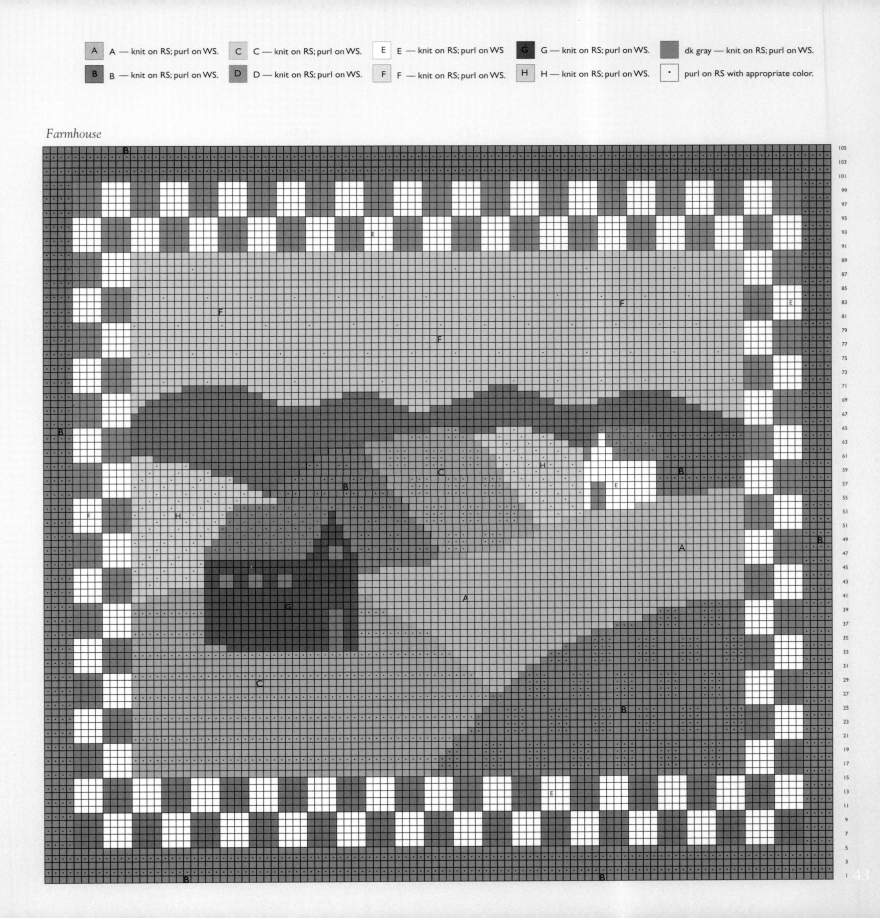

A — knit on RS; purl on WS.
B — knit on RS; purl on WS.
C — knit on RS; purl on WS.
D — knit on RS; purl on WS.
E — knit on RS; purl on WS
F — knit on RS; purl on WS
G — knit on RS; purl on WS.
H — knit on RS; purl on WS.
dk gray — knit on RS; purl on WS.
• purl on RS with appropriate color.

THE KNITTING TREE • Knitters of all ages and from all walks of life are likely to find just what they're looking for when they pass under the bright yellow awning of The Knitting Tree in Madison, Wisconsin. Every one of the scores of yarns—silk, cashmere, fake fur, ribbon, or classic wool or cotton—is accompanied by a swatch or sample. Literally hundreds of sweaters line the walls.

Owner Melissa Matthay's *joie de vivre* is evident throughout The Knitting Tree. Trooper, the store golden retriever, can frequently be found keeping non-knitters occupied, and small children are more than welcome. One visitor wrote, "As a mother, I can't begin to tell you the thrill of watching you cheerfully pull out beautiful handknitted sweaters to make a 'nap nest' for my son."

Melissa is the former owner of New York City's The Yarn Company, picked as a "Best Of New York" shop by *New York Magazine*. In addition to creating just the right designs for her customers in both New York and Madison, Melissa has provided patterns for some of the largest yarn companies in the world.

Because she's adept at designing, Melissa can either write the pattern of her customers' dreams or change a pattern to fit the yarn they just can't live without. To maintain that fresh excitement, she starts a new project almost every Friday evening, and has it ready to display in the store on Tuesday!

THE KNITTING TREE

2614 MONROE STREET
MADISON, WI 53711
PHONE: (608) 238-0121
ORDERS ONLY: (888) 247-7853
WEBSITE: WWW.KNITTINGTREE.COM

LADDERS OF ELEGANCE

Ladders of Elegance is a glitzy sleeveless shell that pairs perfectly with a black skirt or slim black pants. Two strands of yarn are held together, and the unusual laddering technique is as much fun for the knitter to make as it is for a lucky person to wear.

FINISHED SIZE

34 (38)" (86.5 [96.5] cm) bust/chest circumference. Sweater shown measures 34" (86.5 cm).

YARN

Tahki Stacy Charles Annabella (55% viscose, 25% cotton, 20% polyamide; 121 yd [110m]/50 g): #6 multi-color, 4 (5) balls. Tahki Stacey Charles Millefilli Fine (100% cotton; 136 yd [125 m]/50 g): black, 4, (5) balls.

NEEDLES

Ribbing—Size 8 (5.0 mm). Mock turtleneck—Size 8 (5.0 mm): 16" (40-cm) circular (cir). Body—Size 9 (5.5 mm). Adjust needle sizes if necessary to obtain the correct gauge.

NOTIONS

Tapestry needle; size F/5 (4.0-mm) crochet hook; three ½" (1.3-cm) buttons; matching sewing thread.

GAUGE

15 sts and 20 rows = 4" (10 cm) in elegant ladders pattern st, unstretched, on larger needles.

LADDERS OF ELEGANCE
Melissa Matthay

Note This stitch pattern is very loose and stretchy. Work one strand of each yarn together throughout the entire garment. When dropping the ladder stitch, use a crochet hook to gently tug on the running strand between stitches and help the dropped stitch run down all seven rows.

Elegant Ladders Pattern:

Row 1: *P4, k2, p4, k1, M1, k1; rep from * to last 10 sts, p4, k2, p4.

Row 2 and all even-numbered rows: Work sts as they appear.

Rows 3, 5, 7, and 9: *P4, k2, p4, k3; rep from * to last 10 sts, p4, k2, p4.

Row 11: *P4, k1, M1, k1, p4, k1, ladder next st by dropping it down 7 rows, k1, p4, k2; rep from * to last 10 sts, p4, k2, p4.

Rows 13, 15, 17, and 19: *P4, k3, p4, k2; rep from * to last 4 sts, p4.

Row 21: *P4, k1, ladder next st by dropping it down 7 rows, p4, k2; rep from *.

Rep Rows 1–22 for pattern.

Back

With smaller needles, CO 64 (70) sts. Work in p3, k2 ribbing until piece measures 2" (5 cm) from beg. Change to larger needles and work elegant ladders patt until piece measures 12 (13)" (30.5 [33] cm) from beg, ending with a WS row. *Shape armholes:* BO 3 sts at beg of next 2 rows, then dec 1 st at each end of needle every other row 2 times—54 (60) sts rem. Work even in patt until piece measures 20 (22)" (51 [56] cm) from beg and armholes measure 8 (9)" (20.5 [23] cm). BO all sts.

Front

Work as back until piece measures 17 (19)" (43 [48] cm) from beg—54 (60) sts. *Shape neck:* Work 20 (23) sts in patt, join new yarn and work next 14 sts and place on holder for neck, work to end—20 (23) sts each side. Working each side separately, BO 3 sts beg of each neck edge once, then dec 1 st at neck edge every other row 3 times—14 (17) sts rem each side. Work even in patt until piece measures same as back. BO all sts.

Finishing

With yarn threaded on a tapestry needle, sew shoulder seams. Sew side seams. *Armbands:* With crochet hook, holding 2 strands of yarn tog, and beg at underarm, work single crochet (sc; see Glossary) around armhole edge—about 58 (64) sts. *Mock turtleneck:* With smaller cir needle, RS facing, beg at left shoulder seam, and continuing the p3, k2 rib as established, pick up and knit 9 sts along left side front, Work 14 held front sts, pick up and knit 9 sts along right side front, and 21 sts across back neck sts—53 sts total. Match body rib patt as closely as possible. Do not join. Work back and forth in p3, k2 rib patt for 3" (7.5 cm), ending with a WS row. With RS facing, loosely BO all sts in ribbing. Do not cut yarn. **Neck opening:** With crochet hook, 2 strands of yarn held tog, RS facing, and beg at back left side of turtleneck, sc14 sts into the rows of the back neck opening, cont onto front edge and sc1 st into the first row of the lower front edge, then work 3 evenly spaced buttonhole loops along front edge as foll: Ch3, skip 3 rows of knitting, sc1 into each of the next 2 rows; rep from * 2 more times—3 buttonhole loops. Cut yarn, leaving about 5" [13-cm] tails. Thread tails onto a tapestry needle and weave in loose ends to inside of collar to secure. Sew buttons opposite buttonhole loops. Weave in all loose ends and secure them by stitching with sewing thread to prevent raveling.

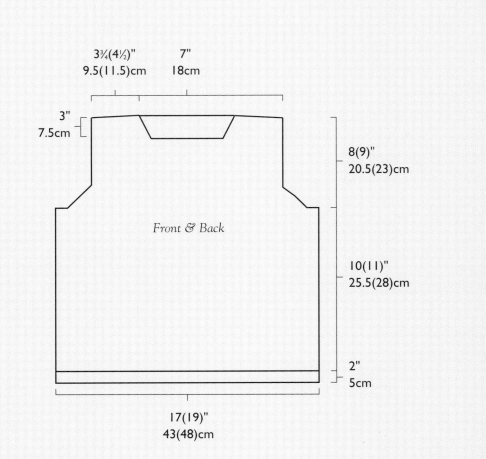

3¾(4½)"
9.5(11.5)cm   7"
18cm

3"
7.5cm

8(9)"
20.5(23)cm

Front & Back

10(11)"
25.5(28)cm

2"
5cm

17(19)"
43(48)cm

LA LANA WOOLS • When fiber aficionados visit Taos, New Mexico, they often find themselves practically living at La Lana Wools. This yarn lover's trove of texture and color is just a short stroll from the main plaza and across the street from the historic Taos Inn. Behind doors framed with vivid blue rustic pillars, skeins of handspun wool, silk, and mohair glow with soft shades of madder, indigo, cochineal, and chamisa. This harmonious and ever-changing natural palette honors centuries of dyeing in the American Southwest. A line of custom-spun yarns from a small mill in the Taos Valley and a couple of carefully selected lines of commercial yarns complement the handspuns, while handcrafted wearables and rugs tempt knitters and non-knitters alike.

Owner Luisa Gelenter fell in love with spinning in Bolivia in the early 1970s—"dancing with wools," she calls that time of exploration. And exploration has become the hallmark of her popular knitters' destination. "We prepare fibers and dyes as best we know how and then let serendipity take over," she says. "We are big fans of random factors." Blending and spinning fibers and experimenting with natural dyes—many of which are gathered locally—to create one-of-a-kind skeins has been the cornerstone of La Lana's longevity and success.

Close relationships with such knitwear designers as Judy Dercum, Valentina Devine, and Linda Romens compensate for Luisa's little secret—she doesn't knit! But the creative partnership among spinners, dyers, and designers fills La Lana with inspiration.

LA LANA WOOLS

136 PASEO NORTE
TAOS, NM 87571
PHONE: (505) 758-9631
ORDERS ONLY: (888) 377-9631
WEBSITE: WWW.LALANAWOOLS.COM
E-MAIL: LALANA@LALANAWOOLS.COM

SONOMA SPRING CANTATA

Soft, earthy pinks, mauves, and greens achieved with nature's dyes play together in Judy Dercum's Sonoma Spring Cantata. This comfortable cardigan uses La Lana Wool's custom-spun knitting worsted and Bombyx Silk, along with splendidly unpredictable Forever Random handspuns. A combination of color stranding and intarsia guarantees a lack of boredom and an invitation to improvise in this intermediate to advanced project.

49

SONOMA SPRING CANTATA
Judy Dercum

FINISHED SIZE
52 (56, 60)" (132 [142, 152.5] cm) bust/chest circumference. Sized for M, L, and XL. Sweater shown measures 52" (132 cm).

YARN
La Lana Wools Solids (100% custom mill spun wool; 200 yd [183 m]/4 oz): madder—pale (A), sea shell (B), sandstone (C), white (E), Indian paintbrush—dark (F), 4 oz each; mullein (D), 4 (8, 8) oz. La Lana Wools Forever Random Blends (100% handspun Romney blends; 200 yd [183 m]/4 oz): Florence's blend (FB), 4 oz; primavera (PR), 2 oz. La Lana Wools Forever Random Blends (handspun obverse blends—60/40% yearling mohair/Romney): spiced mullein (SM), 4 (6,6) oz, sweet Lorraine (SL), 4 oz, faerie queen (FQ) and pastorale (PS), 2 oz each. La Lana Wools Forever Random Blends—Glacé Blends (handspun 60/40% yearling mohair/Romney; 162 yd [149 m]/4 oz): flaminga glacé (FG), 4 (6, 6) oz. La Lana Wools Silk (100% silk; 59 yd [65 m]/1 oz): forest green—Bombyx (G SLK), marigolds/Navajo tea—Bombyx (M SLK), and sandstone—Bombyx (P SLK), 1 oz each. Several yards of smooth cotton yarn for provisional CO.

NEEDLES
Body and Sleeves—Size 9 (5.5 mm): Straight or circular (cir) and set of 4 double-pointed (dpn). Ribbing—Size 8 (5 mm): 32" (80-cm) cir and set of 4 dpn. Adjust needle sizes if necessary to obtain the correct gauge.

Notes The body of this jacket is worked in one large piece, although for space purposes the charts are separated. Begin at the lower back edge, work up to the yoke, then shape the neck and form both fronts.

Many of the yarns are multi-colored, and although represented as solid colors on the chart, you will find the actual yarn colors look somewhat different from the charts. Because of the nature of hand-painted and blended colors, each jacket will have its own unique appearance. While the birds in the "bird and square" motif are shown on the yoke chart, they are easily worked later in duplicate stitch (see Glossary).

The pinwheel design requires moving the yarn a number of stitches to the left. Plan ahead and move the yarn on the preceding row. If you forget and are already working the row where the offset occurs, move the yarn over loosely from the left to the appropriate point and twist it with the yarn from the last stitch worked.

Body
With waste yarn and A, and using the crochet chain method (see Glossary), provisionally CO 96 (104, 112) sts. With larger needles, work Rows 1–66 of Lower Back chart, changing colors and yarns as indicated. Work Rows 67–70 of Fair Isle Back chart. Beg with Row 71, work Yoke Back chart and *at the same time*, inc 8 (inc 0, dec 8) sts evenly spaced—104 sts for all sizes. Work through Row 129 of chart. **Shape neck:** (Row 130 of chart), work 36 sts in patt, join new yarn and BO 32 sts for neck, work to end—36 sts each side. Working each side separately, work Rows 131–194 of Yoke Fronts chart, and *at the same time,* BO 4 sts at neck edge once. Place a safety pin at each outside shoulder edge on Row 132 to mark shoulder line. Dec for neck along front yoke as shown on chart, and at the same time, on Row 194 of chart, dec 4 (dec 0, inc 4) sts evenly spaced each side—48 (52, 56) sts each side. Work Rows 195–198 of Fair Isle Front charts, following right and left front charts as shown. Work Rows 199–264 of Lower Fronts chart. Place sts on holders.

Sleeves
Sleeves are worked from side to side, starting at the underarm. Sleeve shaping and length are worked by casting on sts. With larger needles and Indian paintbrush (F), CO 4 sts. Beg and ending as indicated for your size, work Sleeve chart, following colors, yarns, and shaping as indicated. To mark the halfway point of sleeve, attach a safety pin at the top edge of sleeve while working Row 61 of chart. (This will help you

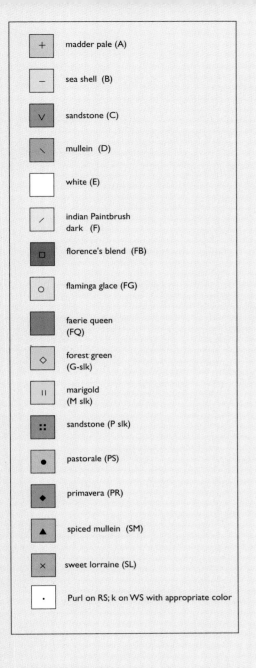

+	madder pale (A)	
−	sea shell (B)	
V	sandstone (C)	
\	mullein (D)	
	white (E)	
/	indian Paintbrush dark (F)	
▫	florence's blend (FB)	
○	flaminga glace (FG)	
	faerie queen (FQ)	
◇	forest green (G-slk)	
‖	marigold (M slk)	
∷	sandstone (P slk)	
●	pastorale (PS)	
◆	primavera (PR)	
▲	spiced mullein (SM)	
×	sweet lorraine (SL)	
·	Purl on RS; k on WS with appropriate color	

Neckband and Facing

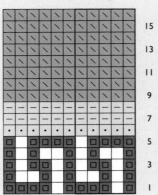

15
13
11
9
7
5
3
1

Cuff and Facing

16
15
14
13
12
11
10
9
8
7
6
5
4
3
2
1

Work 8 (8, 9) patt mutliples

beg all sizes

NOTIONS

Size G/6 (4.25 mm) crochet hook; bobbins (optional); 4 small safety pins (knitter's pins) to use a markers; tapestry needle; six ¾" to 1" (2- to 2.5-cm) buttons.

GAUGE

14¾ sts and 21 rows = 4" (10 cm) in stockinette stitch on larger needles.

Fair Isle Right Front

69
67

End
All sizes

Start
M

Start
L

Start
XL

Fair Isle Left Front

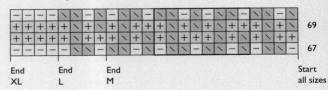

69
67

End
XL

End
L

End
M

Start
all sizes

Fair Isle Back

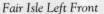

69
67

End
XL

End
L

End
M

Start
M

Start
L

Start
XL

Cont on the 96 (104, 112) stitches from Chart Back, work 4 rows of Fair Isle as shown—Rows 67–70.

Ribbing

BO all sts after rnd 6

5
3
1

SHOULDERS

Stabilizing the back neck and shoulders of a sweater is one of the most effective finishing details, giving a garment a professional handmade instead of "home-made" look. To do this, use a smooth yarn in a color close to that of the sweater itself and work one row of single crochet from shoulder to shoulder across the back neck of the sweater, easing in as you crochet if necessary, to match pattern dimensions.

Tricoter

align the sleeves and armholes later.) The BO rows start at the wrist edge; the sleeve shaping is reversed by working bind-offs every few rows as shown on chart. After completing chart, BO rem 4 sts. Sew sleeves to body matching the safety pins at sleeve center and yoke shoulder. Sew sleeve seams. *Cuff:* With madder pale (A) and larger dpn, pick up and knit 40 (40, 45) sts along lower edge of sleeve. Join and work in the rnd, working Rnds 1–16 of Cuff and Facing chart. *Note:* Rnd 10 is purled on the RS for the turning ridge. Do not BO sts when chart rnds are finished. Fold facing to inside along purl row, and with yarn threaded on a tapestry needle, sew live sts to inside of cuff. Turn sleeve to RS, join mullein (D) or color of your choice, and with smaller needles, work an applied I-cord (see Glossary), attaching I-cord to purl turning rnd, and *at the same time,* [k2tog] 3 times evenly spaced in the purl turning ridge sts (to prevent flaring). Alternatively, you may choose to omit the facing and simply BO the cuff edge and work a row of single crochet to finish.

Finishing

With yarn threaded on a tapestry needle, sew side seams. *Optional pocket(s):* Leave an opening in the side(s) extending up 3½" (9 cm) from bottom edge to 10½" (26.5 cm) from bottom edge for pocket. With larger needles and F (D, D), pick up and knit 28 sts along back edge of opening. Work in St st and *at the same time,* use the knitted method (see Glossary), to CO 2 sts at beg of every 2 rows at lower edge of pocket 3 times, then inc 1 st every 2 rows along lower edge 2 times—36 sts. Work 8 rows even. Reverse shaping for other half of pocket as foll: Dec 1 st every 2 rows 2 times, then BO 2 sts at beg of every 2 rows 3 times—28 sts rem. Cont to dec 2 sts every 2 rows at pocket lower edge until pocket measures about 5½" (14 cm) from beg—about 12 more rows; 16 sts rem. BO all sts. Sew pocket to inside of jacket. With larger needles, RS facing, and pastorale (PS), work attached I-cord (see Glossary)

along the front pocket opening to neaten and strengthen the edge. Sew ends of I-cord securely to inside pocket opening. (You can substitute a row of single crochet for the I-Cord, if you choose.) *Ribbing:* Remove waste yarn of provisional CO from back, and place front, back, front held sts, in that order, onto smaller cir needle—192 (208, 224) sts. Join Indian paintbrush (F), and purl 1 row, dec 10 evenly spaced sts across the back, and 5 evenly spaced sts across each front—172 (188, 204) sts rem. Work Rows 1–6 of Ribbing chart. With madder pale (A), BO all sts loosely. *Neckband:* With sea shell (B), larger needles, RS facing, and beg at front neck, pick up and knit 33 sts to shoulder, 34 sts across back neck to other shoulder, and 33 sts to other front neck—100 sts total. Purl 1 row. Work Rows 1–16 of Neckband and Facing chart. *Loosely* BO all sts. Turn facing to inside along purl ridge and sew in place, leaving about 1" (2.5 cm) at each neck edge open. *Front Bands:* With B, larger needles, and RS facing, pick up and knit 84 sts along right front edge, including neckband. Knit 1 WS row to mark fold line. Cont in St st, work 8 (2, 2) rows in B, then 0 (6, 6) row(s) in D. *Loosely* BO all sts. Work left front edge the same, starting stitch pick-up at RS neckband. Turn facings to inside along purl ridge and tuck under neckband facing. Sew in place. With crochet hook and mullein (D), make 6 evenly spaced crochet chain buttonholes (see Glossary) along right front, starting first buttonhole ¼" (6 mm) from lower edge and ending last buttonhole ¼" (6 mm) from front neckline. Sew buttons on left front opposite buttonholes. *Duplicate stitch birds:* With yarn threaded on a tapestry needle, duplicate stitch (see Glossary) birds on body using a single strand of silk, using colors and placement as indicated on Yoke charts. Weave in loose ends. Use remaining silk to work additional duplicate stitch embellishments, if desired. Wash in mild soap. Dry flat, shaping to correct measurements.

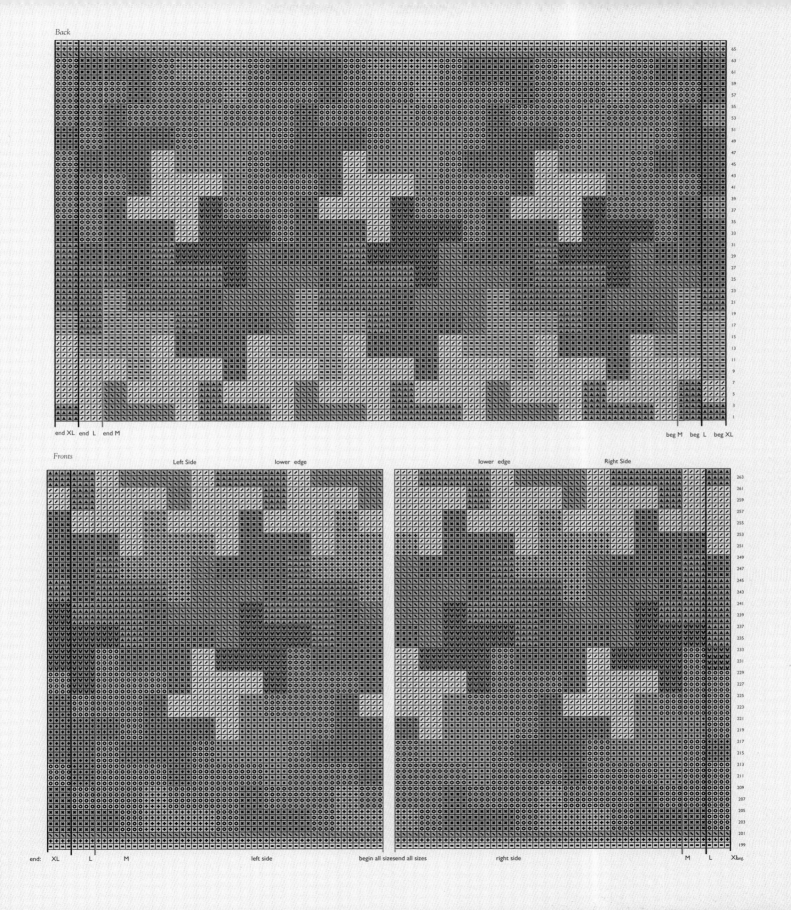

Back

end XL end L end M

beg M beg L beg XL

Fronts

Left Side   lower edge   lower edge   Right Side

end: XL   L   M   left side   begin all sizesend all sizes   right side   M   L   XLbeg.

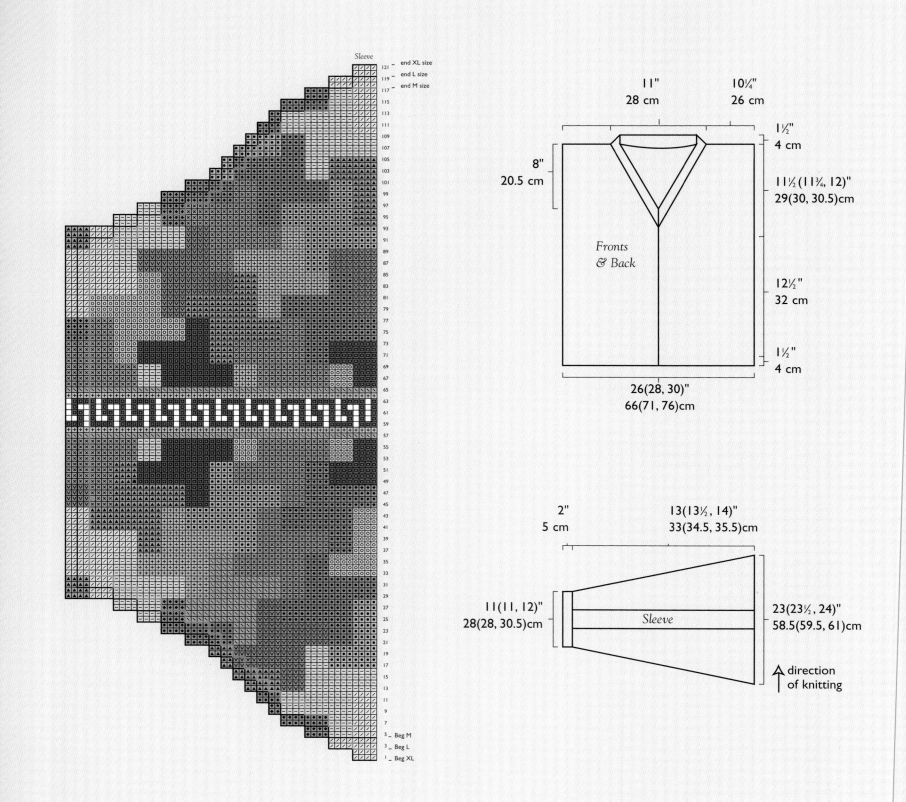

Sleeve

121 — end XL size
119 — end L size
117 — end M size
115
113
111
109
107
105
103
101
99
97
95
93
91
89
87
85
83
81
79
77
75
73
71
69
67
65
63
61
59
57
55
53
51
49
47
45
43
41
39
37
35
33
31
29
27
25
23
21
19
17
15
13
11
9
7
5 — Beg M
3 — Beg L
1 — Beg XL

11"
28 cm

10¼"
26 cm

1½"
4 cm

8"
20.5 cm

11½ (11¾, 12)"
29(30, 30.5)cm

*Fronts
& Back*

12½"
32 cm

1½"
4 cm

26(28, 30)"
66(71, 76)cm

2"
5 cm

13(13½, 14)"
33(34.5, 35.5)cm

11(11, 12)"
28(28, 30.5)cm

Sleeve

23(23½, 24)"
58.5(59.5, 61)cm

↑ direction
of knitting

Yoke Back

BO 32 sts between markers

129
127
125
123
121
119
117
115
113
111
109
107
105
103
101
99
97
95
93
91
89
87
85
83
81
79
77
75
73
71

Adjust stitch count as you work first row (71) of this chart.
Decrease 8 sts evenly spaced across row for size XL, and increase 8 sts evenly spaced for size M.
All sizes now have 104 sts as reflected on Row 71 of this chart.

Yoke Fronts

Size XL   L   M   Center front opening   M   L   XL

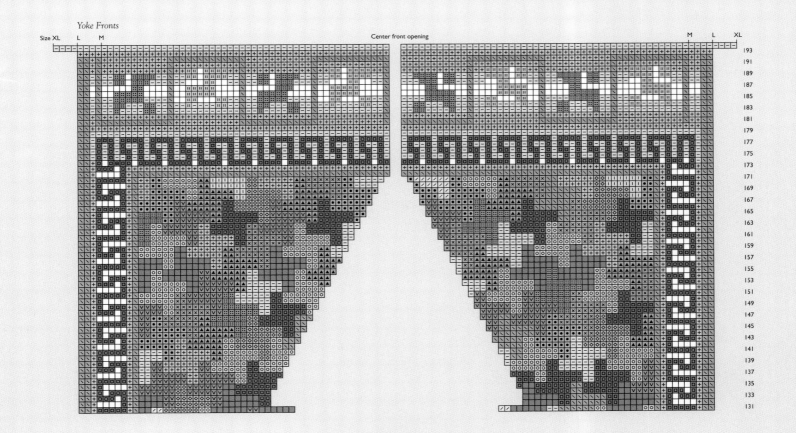

193
191
189
187
185
183
181
179
177
175
173
171
169
167
165
163
161
159
157
155
153
151
149
147
145
143
141
139
137
135
133
131

HANEKE WOOL FASHIONS • At Haneke

Wool Fashions, knitters gather around a cozy wood-burning stove in winter and, in summer, sit out on the deck overlooking an orchard and grazing sheep. Located in a turn-of-the-century school-house west of Boise, Idaho, Haneke offers an abundance of yarn, knitting supplies, looms, spinning wheels, and finished garments in the showroom of this generous two-story building.

Haneke supplies some of the softest yarn in the world, but it's much more than a store—it's a complete "sheep to shawl" experience. Owner Kathy Haneke spent much of her childhood in rural Italy, so raising sheep came naturally when she and her family moved to their Idaho acreage in 1990. She chose Merinos for their fine, soft fleece and legendary status as supplier of the "Golden Fleece" to Jason and the Argo. "It's a wonderful experience to understand each step along the way," she says, "to make the yarn and then the finished project that will be a lifetime treasure."

Kathy is the consummate sheperdess, having tended at one time more than 400 sheep; she has also learned to shear and grade. She keeps alpacas as well, and has traveled to South America to acquire stock and learn about these exotic little creatures. Every Friday, her shop offers its own learning experiences: classes in knitting (by hand and machine), spinning, crocheting, dyeing, button and soap making, and felting. And a couple of times a year, workshops feature some of the most sought-after teachers and designers in the world of fiber.

HANEKE WOOL FASHIONS

630 NORTH BLACK CAT ROAD
MERIDIAN, ID 83642
PHONE: (208)888-3129
FAX: (208)888-2776
WEBSITE: WWW.HANEKEWOOLFASHIONS.COM
E-MAIL: KATHYHANEKE@MSN.COM

HEAVENLY CAMISOLE AND SCARF

Designer Lucky Doan came to the United States from Vietnam when she was twenty-three, bringing six younger siblings with her. She learned to knit when she was seven, and has never really stopped. Because yarn was so scarce in Vietnam, Lucky would wear a sweater for three or four months, then rip it out to create a new design. Now, with Haneke's abundance of lovely, soft yarns, she can let her talents soar. She has created two versions of this soft, light-weight alpaca camisole, one with narrow straps and one with wide. A narrow scarf in the same lacy pattern can be used for sampling.

FINISHED SIZE
Camisole: 34–36(38–40) (86.5/91.5 [96.5/101.5] cm) chest/bust circumference. Scarf: 5" (12.5 cm) wide and 40" (101.5 cm) long.

YARN
Haneke Heaven Sent (70% baby Royal alpaca, 30% wool; 200 yd [183 m]/50 g): Version I: 5 (6) balls, Version II: 4 (5) balls. Shown in natural white and denim.

NEEDLES
Size 3 (3.25 mm): 24" (60-cm) circular (cir). Adjust needle size if necessary to obtain the correct gauge.

NOTIONS
Stitch holders; markers (m); tapestry needle; size C/2 (2.75 mm) crochet hook.

GAUGE
32 sts and 40 rows = 4" (10 cm) in leaf pattern, unstretched; 32 sts and 40 rows = 4" (10 cm) in stockinette stitch, unblocked.

Note Versions I and II are worked the same up to armholes. The back neck is lower in Version II. Refer to separate instructions for the version you are making.

Stitches
Leaf Pattern (worked in the round):
(multiple of 15 sts + 1)
Rnd 1: (RS) *K1, yo, k1, ssk, p1, k2tog, k1, yo, p1, ssk, p1, k2tog, yo, k1, yo; rep from *, end k1.
Rnd 2: *K4, p1, k3, p1, k1, p1, k4; rep from *, end k1.
Rnd 3; *K1, yo, k1, ssk, p1, k2tog, k1, p1, sl 1, k2tog, psso, yo, k3, yo; rep from *, end k1.
Rnd 4: *K4, p1, k2, p1, k6; rep from *, end k1.
Rnd 5: *[K1, yo] 2 times, ssk, p1, [k2tog] 2 times, yo, k5, yo; rep from *, end k1.
Rnd 6: *K5, p1, k1, p1, k7; rep from *, end k1.
Rnd 7: *K1, yo, k3, yo, sl 1, k2tog, psso, p1, yo, k1, ssk, p1, k2tog, k1, yo; rep from *, end k1.
Rnd 8: *K7, [p1, k3] 2 times; rep from *, end k1.
Rnd 9: *K1, yo, k5, yo, ssk, k1, ssk, p1, k2tog, k1, yo; rep from *, end k1.
Rnd 10: *K8, p1, k2, p1, k3; rep from *, end k1.
Repeat Rows 1–10 for pattern.

Leaf Pattern (worked back and forth):
(multiple of 15 sts + 1)
Row 1: (RS) *K1, yo, k1, ssk, p1, k2tog, k1, yo, p1, ssk, p1, k2tog, yo, k1, yo; rep from *, end k1.
Row 2: P1, *p4, k1, p1, k1, p3, k1, p4; rep from *.
Row 3: *K1, yo, k1, ssk, p1, k2tog, k1, p1, sl 1, k2tog, psso, yo, k3, yo; rep from *, end k1.
Row 4: P1, * p6, k1, p2, k1, p4; rep from *.
Row 5: *[K1, yo] 2 times, ssk, p1, [k2tog] 2 times, yo, k5, yo; rep from *, end k1.
Row 6: P1, *p7, k1, p1, k1, p5; rep from *.
Row 7: *K1, yo, k3, yo, sl 1, k2tog, psso, p1, yo, k1, ssk, p1, k2tog, k1, yo; rep from *, end k1.
Row 8: P1, *[p3, k1] 2 times, p7; rep from *.
Row 9: *K1, yo, k5, yo, ssk, k1, ssk, p1, k2tog, k1, yo; rep from *, end k1.
Row 10: P1, *p3, k1, p2, k1, p8; rep from *.
Repeat Rows 1–10 for pattern.

Crocheted Picot Edging:
1 Sc (see Glossary), *3ch, slip st into 3rd ch from hook, sk 1 st or equivalent interval, 1 sc into next stitch; rep from*.

CAMISOLE, VERSION I
Body
CO 270 (300) sts. Place m (pm) and join, being careful not to twist sts. Sl m each rnd. Work 1 rnd St st. Beg with Row 1, work leaf pattern across 136 (151) sts for front (9 [10] leaf patt multiples), pm, work 134 (149) sts in St st for back. Work even in established patt until a total of 14 (15) 10-row leaf patt repeats have been worked, ending with Row 10—piece should measure about 14 (15)" (35.5 [38] cm) from beg. Place 134 (149) back sts onto a holder. From here on, work back and forth in

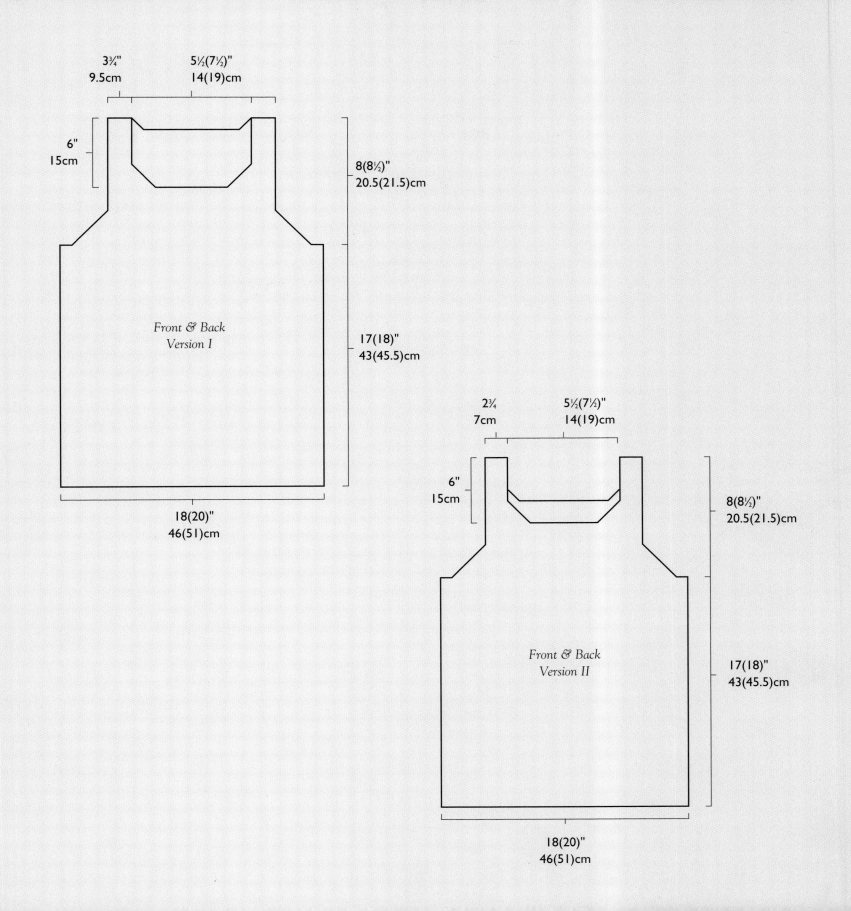

3¾"
9.5cm

5½(7½)"
14(19)cm

6"
15cm

8(8½)"
20.5(21.5)cm

Front & Back
Version I

17(18)"
43(45.5)cm

18(20)"
46(51)cm

2¾
7cm

5½(7½)"
14(19)cm

6"
15cm

8(8½)"
20.5(21.5)cm

Front & Back
Version II

17(18)"
43(45.5)cm

18(20)"
46(51)cm

BINDING OFF

When binding off stitches using the Three-Needle Bind-Off (see Glossary), purl the stitches together instead of knitting them together for a flatter seam.

Kathy's Kreations

SHOULDERS

Knit shoulders together whenever possible. I love using the technique of binding off shoulder stitches together (see Glossary, Three-Needle Bind-Off). It ensures an even, clean "seam" and makes finishing work that much easier. The method is most commonly used in drop-shoulder designs, but can also be used in shaped shoulders if short rows are substituted for a stepped bind-off.

Over the Moon

rows. **Front:** Working 136 (151) front sts only, cont as foll: *Shape armholes:* Cont in patt, BO 7 sts at beg of next 2 rows, then BO 3 sts at beg of foll 4 rows, then BO 2 sts at beg of foll 2 rows—106 (121) sts rem. Dec 1 st each end of needle every other row 5 times—96 (111) sts rem. Work even in patt a total of 16 (17) 10-row leaf patt repeats have been worked, ending with Row 10—armholes should measure about 2" (5 cm). *Shape neck:* (RS) Cont in patt, work 40 sts, join new yarn and BO center 16 (31) sts, work to end. Working each side separately, at neck edge BO 4 sts once, then BO 3 sts twice, then BO 2 sts once—28 sts rem each side. Cont even in patt until a total of 21 (21½) 10-row leaf patt repeats have been worked, ending with Row 10 (5)—piece should measure about 21 (21½)" (53.5 [54.5] cm) from beg. Place sts on holder. **Back:** Place 134 (149) held back sts on needle. With RS facing, join yarn and cont in St st as foll: *Shape armholes:* BO 4 sts at beg of next 4 rows, then BO 3 sts at beg of next 4 rows, then BO 2 sts at beg of next 2 rows—102 (117) sts rem. Dec 1 st each end of needle every other row 4 times—94 (109) sts rem. Work even for 62 (67) more rows, or until armholes measure about 6¼ (6¾)" (16 [17]

cm), ending with WS row. *Shape neck:* (RS) K35, join new yarn and BO center 24 (39) sts, knit to end. Working each side separately, at neck edge BO 3 sts once, then BO 2 sts once—30 sts rem each side. Dec 1 st at neck edge every other row 2 times—28 sts rem each side. Place sts on holder.

Finishing

Using the three-needle bind-off (see Glossary), join front to back at shoulders. Steam-block lightly to measurements, allow to dry completely. *Edging:* With RS facing and crochet hook, join yarn to lower edge of sweater. Work 1 row single crochet (sc; see Glossary) evenly around sweater. Work 1 row picot edging on top of sc, skipping 1 st now and then to prevent edge from flaring. Repeat for armhole and neck edges. Weave in loose ends.

CAMISOLE VERSION II

Body

Work same as Version I to armhole. Place back 134 (149) sts on holder. From here on, work back and forth in rows. **Front:** Working 136 (151) front sts only, cont as foll: *Shape armholes:* (RS) BO 7 sts at beg of next 2 rows, then BO 5 sts at beg of foll 2 rows, then BO 3 sts at beg of foll 4 rows,

then BO 2 sts at beg of foll 4 rows—92 (107) sts rem. Dec 1 st each end of needle every other row 6 times—80 (95) sts rem. Work even in patt until a total of 16 (17) 10-row leaf patt repeats have been worked, ending with Row 10—armholes should measure about 2" (5 cm). *Shape neck:* (RS) Work 34 sts in leaf patt, join new yarn and BO center 12 (27) sts, work to end. Working each side separately, BO 5 sts once, then BO 4 sts once, then BO 3 sts once, then BO 2 sts once—20 sts rem each side. Work in patt for a total of 21 (21½) leaf patt reps from CO edge, ending with Row 10 (5)—70 (75) rows total; piece should measure about 21 (21½)" (53.5 [54.5] cm) from beg. Place sts on holder. *Back:* Place 134 (149) held back sts on needle. *Shape armholes:* With RS facing, join yarn and cont in St st as foll: BO 5 sts at beg of next 2 rows, then BO 4 sts at beg of foll 4 rows, then BO 3 sts at beg of foll 4 rows, then BO 2 sts at beg of foll 4 rows—88 (103) sts rem. Dec 1 st at each end of needle every other row 5 times—78 (93) sts rem; armholes should measure about 2" (5 cm). *Shape neck:* (RS) K34, join new yarn and BO center 10 (25) sts, knit to end. Work-

ing each side separately, at neck edge BO 5 sts once, then BO 4 sts once, then BO 3 sts once, then BO 2 sts once—20 sts rem each side. Work even for 50 (55) rows or until armholes measure 7 (7½)" (18 [19] cm), ending with a WS row. Place sts on holders.

Finishing
Finish as for Version I.

Scarf

CO 35 sts. Purl 1 row. *Next row:* (RS) Sl 1 kwise tbl, k1, work Row 1 of leaf pattern to last 2 sts, k2. To maintain double garter-st selvedges, cont to work the first 2 and last 2 sts of each row as above, and work center 31 sts in leaf patt. Work even in patt until 32 ten-row leaf patt repeats have been worked, ending with Row 10 of patt—piece should measure about 32" (81.5 cm) from beg. Knit 1 row. BO off all sts.

Finishing
Work picot edging as for camisoles at each end of scarf. Weave in loose ends. Steam-block lightly to measurements.

PINE TREE YARNS • Elaine Eskesen has always had an artistic flair, but it was her children's paintings that first inspired her to combine colors in new and different ways in the yarns she hand-dyes in her shop. The path to owning a yarn shop and creating custom-dyed yarns had many twists and turns, from living on a Greek island to a farm in Maine to giving up a career in counseling to stay home with her four children to designing knitwear for a Madison Avenue boutique. Not happy with the range of colors she found in commercial yarn for these pieces, Elaine began to dye her own in the summer kitchen of the farm.

At first, Elaine used all her yarns to knit her own pieces; the business grew from there to a full-service shop full of natural fibers, many hand-dyed and -painted, in a historic house in downtown Damariscotta. Color inspiration for Pine Tree's yarns comes from daily walks in the woods and an abundance of Maine wildflowers that fill the shop's courtyard in summer. "I love every single skein that I have ever made," Elaine says.

Pine Tree Yarn's dye studio is set up for visitors to see solar dyeing, hand-painting on wool, or space-dyeing. Elaine teaches workshops in her store and around the country.

PINE TREE YARNS

74 MAIN STREET
DAMARISCOTTA, ME 04543
PHONE: (207) 563-8909
WEBSITE: WWW. PINETREEYARNS.COM
E-MAIL: ELAINE@PINETREEYARNS.COM

PENELOPE'S PILLOWS

Ingenious construction and frequently changing colors make these easy pillows lots of fun to knit. The ruffled stripes are deceptively simple, created with increases and decreases and two sizes of needles used alternately.

FINISHED SIZE

16" (40.5 cm) square.

YARN

Pine Tree Yarns Rainbow-Dyed sport weight (100% wool; 350 yd [320m]/ 100 g): wild berries (A),1 skein. Pine Tree Yarns Watercolor Wool worsted weight (100% wool; 250 yd [228m]/100 g): 1 skein each of 3 colors (Pillow 1: pines by the sea, autumn sunset, and maple leaf; Pillow 2: pines by the sea, tidal pool, and autumn sunset).

NEEDLES

Flat stripes—Size 7 (4.5 mm): 14" (35-cm) straight. Gathered Stripes—Size 9 (5.5 mm): 14" (35-cm) straight or 24" (60-cm) circular. Adjust needle sizes if necessary to obtain the correct gauge.

NOTIONS

Tapestry needle; ten ½" (1.3-cm) buttons for each pillow; 16" (40.5-cm) square pillow form for each pillow.

GAUGE

18 sts and 22 rows = 4" (10 cm) in stockinette stitch on larger needles, using worsted weight yarn.

PENELOPE'S PILLOWS
Elaine Eskesen

Pillow Front

Flat Stripe: With A and smaller needles, CO 72 sts. Work garter st (knit every row) for 6 rows (3 ridges). *Inc row:* K1f&b in each st—144 sts. *Gathered Stripe:* Change color (your choice) and with larger needles, work St st for 6 rows, ending with a WS row. *Dec row:* (RS) With A and smaller needles, *k2tog; rep from *—72 sts rem. This will be the first row of the second flat stripe. Cont to alternate flat and gathered stripes, carrying A along edge of work, and changing to smaller needles for flat stripes and larger needles for gathered. When 10 gathered stripes have been completed, work final flat stripe with A and smaller needles. BO off all sts.

Pillow Back

With A and smaller needles, CO 72 sts.

Work 6 rows garter st. Change to larger needles and without inc or dec, work a 6-row flat stripe to match the color selected on the front. Cont to change needle size while working garter st and St st stripes in same color sequence as for front, ending with 6 rows of A. BO all sts.

Finishing

With yarn threaded on a tapestry needle, sew front to back along 3 sides, matching color stripes, and allowing a bit of the gathered stripe to hang over the edge to create an attractive little ruffle. Insert pillow form and sew remaining seam. Along one side, sew a button to the center of each ruffle to give the appearance of a buttoned opening.

COUNTRYWOOL • Located in the scenic Hudson Valley between the Berkshire and Catskill Mountains, Countrywool provides a perfect, wooded, out-of-the-way setting for a knitting and spinning shop that also is home to fluffy long-haired angora bunnies. Owner Claudia Krisniski, who started the business in the 1980s, has made sure that the shop has stuck to its original mission of promoting natural fibers as a renewable resource. Today the shop boasts more than forty lines of yarn for knitters, crocheters, and weavers, and fifteen different kinds of wool, mohair, angora, alpaca, llama, and silk fibers for spinning. Many of the fibers come from local sources. And in the airy bunny barns, a lot of fiber is hopping around!

Visitors are greeted by a rustic carved wooden sign; inside, wooden shelves and baskets display an abundance of yarn and unspun fibers. Lots of knitting supplies and accessories, spinning wheels, handspindles, and other spinning tools add to the homey feel. The shop offers classes and workshops in knitting and spinning, as well as instruction on raising and caring for angora bunnies. For those looking for a getaway fiber weekend in the country, a cozy cottage is available for rent.

Countrywool hosts a charity knitting group (The Neighborhood Knitters) that knits for Children in Common, an international adoption agency, and another group, The Neighborhood Spinners, meets at the shop monthly. In addition to reaching out to the local community, Claudia enjoys the chatty cyber-community of thousands of knitters on fiber lists as well as those who visit Countrywool's website where she offers a sampling of her special blend of savvy country know-how about fiber, knitting, and angora.

COUNTRYWOOL

59 SPRING ROAD
HUDSON, NY 12534
PHONE: (518) 828-4554
WEBSITE: COUNTRYWOOL.COM
E-MAIL: COUNTRYWOOL@BERK.COM

ANGORA FURRED TEDDY HOOD

Luxurious fibers make this easy, snuggly hood a pleasure to knit. Designer Claudia Krisniski reports that when she was first learning to spin and had only one rabbit, twenty yards of angora yarn was a lot. She created this hood because it beautifully shows off just a little bit of fiber. It was one of the first patterns that Claudia designed for her shop and she displayed it on a huge teddy bear—thus its name.

67

ANGORA FURRED TEDDY HOOD
Claudia Krisniski

Note The angora yarn used in this pattern is available through Countrywool, or you can substitute 2 strands (knit together) of worsted weight (1000 yd/lb) or 1 strand of bulky (500 yd/lb) brushed mohair (such as La Gran from Classic Elite).

If you'd like to spin your own angora yarn, use premium angora with at least a 4" (10 cm) staple for maximum fluff. Spin thickly with low twist and ply 2 strands for strength. The 20 yards needed for this pattern can be quickly spun with a handspindle. It requires just ½ ounce of plucked angora, which is available from Countrywool.

Hood: With MC, loosely CO 110 sts. Place marker (pm) and join, being careful not to twist sts. Work k1, p1 ribbing for 4 rnds. Join CC and cont in rib for 6 rnds. Change to MC and cont in rib until piece measures 21" (53.5 cm), or until 6 yd (5.5 m) of MC rem. Loosely BO all sts kwise. Weave in loose ends. Hand wash and dry flat. To maximize fluffiness, toss *dry* hood in hot dryer for 5 minutes.

SPINNING ON A HANDSPINDLE

What you need: A handspindle, a length of commercially spun plied yarn for leader, wool roving to practice with.

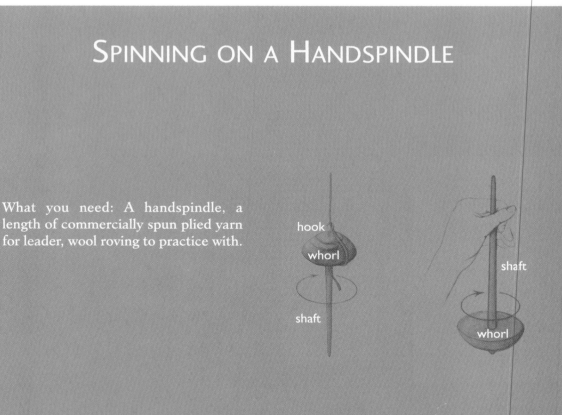

Attaching the Leader
Cut 2-3 yards of plied commercial yarn and fold in half. Thread both yarn ends through the fold, making a loop, and slip it over the whorl onto the shaft, pull both ends tightly to close loop. Place the leader ends to the right of the hook on the whorl and turn the shaft clockwise, securing the leader under the hook.

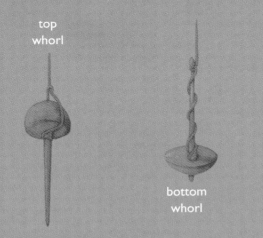

top
whorl

bottom
whorl

Spin the yarn
Hold a small amount of fiber in one hand, and using the forefinger and thumb of the other hand, gently pull out a few fibers for an inch or two. With the thumb and forefinger, twist a few fibers around the leader ends to secure. Quickly roll the shaft up the outside of your right thigh and release it. Keeping the shaft upright, allow the spindle to drop and spin so that the fibers you've pulled out begin to twist into yarn. Check the yarn for strength. Holding one end in each hand, tug gently. If the yarn breaks, it doesn't have enough twist; if it kinks tightly, you may have too much twist. Learning how much twist is enough will come with practice. Continue pulling out more fibers and spinning until the spindle reaches the ground.

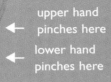

← upper hand
pinches here

← lower hand
pinches here

Winding on: With the spindle in one hand and the yarn in the other, release the leader from the hook. Turn the spindle shaft, winding on the new yarn directly above the whorl. Leave a few yards to thread through the hook and begin spinning again. When the spindle is full, remove the spun yarn by winding it from the spindle onto a tennis ball or a small ball of waste yarn. If you plan to make a plied yarn, divide the yarn into two balls.

Plying: Take one end from each ball and attach to the leader as before. Roll the shaft quickly *down* the right thigh, the opposite direction from when you were spinning. The plying process is much the same as spinning, but twists in the opposite direction. Wind on as before, and as the spindle fills, wind off into a ball or start a skein.

Making a skein: When your yarn gets long, you need to wind on. To keep the strand from tangling while you wind on, catch it behind your elbow. Release the end nearest the spindle and wind the yarn around the spindle shaft.

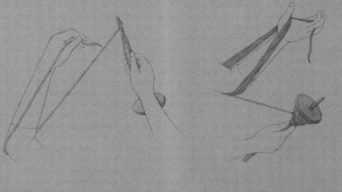

Wash skein in warm water with a little dish detergent, and hang to dry. Wind the yarn into a center-pull ball and it's ready for knitting.

RUMPELSTILTSKIN • It was the early 1970s, and Linda Urquhart had just graduated with a design degree from the University of California at Davis. A course in weaving inspired her to open a shop devoted to her newfound and "happening" hobby. Working on a shoestring budget, she moved, along with some other arty alternative businesses, into a brick building near the state capitol where the shop still operates today. While the vibrant hippy fiber scene of thirty years ago has faded, Rumpelstiltskin continues to be a guiding light in the Northern California craft world.

In response to exciting new knitwear designers and yarn lines, Linda, a longtime knitter like her mother, began to shift the shop's emphasis from weaving and spinning toward knitting in the mid-1980s. Today, the store is crammed to the ceiling with yarn, books, patterns, and bright Guatemalan handwoven fabrics. Linda says she has stayed in the business for so long because the "knitting industry has nice customers who are fun people to get to know."

A favorite shop tradition is Rumpelstiltskin's Show Your Hand open house, held every first Sunday in February for the past fifteen years, where customers wear the items they have knitted, crocheted, or woven during the past year. The store supplies cookies, wine, punch, and a discount on purchases while fiber enthusiasts admire each other's creations and share ideas and inspiration.

RUMPELSTILTSKIN

1021 R Street
Sacramento, CA 95814
Phone: (916) 442-9225
E-mail: lurumpel@home.com

TODDLER JACKET

This cozy jacket is so quick and easy, even a beginner can finish it in a weekend. Designed by Linda Urquhart, it's a hit with toddlers because it is roomy, lightweight, and soft. Here it is shown in a cheerful multi-colored chenille tape, but it can be knitted in any super-chunky yarn or with a double strand of worsted-weight. Interesting buttons jazz it up.

Sleeve

10⅞(12⅔, 13¼)"
27.5(32.5, 33.5)cm

9(9½, 10½)"
23(24, 26.5)cm

6(6⅔, 7¼)"
15.25(17, 18.5)cm

RUMPELSTILTSKIN'S TODDLER'S JACKET
Linda Urquhart

FINISHED SIZE
29 (31, 33)" (74 [79, 84] cm) chest circumference, buttoned. Oversize fit for about 2 (4, 6) years.

YARN
The Drop Spindle Chenille Tape (100% cotton; 160 yd [146 m]/12 oz): autumn leaves, 1 (2, 2) skeins. (You can substitute any worsted-weight yarn, used double.)

NEEDLES
Size 13 (9 mm). Adjust needle size if necessary to obtain the correct gauge.

NOTIONS
Tapestry needle; three or four ⅝" (1.5-cm) buttons.

GAUGE
6¾ sts and 9 rows = 4" (10 cm) in stockinette stitch.

Seed Stitch:
(worked on an even number of sts)
Row 1: (RS) *K1, p1; rep from *.
Row 2: *P1, k1; rep from *.
Repeat Rows 1 and 2 for pattern.

(worked on an odd number of sts)
Row 1: (RS) *K1, p1; rep from *, end k1.
Row 2: K1, *p1, k1; rep from *.
Repeat rows 1 and 2 for pattern.

Back
Loosely CO 24 (26, 27) sts. Work seed st for 2 rows. Work St st until piece measures 12 (14, 16½)" (30.5 [35.5, 42] cm) from beg. Loosely BO all sts.

Right Front
Loosely CO 12 (13, 14) sts. Work seed st for 2 rows. *Set up for front band:*
Row 1: K10 (11, 12), p1, k1.

Row 2: K1, p1, p10 (11, 12).
Rep Rows 1 and 2 until piece measures 9 (11, 13)" (23 [28, 33] cm) from beg, ending with a WS row. *Shape neck:* At beg of next row loosely BO 6 (7, 7) sts—6 (6, 7) sts rem. Cont in St st until piece measures 12 (14, 16½)" (30.5 [35.5, 42] cm) from beg. Loosely BO all sts.

Left Front
Loosely CO 12 (13, 14) sts. Work seed st for 2 rows. *Set up for front band:*
Row 1: K1, p1, k10 (11, 12).
Row 2: P10 (11, 12), p1, k1.
Rep Rows 1 and 2 until piece measures 9 (11, 13)" (23 [28, 33] cm) from beg, ending with a RS row. *Shape neck:* At beg of next row loosely BO 6 (7, 7) sts—6 (6, 7) sts rem. Cont in St st until piece measures 12 (14, 16½)" (30.5 [35.5, 42] cm) from beg. Loosely BO all sts.

Sleeves

Loosely CO 10 (11, 12) sts. Work seed st for 2 rows. Change to St st, inc 1 st on each end of needle on next row, then every 4 (3, 3) rows 3 (4, 4) times—18 (21, 22) sts. Work even until piece measures 9 (9½, 10½)" (23 [24, 26.5] cm) from beg, or desired total length. Loosely BO all sts.

Finishing

With yarn threaded on a tapestry needle, join fronts to back at shoulders. *Collar:* With RS facing and beg at right front neck, pick up and knit 6 (6, 7) sts along right front neck edge, 11 (12, 12) sts along back neck edge, and 6 (6, 7) sts along left front neck edge—23 (24, 26) sts total. Work 4 rows seed st. Loosely BO all sts. Sew sleeves into armholes. Sew side and sleeve seams. Weave in loose ends. Sew 3 (4, 4) buttons evenly spaced on right front band. *Note:* The stitches are large enough to accommodate the buttons; there's no need to make buttonholes.

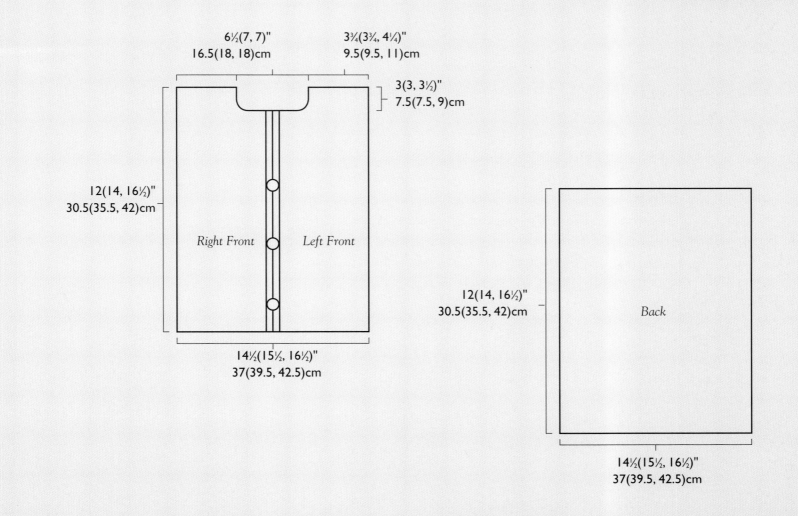

6½(7, 7)"
16.5(18, 18)cm

3¾(3¾, 4¼)"
9.5(9.5, 11)cm

3(3, 3½)"
7.5(7.5, 9)cm

12(14, 16½)"
30.5(35.5, 42)cm

Right Front   *Left Front*

14½(15½, 16½)"
37(39.5, 42.5)cm

12(14, 16½)"
30.5(35.5, 42)cm

Back

14½(15½, 16½)"
37(39.5, 42.5)cm

THE YARNERY • A quaint old house with odd doorways and a built-in buffet is home to The Yarnery, a lively old-timer on the St. Paul craft scene. Located in the trendy Victoria Crossing area just west of downtown, The Yarnery is surrounded by great restaurants, a children's bookstore, boutiques, and coffee shops—a perfect destination neighborhood.

Customers are likely to find the bustle and activity of a room full of beginners, or advanced knitters engrossed in constructing intricate Norwegian sweaters. The Yarnery has classes almost every night and weekend day. A big surge in interest among their college-age customers has prompted the shop to offer continuous classes for beginners, and older people who used to knit are coming back to the craft after decades—sometimes to finish projects they started twenty years ago.

The Yarnery offers a wide variety of yarns, mostly natural fibers, and co-managers Theresa Gaffey and Lynn VanderHaar have been adding high-end yarns that their customers appreciate. Open seven days a week, the shop is staffed mostly by enthusiastic part-time employees who all love yarn, love knitting, and tend to have other jobs outside The Yarnery to help support their knitting habit. In fact, one employee is a doctor!

THE YARNERY

840 GRAND AVENUE
ST. PAUL, MN 55105
PHONE: (651) 222-5793

EIGHT LINEN WASHCLOTHS

Theresa Gaffey likes to knit with a project in mind, so when she found herself with a stack of linen test swatches in one hand and a bar of homemade soap in the other, the swatches were magically transformed into washcloths. The sheen and drape of linen is appealing, the washcloths make good portable projects, and with the yarn used here, you can get two cloths from one skein. Knitting them is practically addictive.

(left to right: lacy vine, feather and fan, basket weave, tile stitch, garter ridge, dragon scales)

YARN

Louet Euroflax Linen Yarn (100% linen; 325 yd [298 m]/114 g): ½ skein for each washcloth. Shown in #18.50 sage, #18.35 mustard, #18.47 terra cotta, #18.52 grape, #18.09 lavender, and #18.15 neptune.

NOTIONS

Tapestry needle.

NOTE Euroflax Linen Yarn is machine-washable, and softens with every washing.

EIGHT LINEN WASHCLOTHS
Theresa Gaffey

BASKET WEAVE WASHCLOTH

FINISHED SIZE
11" (28 cm) square.

YARN COLOR
#18.50 sage.

NEEDLES
Size 4 (3.5 mm). Adjust needle size if necessary to obtain the correct gauge.

GAUGE
23 sts and 38 rows = 4" (10 cm) in basket weave pattern.

CO 63 sts. Knit 6 rows. Change to basket weave patt as foll:

Rows 1, 3, and 5: (WS) K6, *p6, k3; rep from * to last 3 sts, k3.
Rows 2, 4, and 6: K3, p3, *k6, p3; rep from * to last 3 sts, k3.
Rows 7 and 9: K3, p3, *k6, p3; rep from * to last 3 sts, k3.
Rows 8 and 10: K6, *p6, k3; rep from * to last 3 sts, k3.
Work Rows 1–10 ten times more, then work Rows 1–6 once, or until piece measures 10½" (26.5 cm) from beg. Knit 6 rows. BO all sts. With yarn threaded on a tapestry needle, weave in loose ends.

DRAGON SCALES WASHCLOTH

CO 71 sts. Knit 6 rows. Change to dragon scales patt as foll:

Row 1: K4, M1, ssk, k4, k2tog, k3, M1, k1, *k1, M1, k3, ssk, k4, k2tog, M1, k2, M1, ssk, k4, k2tog, k3, M1, k1; rep from * once, k3.
Row 2 and all even-numbered rows: K3, purl to last 3 sts, k3.
Row 3: K4, M1, k1, ssk, k2, k2tog, k4, M1, k1, *k1, M1, k4, ssk, k2, k2tog, k1, M1, k2, M1, k1, ssk, k2, k2tog, k4, M1, k1; rep from * once, k3.
Row 5: K4, M1, k2, ssk, k2tog, k5, M1, k1, *k1, M1, k5, ssk, k2tog, k2, M1, k2,

FINISHED SIZE
10½" (26.5 cm) square.

YARN COLOR
#18.35 mustard.

NEEDLES
Size 4 (3.5 mm). Adjust needle size if necessary to obtain the correct gauge.

GAUGE
26 sts and 42 rows = 4" (10 cm) in dragon scales pattern.

M1, k2, ssk, k2tog, k5, M1, k1; rep from * once, k3.

Row 7: K4, M1, k3, ssk, k4, k2tog, M1, k1, *k1, M1, ssk, k4, k2tog, k3, M1, k2, M1, k3, ssk, k4, k2tog, M1, k1; rep from * once, k3.

Row 9: K4, M1, k4, ssk, k2, k2tog, k1, M1, k1, *k1, M1, k1, ssk, k2, k2tog, k4, M1, k2, M1, k4, ssk, k2, k2tog, k1, M1, k1; rep from * once, k3.

Row 11: K4, M1, k5, ssk, k2tog, k2, M1, k1, *k1, M1, k2, ssk, k2tog, k5, M1, k2, M1, k5, ssk, k2tog, k2, M1, k1; rep from * once, k3.

Rep Rows 1–12 until piece measures 10" (25.5 cm) from beg. Knit 6 rows. BO all sts. With yarn threaded on a tapestry needle, weave in loose ends.

FEATHER AND FAN WASHCLOTH

FINISHED SIZE
11" (28 cm) wide and 13" (33 cm) long.

YARN COLOR
#18.47 terra cotta.

NEEDLES
Size 3 (3.25 mm). Adjust needle size if necessary to obtain the correct gauge.

GAUGE
28 sts and 30 rows = 4" (10 cm) in feather and fan pattern.

CO 78 sts. Knit 6 rows. Change to feather and fan patt as foll:

Row 1: Knit.
Row 2: K3, purl to last 3 sts, K3.
Row 3: K3, [k2tog] 3 times, *[yo, k1] 6 times, [k2tog] 6 times; rep from * 2 more times, [yo, k1] 6 times, [k2tog] 3 times, k3.

Row 4: Knit.
Repeat Rows 1–4 a total of 21 more times. Knit 6 rows. BO all sts. With yarn threaded on a tapestry needle, weave in loose ends.

GARTER RIDGE WASHCLOTH

FINISHED SIZE
11" (28 cm) square.

YARN COLOR
#18.52 grape.

NEEDLES
Size 4 (3.5 mm). Adjust needle size if necessary to obtain the correct gauge.

GAUGE
21 sts and 32 rows = 4" (10 cm) in garter ridge pattern.

CO 62 sts. Knit 6 rows. Change to garter ridge patt as foll:

Rows 1, 3, and 4: Knit.
Row 2: K3, purl to last 3 sts, k3.
Rep Rows 1–4 until piece measures 10½" (26.5 cm) from beg. Knit 6 rows. BO all sts. With yarn threaded on a tapestry needle, weave in loose ends.

HORSESHOE LACE WASHCLOTH

CO 67 sts. Knit 6 rows. Change to horseshoe lace patt as foll:

Row 1: K4, *yo, k3, sl 1, k2tog, psso, k3, yo, k1; rep from* to last 3 sts, k3.
Rows 2, 4, 6, and 8: K3, purl to last 3 sts, k3.
Row 3: K4, *k1, yo, k2, sl 1, k2tog, psso, k2, yo, k2; rep from * to last 3 sts, k3.
Row 5: K4, *k2, yo, k1, sl 1, k2tog, psso, k1, yo, k3; rep from * to last 3 sts, k3.

FINISHED SIZE
10½" (26.5 cm) square.

YARN COLOR
#18.52 grape.

NEEDLES
Size 4 (3.5mm). Adjust needle size if necessary to obtain the correct gauge.

GAUGE
26 sts and 32 rows = 4" (10 cm) in horse-shoe lace pattern.

Row 7: K4, *k3, yo, sl 1, k2tog, psso, yo, k4; rep from * to last 3 sts, k3.
Rep Rows 1–8 rows a total of 10 more times, or until piece measures 10" (25.5 cm) from beg. Knit 6 rows. BO all sts. With yarn threaded on a tapestry needle, weave in loose ends.

LACY VINE WASHCLOTH

FINISHED SIZE
11½" (29 cm) square.

YARN COLOR
#18.09 lavender.

NEEDLES
Size 4 (3.5 mm). Adjust needle size if necessary to obtain the correct gauge.

GAUGE
22 sts and 34 rows = 4" (10 cm) in lacy vine pattern.

CO 62 sts. Knit 6 rows. Change to lacy vine patt as foll:
Row 1: (WS) Knit.
Row 2 and all even numbered rows: K3, purl to last 3 sts, k3.

Row 3: K3, *k2, k2tog, yo, k3; rep from * to last 3 sts, k3.

Row 5: K3, *k1, k2tog, yo, k4; rep from * to last 3 sts, k3.

Row 7: Knit.

Row 9: K3, *k3, yo, ssk, k2; rep from * to last 3 sts, k3.

Row 11: K3, *k4, yo, ssk, k1; rep from * to last 3 sts, k3.

Rep Rows 1–12 until piece measures 11" (28 cm) from beg. Knit 6 rows. BO all sts. With yarn threaded on a tapestry needle, weave in loose ends.

TILE STITCH WASHCLOTH

FINISHED SIZE
11" (28 cm) square.

YARN COLOR
#18.15 neptune.

NEEDLES
Size 4 (3.5 mm). Adjust needle size if necessary to obtain the correct gauge.

GAUGE
21 sts and 36 rows = 4" (10 cm) in tile stitch pattern.

CO 65 sts. Knit 6 rows. Change to tile stitch patt as foll:

Rows 1, 3, 5, and 7: Knit.

Rows 2, 4, and 6: K3, *p4, k1; rep from * to last 7 sts, p4, k3.

Row 8: Knit.

Rep Rows 1–8 until piece measures 10½" (26.5 cm) from beg. Knit 6 rows. BO all sts.

With yarn threaded on a tapestry needle, weave in loose ends.

SEED STITCH STRIPE WASHCLOTH

FINISHED SIZE
11" (28 cm) square.

YARN COLOR
#18.15 neptune.

NEEDLES
Size 4 (3.5 mm). Adjust needle size if necessary to obtain the correct gauge.

GAUGE
23 sts and 40 rows = 4" (10 cm) in seed stitch stripe pattern.

CO 65 sts. Knit 6 rows. Change to seed st stripe patt as foll:

Row 1: K3, *[p1, k1] 3 times, p1, [p1, k1] 3 times; rep from * to last 10 sts, [p1, k1] 3 times, p1, k3.

Row 2: K3, *[k1, p1] 6 times, k1; rep from * to last 10 sts, [k1, p1] 3 times, k4.

Row 3: K3, *[p1, k1] 6 times, p1; rep from * to last 10 sts, [p1, k1] 3 times, p1, k3.

Row 4: K3, *[k1, p1] 3 times, k1, [k1, p1] 3 times; rep from * to last 10 sts, [k1, p1] 3 times, k4.

Rep Rows 1–4 until piece measures 10½" (26.5 cm) from beg. Knit 6 rows. BO all sts. With yarn threaded on a tapestry needle, weave in loose ends.

(top to bottom: seed stitch stripe, horseshoe lace)

AMAZING YARNS • A sunny log cabin complete with a creek, two-story stone waterfall, stained glass windows, and balcony decks is home to Amazing Yarns, a West Coast fiber and textile boutique. Andrea Niehuis and her husband spent seven years adding on to the 1910 redwood lodge, bringing all the color and exciting activity of a busy yarn shop to the vintage structure. As knitters browse, they may catch a glimpse of a deer running by and Emerald Lake sparkling in the distance.

The shop specializes in exclusive hand-dyed yarns and carefully selected complementary yarns, as well as fleece, silk top, and mohair for handspinners. Classes are offered in knitting, crocheting, and weaving.

Andrea and her business partner, Ed Callender, both have eclectic backgrounds and boundless energy. Ed is a former nuclear engineer; besides his work at Amazing Yarns, he sells commercial real estate and dances—with a specialty in Argentine tango! Andrea taught elementary school for thirty-four years and also ran a catering business. She is currently in the shop four days a week and teaches the other three days. "I love the excitement and variety of two completely different careers," she says.

While both partners design knitwear, the shop's goal is to help its customers create their own designs. Their philosophy is that anyone can become a designer! Customers are encouraged to call ahead before visiting to make sure that the dynamic duo is in the shop. This practice allows the owners to pursue their other careers, do some designing, and have rich and creative lifestyles.

Recently the Amazing Yarns team began producing "Amazing Buttons"—one-of-a-kind accessories in glass, semi-precious stones, wood, or more surprising materials. Customers have been known to design a garment to complement a button they love.

AMAZING YARNS

2559 WOODLAND PLACE
EMERALD HILLS, CA 94062
PHONE: (650) 306-9218
E-MAIL: AMAZINGYARNS@IX.NETCOM.COM
WEBSITE: WWW.AMAZINGYARN@NETCOM.COM

FOG CHASER JACKET

Andrea Niehuis based the Fog Chaser Jacket on a design by her partner, Ed Callender, and it has become a favorite in their shop. It's all about versatility—it can go from work and errand-running to a dressy night out, and from chilly, foggy mornings to crisp, sunny afternoons. Best of all, it knits up on jumbo needles with multiple strands of yarn.

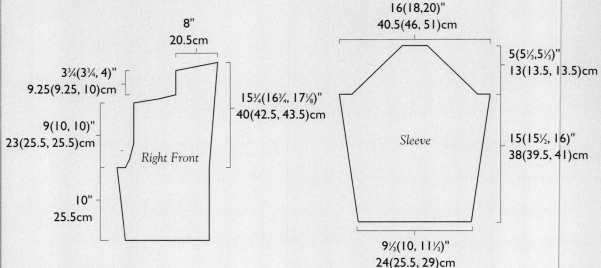

Right Front

Sleeve

16(18,20)"
40.5(46, 51)cm

5(5⅓,5⅓)"
13(13.5, 13.5)cm

15(15½, 16)"
38(39.5, 41)cm

9⅓(10, 11⅓)"
24(25.5, 29)cm

8"
20.5cm

3¾(3¾, 4)"
9.25(9.25, 10)cm

9(10, 10)"
23(25.5, 25.5)cm

15¾(16¾, 17⅛)"
40(42.5, 43.5)cm

10"
25.5cm

FINISHED SIZE

46 (51, 57)" (117 [129.5, 145] cm) bust/chest circumference, unbuttoned. Jacket shown measures 46" (117 cm).

YARN

Mountain Colors Merino Ribbon (80% Merino, 20% nylon; 245 yd [225 m]/4 oz) Ruby River, Mountain Colors Mohair (78% mohair, 13% wool, 9% nylon; 225 yd [205m]/4 oz) Ruby River, Mountain Colors 4/8 Wool (100% worsted-spun wool; 350 yd [320 m] /4 oz) Ruby River, Mountain Colors Wool Crepe (100% Merino; 1450 yd [1326m]/ 12oz), Ruby River, and Dale of Norway Kolibri (100% cotton; 114yd [105m]/50 g), New Wine, 575 (675, 775) yd (526 [618, 709] m) each.

NEEDLES

Size 19 (15 mm). Adjust needle size if necessary to obtain the correct gauge.

NOTIONS

Tapestry needle; size H/8 (4.75-mm) crochet hook; two, four, or six ⅞"(2.25cm) buttons (optional).

GAUGE

6 sts and 9 rows = 4" (10 cm) in seed stitch with one strand of each yarn held together.

FOG CHASER JACKET
Ed Callender and Andrea Niehuis

Seed Stitch:
(odd number of sts)
Row 1: *K1, p1; rep from *, end k1.
Row 2: *P1, k1; rep from *, end p1.
Rep Rows 1 and 2 for pattern.

Back
Holding 1 strand of each yarn tog, loosely CO 27 (31, 36) sts. Work seed st for 2 rows. Cont in seed st and *at the same time,* inc 1 st each end of needle every 3 rows 3 times—33 (37, 42) sts. Work even until piece measures 10" (25.5 cm) from beg, or desired length to armhole, ending with a WS row. *Shape armholes:* BO 3 (4, 5) sts at beg of next 2 rows—27 (29, 32) sts rem. Dec 1 st each end of needle every other row 3 times—21 (23, 26) sts rem. Work even until armholes measure 9 (10, 10)" (23 [25.5, 25.5] cm), ending with a WS row. *Shape shoulders:* BO 3 (3, 4) sts at beg of next 2 rows, then BO 2 (3, 3) sts at beg of foll 2 rows—11 (11, 12) sts rem. Loosely BO rem sts.

Right Front
Holding 1 strand of each yarn tog, loosely

CO 15 (17, 19) sts. Work seed st for 2 rows. Cont in seed st and *at the same time,* inc 1 st at side edge (end of RS rows; beg of WS rows) every 3 rows 3 times—18 (20, 22) sts. Work even until piece measures same as back to armhole ending with a RS row. *Shape armhole:* BO 3 (4, 5) sts at beg of row (armhole edge)—15 (16, 17) sts rem. Dec 1 st at armhole, edge every other row 3 times—12 (13, 14) sts rem. *Shape neck:* Beg collar same time as armhole shaping, work 1 row even. Inc 1 st at front edge (beg of RS rows; end of WS rows) on next row, then every third row 4 times more—17 (18, 19) sts. (For a wider shawl collar, inc 1 to 2 sts more and work all inc every other row.) Work even until armhole measures 9 (10, 10)" (23 [25.5, 25.5] cm), ending with a RS row. *Shape shoulder:* (WS) BO 3 (3, 4) sts at armhole edge once, then BO 2 (3, 3) sts at armhole edge once—12 sts rem. Work even in patt for 5 rows. *Back collar short rows:* *Beg at outside collar edge, work to last 4 sts. Turn, and work next row leaving 4 sts on needle unworked. Rep from *, working to last 8 sts, turn, and work next row. Work even in patt on all sts until collar meets neckline at center back. BO all sts.

Left Front
Work as for right front, reversing shaping by working armhole shaping at beg of RS rows and end of WS rows and working neck shaping at end of RS rows and beg of WS rows.

Sleeves
Holding 1 strand of each yarn tog, loosely CO 14 (15, 17) sts. Work seed st for 5 rows. Cont in patt, inc 1 st each end of needle every 4 rows 5 (6, 7) times—24 (27, 30) sts. Work even until piece measures 15 (15½, 16)" (38 [39.5, 41] cm) from beg, or desired length to underarm, allowing for sleeve to stretch about 1" (2.5 cm) due to weight and drape when worn. *Shape cap:* BO 3 (4, 5) sts at beg of next 2 rows—18 (19, 20) sts rem. Dec 1 st each end of needle every other row 3 times—12 (13, 14) sts rem. Work even for 11 (12, 12) rows or until sleeve cap depth measures 5 (5⅓, 5⅓)" (13 [13.5, 13.5] cm) from beg of cap shaping. BO all sts.

Finishing
With yarn threaded on a tapestry needle, sew shoulder seams. Sew sleeves into armholes. Sew shawl collar tog at center back and attach to neckline. Sew side and sleeve seams. *Optional edging:* With crochet hook, and 1 strand of chenille or ribbon, work single crochet (see Glossary) around entire edge of front, neckline, and collar. Work single crochet around lower edges of body and sleeves. Weave in loose ends. *Note:* Add 2, 4, or 6 buttons if desired. The stitch gauge is large enough to accommodate ⅞" (2.25-cm) buttons, so no buttonholes are needed.

SENSATIONAL SLEEVES

Make both sleeves at once. Not only will your sleeves be the same length, the gauge and shaping will also be consistent.

Green Mountain Spinnery

When using a back stitch to sew on sleeves, be sure to get under all of the bound-off stitch from the sleeve and under one complete stitch from the body of the sweater.

Northampton Wools

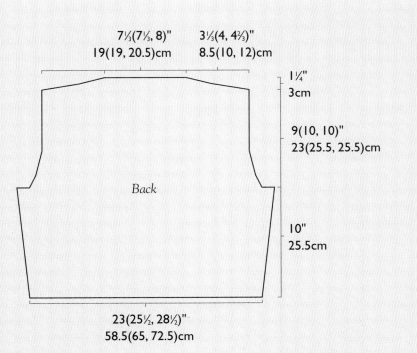

7⅓(7⅓, 8)"
19(19, 20.5)cm

3⅓(4, 4⅔)"
8.5(10, 12)cm

1¼"
3cm

9(10, 10)"
23(25.5, 25.5)cm

Back

10"
25.5cm

23(25½, 28½)"
58.5(65, 72.5)cm

IDLE HOURS NEEDLE ART • In a subtropical southwest Florida paradise of beautiful beaches and balmy weather, knitters tend to want quick and easy projects that travel easily to the beach or pool. Barbara Boulton and Vicki McEntaffer understand this well, and have filled their shop with bright, festive yarns in interesting textures, and patterns for sleeveless shells, vests, scarves, bags, caps, and other smaller items. Idle Hours Needle Art also offers hand-painted needlepoint canvases and cross-stitch charts in tropical themes—shells, birds, fish, and flowers—sometimes it's difficult for customers to decide whether they want to knit or stitch.

Barbara opened her shop originally on Sanibel Island in 1976. In 1997, she and Vicki moved the business to a larger space in Fort Myers. A prolific designer, Barbara has created hundreds of knitting patterns—many of which have evolved from customer requests—for Leisure Arts and for magazines and newspapers. Vicki grew up in Norway, and knitted intricate sweaters for Stein Erikson of Oslo. She currently focuses on beadwork and cross-stitch.

IDLE HOURS NEEDLE ART

8595 COLLEGE PARKWAY
FORT MYERS, FL 33919
PHONE: (941) 481-1947
WEBSITE: WWW.STITCHING.COM/IDLEHOURS
E-MAIL: IDLEHRS@AOL.COM

Magic Friends

This soft, furry yarn insisted on becoming a teddy bear—but not just any teddy bear—and then a cat, and then a bunny. Barbara Boulton's clever design is knitted as a seamless tube on just two straight needles, making it a magical project indeed, and one that invites many variations.

FINISHED SIZE
Each animal is about 12" (30.5 cm) tall.

YARN
Marks & Kattens Peluche (from Swedish Yarn Imports) (100% polyester; 71 yd [65 m]/ 50 g): 1 ball for each animal. Shown in #263 for Teddy; #1101 for Bunny; #253 for Kitty.

NEEDLES
Size 9 (5.5 mm): Straight and set of 2 double-pointed (dpn). Adjust needle size if necessary to obtain the correct gauge.

NOTIONS
Tapestry needle; about 2 oz fiberfill; ribbon to tie around necks of animals; black embroidery floss or yarn for eyes and nose on Teddy and Kitty and eyes on Bunny; several 1½–2" (3.8–5 cm) lengths of black sparkly thread for whiskers on Kitty; 2 yd (2 m) pink yarn for Bunny's ears and nose.

GAUGE
About 14 sts and 24 rows = 4" (10 cm) in k1, sl 1 pattern.

MAGIC FRIENDS
Barbara Boulton

Note All sl sts are slipped pwise. The bodies, arms, and legs are identical for all animals; separate instructions are given for specific features.

ALL ANIMALS
Legs: With straight needles, CO 16 sts.
Rows 1–36: *K1, sl 1; rep from *.
Cut off yarn, leaving a 4" (10-cm) tail. Push sts to back end of needle. With same needle, CO 16 sts again and rep for second leg—32 sts total. Do not cut yarn. *Body:* *K1, sl 1; rep from * across all 32 sts. Work 28 rows in established patt. *Arms:* Using the cable method (see Glossary), CO 20 sts at beg of row, then work as established across all 52 sts. CO 20 sts at beg of next row, then cont in patt across all 72 sts. Work 22 rows even in patt. *Head:* BO 22 sts beg of next row, work in patt to end—50 sts rem. On next row, BO 22 sts, work in patt to end—28 sts rem. Work 24 rows in patt.

TEDDY
Ears: CO 2 sts at beg of next 2 rows—32 sts. Work k1, sl 1 patt for 6 rows. *Work patt across first 10 sts only for 6 rows. *Next row:* [K2tog] 5 times—5 sts rem. BO 5 sts. Cut yarn leaving about 4" (10-cm) tail. Slide sts to opposite end of needle. Join yarn and rep from * for second ear.
Form top closing: Sl every other st onto one dpn (6 sts), then sl rem 6 sts to another dpn. Align dpn side by side with sts facing each other. Thread 12" (30.5-cm) yarn on a tapestry needle, sl needle through sts on first dpn, pull yarn halfway through, turn piece and sl needle through sts on second dpn, pull yarn through, sl 12 sts off needles.

KITTY
Knit 6 more rows in patt after the 24 head rows. *Ears:* *Work patt on first 8 sts only, leaving the other sts on the needle. After 8 rows, [k2tog] 4 times. *Next row:* [K2tog]

twice. *Next row:* K2tog, cut yarn and pull through last loop. Slide the sts to the opposite needle and tie on a new yarn; rep from *. Form top closing as for teddy. *Tail:* Leave about 4" (10 cm) of yarn, then CO 25 sts for tail, knit 2 rows. BO sts. Thread yarn tail on a tapestry needle and sew animal tail to body. Weave in rem yarn end. *Whiskers:* Thread tapestry needle with black sparkly yarn and attach to head as whiskers.

BUNNY

Rows 1–4: Work in established patt.
Row 5: K3tog, return st back to left needle—26 sts.

CO 19 sts—45 sts. *Next row:* K3tog, k17—18 sts on right needle, 25 sts on left needle. *First Ear:* *Working 18 sts on right needle only, turn work, k16, k2tog, turn, k18 (the 18th st is the first st on left needle), turn, with pink yarn k14, turn, k14, drop pink yarn, k2 from left needle, turn, k18, k2tog, turn, k20 (includes 1 st from left needle), turn, k18, k2tog, turn,

BO 20 sts, *sl 1, k1; rep from * to end of row—20 sts rem. *Second ear:* K3tog, return st to left needle—18 sts. CO 19 sts—37 sts. K3tog, k17—18 sts on right needle; 17 sts on left needle. Rep from *, ignoring the st counts of first ear. Form top closing as for teddy. *Tail:* CO 6 sts. Knit 5 rows. BO all sts. Stuff center of tail with a small amount of fiberfill. Use yarn threaded on tapestry needle to close tail around fiberfill and attach to body.

Finishing

Weave in loose ends. Gently push a small amount of fiberfill through the top hole and into the legs. Tie a piece of yarn (not too tightly) around the top of each leg to segment it. Stuff and segment arms, body, and neck in the same manner. Cinch tog the yarn ends holding the top sts. With yarn threaded on a tapestry needle, sew tog any holes. Stitch on eyes and nose. Connect the eyes together with a thread so the nose will push forward. With ribbon, tie a bow around neck.

GREEN MOUNTAIN SPINNERY • The sweet, peaty aroma of wool and lanolin permeates the air and if you listen carefully, you'll hear the hum and thrum of yarn being made all around you when you visit Green Mountain Spinnery. Unlike most yarn shops, Green Mountain Spinnery produces all its yarn on the premises using vintage spinning machines. Visitors are immediately struck by the spinnery's compact size, the brilliant range of color, and the variety of yarn showcased in wooden cubbies. Samples of the store's exclusive Vermont Designer patterns are also on display along with knitting accessories, blankets, and a wide selection of knitting and fiber books.

Green Mountain Spinnery was founded in 1981 to encourage and support local agriculture. Their wool blend yarns use alpaca, mohair, and organic cotton to create a color palette of over fifty spectacular natural and dyed colors. The 100 percent wool yarns come entirely from New England fleeces. All fibers for Spinnery yarns are washed and spun with vegetable-based soaps and oils rather than with the petroleum-based products frequently used in the textile industry, and no chemicals are used to bleach, mothproof, shrink proof, or remove chaff. The ultimate goal is to produce yarn that is environmentally friendly and to preserve the best qualities of the natural fiber. The Spinnery's newest line is 100 percent Wool Vermont Organic.

Tours of the production process take place a couple times a month and "impromptu tours for ingenuous and interested parties (or their restless significant others)" are accommodated when possible, though advance notice is always appreciated. The Spinnery is located at the gateway to the town of Putney, a lively rural community where travelers are welcome and writers, artists, and craftspeople find inspiration and support.

GREEN MOUNTAIN SPINNERY

Box 568
PUTNEY, VT 05346
PHONE: (802) 387-4528
FAX: (802) 387-4841
WEBSITE: WWW.SPINNERY.COM
E-MAIL: SPINNERY@SOVER.NET

CELTIC CARDIGAN

Designer Melissa Lumley's love of Celtic motifs inspired this comfy, cozy Celtic Cardigan perfect for those chilly Vermont days. The Spinnery's Mountain Mohair line offers many rich color possibilities for working her favorite braid motif into the design. The intricate multicolored yoke features crosses in reverse stockinette stitch for extra texture. A single body color provides a great framework for all these pattern elements.

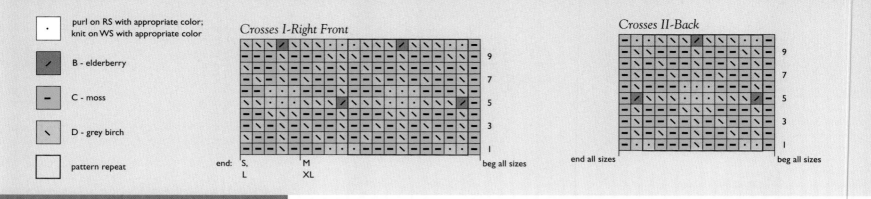

Legend:

- · purl on RS with appropriate color; knit on WS with appropriate color
- ╱ B - elderberry
- — C - moss
- ╲ D - grey birch
- ☐ pattern repeat

Crosses I-Right Front

end: S, L, M, XL · beg all sizes

Crosses II-Back

end all sizes · beg all sizes

FINISHED SIZE

42 (46, 50, 54)" (106.5 [117, 127, 137] cm) chest/bust circumference. To fit size S (M, L, XL). Sweater shown measures 46" (117 cm).

YARN

Green Mountain Spinnery Mountain Mohair, worsted weight (30% mohair, 70% wool; 140 yd [128 m]/2 oz): #5-A alpenglo (A), 5 (6, 6, 7) skeins, #5-EB elderberry (B), 1 (2, 2, 2) skeins. #5-MO moss (C), 4 (4, 5, 5) skeins, #5-GB grey birch (D), 2 (2, 3, 3) skeins.

NEEDLES

Front and Neckband Facing—Size 4 (3.5 mm): 24" or 29" (60- or 80-cm) circular (cir). Lower Edging, Sleeves, Front Bands and Neckband—Size 6 (4.0 mm) 29" or 36" (80-cm) cir. Body— Size 7 (4.5 mm) 29" or 36" (80-cm) cir. One extra cir needle (size 6 or smaller) to use as a stitch holder. Adjust needle sizes if necessary to obtain the correct gauge.

NOTIONS

Stitch holders; markers (m); tapestry needle; 6 to 8 hook and eyes or heavy zipper.

GAUGE

20 sts and 22 rows = 4" (10 cm) in both charted color pattern and solid color. It may be necessary to change needle sizes when going from charted to solid-color work.

CELTIC CARDIGAN
Melissa Lumley

Note The back and both sides of the front are worked as one piece for this cardigan, eliminating side seams. Because of the large number of sts, it is made on a long circular needle, working back and forth.

Body

With medium needle and C, CO 202 (222, 242, 262) sts. Work 5 rows garter st (knit every row). Change to largest needle and A, and work 2 rows in St st. Work Braid I chart, inc 4 sts evenly spaced in Row 2 for sizes M and XL—202 (226, 242, 266) sts. After completing chart, change to A (and medium needle if necessary to retain gauge in solid-color knitting). Work St st until piece measures 14 (14, 16, 16)" (35.5 [35.5, 40.5, 40.5] cm), or 2" (5 cm) less than desired length to underarm, ending with a WS row. Change back to largest needle, if necessary. Repeat Braid I chart, and on Row 12, inc 1 st for sizes S and L, and dec 3 sts for sizes M and XL—203 (223, 243, 263) sts.

Right Front Yoke

Starting with Row 1 at st marked for beg of Crosses I chart, work 50 (55, 60, 65) sts. *Note:* To avoid bi-color purl ridges in the very first row, do not work the rev St sts of color D, work them in rev St st only in sub-

sequent repeats of Row 1. Place rem sts on extra cir needle. Work Rows 1–10 of Crosses I chart 3 times, then work Rows 1–9—39 rows total. Break off all colors. Join C at neck edge and BO 16 sts—34 (39, 44, 49) sts rem. Work 12 rows of Braid II chart, and *at the same time,* inc 2 sts in Row 2 for sizes M and XL—34 (41, 44, 51) sts, and dec 1 st in Row 12 for sizes M and XL—34 (40, 44, 50) sts rem. Change to medium needles and work 6 rows garter st, dec 1 st at neck edge 4 times for sizes L and XL—34 (40, 40, 46) sts. Place sts on holder.

Back Yoke

Work Row 1 of Crosses II chart over 103 (113, 123, 133) held sts (to avoid bi-color purl ridges of Row 1 the first time the row is worked; work rev St st on subsequent repeats of Row 1), place rem 50 (55, 60, 65) sts on holder for left front yoke. Work Rows 1–10 of Crosses II chart 3 times, then work Rows 1–9—39 rows total. Break off all colors so Braid III chart can begin with RS facing. With RS facing, work Braid III chart, and *at the same time,* on Row 2, dec 1 st for sizes S and L, and inc 1 st for sizes M and XL—102 (114, 122, 134) sts. Change to medium needle and C, and work 6 rows garter st. Place sts on extra circular needle.

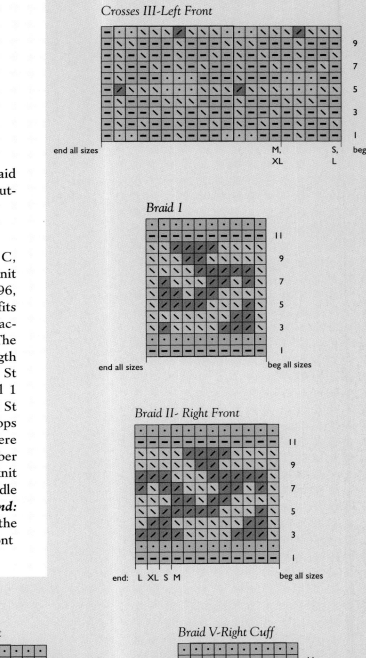

Crosses III-Left Front

end all sizes — M, XL — S, L — beg

Braid 1

end all sizes — beg all sizes

Braid II- Right Front

end: L XL S M — beg all sizes

Left Front Yoke

Place held left front yoke sts on same size needle used for back and right front yokes. Work Crosses III chart. With C, BO 16 sts—34 (39, 44, 49) sts rem. Break off all colors. With RS facing, work Braid IV chart, inc or dec as for right front yoke. Work as for right front yoke, reversing shaping. Place sts on holder.

Right Sleeve

With medium needle and C, CO 42 (42, 50, 50) sts. Work garter st for 5 rows. Change to largest needle and A, and work 2 rows St st. Work Rows 1–12 of Braid V chart. With A, work St st, and *at the same time,* on the third row, inc 1 st bet every 2 sts—63 (63, 75, 75) sts. Cont in St st, inc 1 st each end of needle every 3 (3, 4, 4) rows, until there are 103 sts. Work even until piece measures 2" (5 cm) less than desired total sleeve length. Work Rows 1–12 of Braid VI chart, inc 1 st in Row 2—104 sts. With C, BO all sts.

Left Sleeve

Work as for right sleeve, substituting Braid VII chart for Braid V chart and substituting Braid VIII chart for Braid VI chart.

Finishing

Left Front Band: With medium needle, C, and beg at neck edge, pick up and knit about 3 sts for every 4 rows—about 96 (96, 101, 101) sts, or whatever number best fits the length of your garment. With WS facing, knit 1 row. Work Band I chart. The number of reps will depend on the length of your garment. With C, work 2 rows St st. Change to smallest needle and purl 1 (RS) row for turning ridge. Work 7 rows St st. With spare needles, pick up the loops formed when sts for front band were picked up. Pick up the exact same number as for front band. With largest needle, knit the 2 sets of sts tog using the three-needle bind-off (see Glossary). *Right Front Band:* Starting at the bottom edge, pick up the same number of sts used for the left front

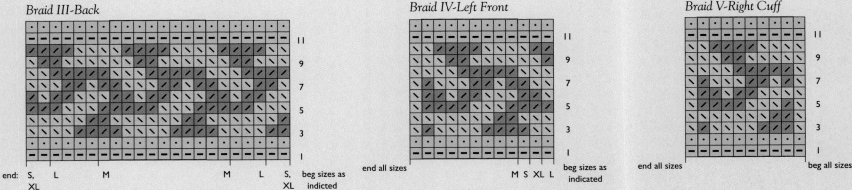

Braid III-Back

end: S, XL — L — M — M — L — S, XL — beg sizes as indicted

Braid IV-Left Front

end all sizes — M S XL L — beg sizes as indicated

Braid V-Right Cuff

end all sizes — beg all sizes

Braid VI-Right Sleeve Top

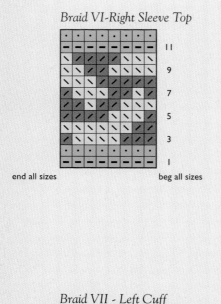

end all sizes   beg all sizes

Braid VII - Left Cuff

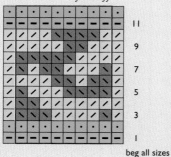

end all sizes   beg all sizes

Braid VIII-Left Sleeve Top

end all sizes   beg all sizes

band. Turn and knit second row. Break yarn, Beg Band II chart at top neck edge with a WS purl row. Complete as for left front band. ***Assembly:*** Using the three-needle bind-off, join the front to back at shoulders. Place rem 34 (34, 42, 42) back neck sts on holder. With yarn threaded on a tapestry needle, sew sleeve seams. Sew sleeves into armholes. ***Neckband:*** With medium needle, C, and RS facing, pick up and knit 5 sts at top of front band, 16 sts through BO sts of neck, 1 st in corner, 12 sts (3 sts for every 4 rows) along right neck edge, and 1 st at shoulder seam, k34 (34, 42, 42) held back neck sts, pick up and knit 1 st at shoulder seam, 12 sts along left edge, 1 st in corner, 16 sts through BO sts of neck, and 5 sts at top of front band—104 (104, 112, 112) sts total. With WS facing, k22, place marker (pm),

k13, pm, k35 (35, 43, 43), pm, k13, pm, k21. Slip markers every row. Work 5 rows St st, and *at the same time,* dec 2 sts at each corner every RS row as foll: Ssk, sl 1, k2tog. Change to smallest needle. With WS facing, knit 1 row for turning ridge. Work 6 rows St st, and *at the same time,* inc 1 st each side of each corner st every RS row. BO all sts as for front band. With yarn threaded on a tapestry needle, sew open ends of neckband and front bands shut. Place hooks and eyes evenly along front bands or hand-sew zipper in place. Weave in loose ends. Wash garment gently by hand in warm water with mild soap or detergent. Rinse well. Roll sweater in a towel to remove excess moisture, or spin dry in washing machine (10 seconds only). Lay flat to dry, shaping to correct measurements.

Band I

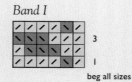

beg all sizes

Band II

beg all sizes

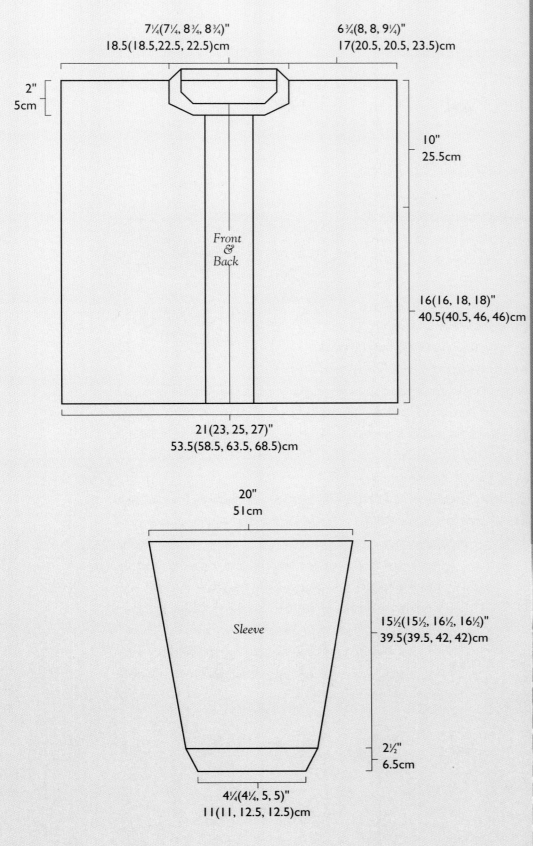

7¼(7¼, 8¾, 8¾)"
18.5(18.5,22.5, 22.5)cm

6¾(8, 8, 9¼)"
17(20.5, 20.5, 23.5)cm

2"
5cm

10"
25.5cm

*Front
&
Back*

16(16, 18, 18)"
40.5(40.5, 46, 46)cm

21(23, 25, 27)"
53.5(58.5, 63.5, 68.5)cm

20"
51cm

Sleeve

15½(15½, 16½, 16½)"
39.5(39.5, 42, 42)cm

2½"
6.5cm

4¼(4¼, 5, 5)"
11(11, 12.5, 12.5)cm

tips

WEAVING IN ENDS

To work in the "tails" when finishing a garment, duplicate-stitch the ends on the purl side. If you're using wool, the stitches generally stay in place with no problem. If you're using cotton or a slippery yarn like rayon, it's helpful to separate the yarn strand into two plies and duplicate stitch in opposite directions or work diagonally.

Kathy's Kreations

FIBERSPACE • Located on the wide open plains of eastern Colorado, FiberSpace is the only "real" yarn shop for at least a hundred miles in all directions. As its name implies, it offers more than just yarn, though. In addition to natural fiber yarns, Fiber-Space is chockfull of books, patterns, magazines, carded wool, looms, spinning wheels, beads, basketry, paper- and soap-making supplies, fiber art, fine art, and a work area where knitters bring their problems and successes.

Owner Linda Taylor is originally from Sterling. She spent thirteen years playing bass guitar and singing in the Colorado Sunshine Company band, after which she worked as an addictions counselor for nine years, and then in real estate for a time. In 1996, she and her husband decided to move back to her hometown and open a yarn shop and a fiber arts gallery. Both of her parents, who are "seventy-something," knit and weave for the shop, and getting to see that "man who knits" draws visitors.

The fiber and fine art gallery portion of this space-efficient shop showcases their finished knitted and woven pieces as well as the work of local potters, painters, jewelry makers, and fine artists; it's a popular stop for purchasing quality handcrafts. Linda reports that developing a customer base has taken a little time because she has had to lure back people who once knit but quit after supplies became scarce; she also offers frequent classes to introduce even more people to the craft. Linda's customers are big fans of sock knitting and felting, and a small group of the more expert knitters love the challenge of Nordic sweaters.

FiberSpace

113 North Second Street
Sterling, CO 80751
Phone: (970) 521-9041
Orders only: (877) 467-0382
Website: www.suite101.com/
myhome.cfm/fiberspaceofcolorado
E-mail: fiberspace@rmi.net

FELTED FISH

It's hard to believe that these fanciful tropical fish are from a designer based in land-locked Colorado. Shop owner and designer Linda Taylor developed the pattern at the request of a ten-year-old in home schooling who spent several days a week in her shop to learn fiber arts. The pattern is a wonderful way to learn knitting in the round on both circular and double-pointed needles, as well as color work: It's a great project for learning new techniques without a lot of pressure, because the felting covers any minor flaws. These fish are equally at home swimming over a baby's crib or the desk of an ocean-loving executive.

FINISHED SIZE

About 9" by 5" (23 by 12.5 cm), including fins, after felting. About 13½" by 8½" (34.5 by 21.5 cm), including fins, before felting.

YARN

Brown Sheep Nature Spun Sport (100% wool; 184 yd [168 m]/50 g): assorted colors (good choices are #861 orange crush, #N78 turquoise wonder, #308 sunburst gold, #N19 harlan's forest, #42 royal purple, #46 red fox, #116 blue boy), 3 to 4 ounces total. *Note:* You can substitute any sport or worsted weight wool, except superwash. Do not substitute synthetic yarn.

NEEDLES

Size 8 (5 mm): 16" (40-cm) circular (cir) and set of 5 double-pointed (dpn). For worsted weight yarn, substitute size 10.5 (6.5 mm) needles.

NOTIONS

Coiless brass pin; markers (m); tapestry needle; fishing leader to hang fish; fiberfill stuffing; one ½" (1.3-cm) button; one button same size as desired eye diameter.

GAUGE

4 sts = 1" (2.5 cm) before felting. As with all felted projects the gauge is very loose and irregular stitches do not pose a problem.

NOTES

Switch from dpn to cir and back as needed. Always break the yarn when changing colors—cut ends tend to be blunt and will not blend in well when felted. Weave in ends as you go—parts of the fish are difficult to get to once the knitting is completed.

FELTED FISH PATTERN
Linda Taylor

Body

Mouth: With A and dpn, loosely CO 16 sts. Divide sts evenly onto 3 or 4 dpn. Join into a rnd being careful not to twist sts. Knit 12 rnds, placing brass pin at beg of rnd and moving it up every 4 to 6 rnds. (This pin marks the bottom edge of fish and beg of rnd.) Break yarn and weave in ends. *Head and body:* Join B and work 1 rnd as foll: *K1, M1; rep from *—32 sts. Knit 6 rnds. *Next rnd:* *K2, M1; rep from *—48 sts. Knit 3 rnds. Break yarn and weave in ends. Join C and knit 3 rnds. *Next rnd:* *K3, M1; rep from *—64 sts. Knit 1 rnd. Break yarn and weave in ends. Join B and D, and work 3 or 4 rnds as foll: *K2 with D, k2 with B; rep from *. Break off B and weave in ends. Join A and work 3 or 4 rnds as foll: *K2 with D, k2 with A; rep from *. Cont changing one color every 3 to 4 rnds in this manner until this patt

section measures 3"–6" (7.5–15 cm) from beg (5"–7" [12.5–18 cm] for worsted-weight yarn).
Set-up for tail: (*Note:* Instructions are for a single-color, add colors as desired.)
Rnd 1: K1, *k2tog, k1; rep from *—43 sts rem.
Rnds 2 and 4: Knit.
Rnd 3: K1, *ssk, k1; rep from *—29 sts rem.
Rnd 5: K4, *k2tog, k3; rep from *—24 sts rem.
Rnds 6–10: Knit.
Tail: (For a colorful tail, work all M1 sts with a contrasting color).
Rnd 1: *K2, M1; rep from *—36 sts.
Rnds 2 and 4: Knit.
Rnd 3: *K3, M1; rep from *—48 sts.
Rnd 5: *K4, M1; rep from *—60 sts.
Rnd 6: Knit.
Change color and knit 4–6 rnds, depend-

felt happens

When a knitted piece made of 100-percent wool is washed in hot water with lots of agitation, felt happens. The fibers lock together under these conditions and, as you may know from experience, felt is forever!

Pieces knitted for felting start out loose and large and end up dense and fuzzy, warm and durable. Superwash wools, synthetics, and cottons will not felt. If you are not sure about the properties of a specific yarn or yarn color, try felting a swatch first. The swatch will also give you an idea of how much smaller your piece will be after felting.

Knitting for Felting
Aside from following the pattern directions, make sure your stitches are *not too tight*. The wool fibers need room to move during felting.

If you are like me and tend to knit tightly, use a needle one or more sizes larger than the pattern recommends. Most of my felt projects are knitted on size 13 needles. When I use smaller needles, I make sure that my tension is loose.

Finishing
It's very important to weave in tails securely. Break the yarn instead of cutting it, since a ragged end blends into the fabric better.

Joining knots should be untied and retied with a half knot, and the tails should be woven in opposite directions. If you leave a knot in the piece, it will felt into a tight little wad that can't be removed.

On to the Washer
Put your piece(s) to be felted in a lingerie bag or an old pillow case. Do not add a towel or a pair of blue jeans as some patterns suggest—they can shed cotton lint that gets trapped in the felt and is nearly impossible to get out.

Hot Water—If you don't think your hot water is at least 120°F, boil a big pot and add it to the wash water to bring up the temperature.

Low Water Level—You want the pieces to slosh, not float.

Liquid Soap—Add a drop or two of liquid soap to the water.

Lots of Agitation—You may have to repeat the machine's agitation cycle several times before your piece is felted. Smaller items like children's slippers seem to take the longest. Do not let your washer spin out the hot water until you are finished felting.

Stay Near the Washer—At the beginning of the process, it's safe to agitate for about 10 minutes before you check on the size of your piece. After that, it's best to check every 5 minutes. When the piece is nearly ready, check every minute.

Monitor Your Progress—If you need to try the piece on, squeeze (don't wring) the water out, and blot it on a towel. (If it's a knitted fish, never mind.)

If the piece is too small, or it's small in one spot and big in another, stretch it. The fibers will give somewhat while warm and wet.

Rinsing
When the piece is felted to your satisfaction, let the washer drain and spin for only a minute. Take your piece(s) out, let the spin cycle finish, and fill for the rinse.

Put your pieces back in the full tub. Let them agitate about 10 seconds and reset the washer to spin. Let the water pump out and listen for the spinning to begin. Stop the washer after about 10 seconds of dry spinning. Reposition the pieces in the tub. Give them another 10 seconds of spinning and remove. Too much spinning can cause nasty felted welts that usually end up in the worst places.

If you are worried about welts or additional felting from rinsing and spinning, rinse your pieces by hand in cool water and blot them with towels. (Do not wring.)

Air-dry your pieces with plenty of free circulation, or place them on an absorbent towel to flat-dry.

Linda Taylor, FiberSpace

tips

Here are ideas for your knitting bag—some are essential and some simply a pleasure to have readily available.

- Pen or pencil (our favorite is a mechanical pencil)

- Tape measure, preferably retracting, or a six-inch ruler

- Small scissors; we like the folding type, tied to the strap of our knitting bag and dropped into the pocket

- A couple of yarn needles threaded and poked into the felted fabric of the bag

- Small pocket calculator

- An assortment of double-pointed needles in favorite sizes, to test new patterns or try out new ideas (tightly fitting point protectors placed on one end turn double-pointed needles into straight needles for swatches or scarves)

- A small assortment of favorite yarns, useful for marking your place, holding stitches or test-knitting a new cast-on or pattern

- A notebook dedicated to knitting

- Post-It notes, invaluable for marking our place on a pattern and measuring short lengths of knitting; for measuring fingers for gloves or the length of a cuff; to wind a small tassel for the top of a hat or the edge of a scarf; as bookmarks, or to jot down pattern changes, friends' measurements, favorite colors, new yarn names, yardages, e-mail addresses of new knitters, websites

ing on tail length desired. Divide sts evenly onto 2 dpn and join tog using the three-needle bind-off (see Glossary). Work yarn tail into fin.

Fins: Lay fish flat and choose placement of dorsal fin. Join yarn at the tail end of fin and weave yarn tail to inside of fish. Using 2 dpn and your choice of color, pick up and knit 28 sts as foll: pick up 14 sts on each needle, each side of the center top of the fish, leaving one row of sts between the 2 parallel needles. With a third needle, knit across first needle where yarn is attached, turn, and knit sts on other needle to complete rnd. Don't worry about the gap between the needles—it will all come out in the wash.

Rnd 1: Knit.

Rnd 2: K12, [k2tog] 2 times, k12—26 sts rem.

Rnd 3: K1f&b, k10, [k2tog] 2 times, k10, k1f&b.

Rnd 4: K11, [k2tog] 2 times, k11—24 sts rem.

Rnd 5: K2tog, k8, [k2tog] 2 times, k8, k2tog—20 sts rem.

Rnd 6: K2tog, k16, k2tog—18 sts rem.

Rnd 7: K7, [k2tog] 2 times, k7—16 sts rem.

Rnd 8: *K2tog; rep from *—8 sts rem. Place 4 sts on each of 2 needles and BO sts tog using three-needle method as before. Work yarn tail into fin.

Flippers: Mark placement of flippers, about 2" (5 cm) up from bottom edge of fish and at 45-degree angle to tail. Sts are picked up and worked on 2 parallel needles as for dorsal fin.

Left side: Using 2 dpn, join yarn at fin *underside,* near tail end, and pick up and knit 8 sts—4 sts on each needle, parallel to each other.

Rnd 1: *K1f&b; rep from *—16 sts.

Rnd 2: K1f&b, k14, k1f&b—18 sts.

Rnd 3: K7, [k2tog] 2 times, k7—16 sts rem.

Rnds 4, 6, and 8: Knit.

Rnd 5: K2tog, k4, [k2tog] 2 times, k4, k2tog—12 sts rem.

Rnd 7: K4, [k2tog] 2 times, k4—10 sts rem.

Rnd 9: K3, [k2tog] 2 times, k3—8 sts rem. BO rem sts tog as before.

Right side: To mark position of right flipper, lay fish flat, flipper side up. Pass dpn through fish at points where left flipper is attached, turn fish over, and pick up sts between the 2 dpns. Pick up and knit

8 sts as for left side, joining yarn at *topside* of flipper, near tail end. Work as for left flipper.

Finishing

Eyes can be sewn on before or after felting. If sewn on before, remember to keep sts loose. Fine lines can be added to emphasize shapes or to suggest gills or scales. Try out different ideas and see what works best for you. *Felting:* Stretch fish in all directions and pull base of dorsal fin lengthwise to cause errant yarn tails to pop out. Sew tails back to inside of fish if necessary. Set washing machine for heavy-duty cycle, low water level, and hot water. Add a few drops of liquid laundry soap. Place fish in a lingerie bag and drop in washer. Machine agitate for about 10 minutes. Check size of fish and cont machine agitation as necessary, checking every 5 minutes until fish is desired size. (Because size and fit are not considerations, you can let the fish swim through the entire wash cycle, though there is a chance that a permanent crease may form from too much spinning.) Spin out most of water, then remove fish from washer and blot excess moisture with a towel. Shape fish and let dry. (To dry the fish quickly, place it on an old oven rack over a heat register.) Stuff fish firmly with fiberfill, working from tail to mouth. Sew mouth closed, and then push sewn edge to inside to form mouth opening. With matching yarn sew around inside edge of the mouth to secure and shape. Pull up gently on yarn, tie a knot and hide yarn tail by threading into fish. *Eyes:* Temporarily secure button at desired place on fish by sticking 2 tapestry needles through the button holes (the needles will hold the button in place but will not pass completely through the holes). With the button as a guide, use a running st to embroider around outside edge of button. Remove button and finish eye as desired, using French knots for pupils. Embellish fish as desired with embroidery, beads, or sequins. *Hanger:* To hang your fish, find its balance point and mark with a coiless pin. Place a button at center underside of fish, and leaving a 6" to 8" (15- to 20.5-cm) tail thread a length of fishing leader through 1 hole of button, then up through center of fish to balance point. Rethread needle and sew yarn tail through second hole of button, up through to balance point. Adjust length of leader as desired and tie knot close to upper body, being careful not to pull too tightly. Tie overhand knot at other end of fishing leader close.

- Good hand lotion
- Magnifying glasses
- One extra needle of the size you're using in your current project
- A couple of crochet hooks
- A bit of fine sandpaper or emery board to smooth a rough spot on a needle
- Waxed paper for buffing up a hand-made needle or repairing one that gets sticky or nicked

My Yarn Shop

Books on tape make great knitting companions even while knitting a challenging project.

Northampton Wools

Always have a second project to work on in the event that you get stuck, run out of yarn, lose your pattern, etc. There is nothing worse than having the time to knit and no knitting!

Tricoter

NORTHAMPTON WOOLS • Only
a mile from Smith College, Northampton Wools
has always enjoyed a population of student
knitters, but in the last few years this group
has really grown, thanks to a full schedule of
knitting classes. Shop owner Linda Daniels
started by offering five classes a week, now she's
up to ten, and she recently hired two new teachers and
rented a second classroom space.

Service has always been the main goal of this cozy nook of a shop. It's located in a 150-year-old building with beautiful tin ceilings and patinaed walls that provide a charming background for the abundance of yarn. Every once in a while someone suggests moving to a larger space, but Linda believes that the shop's charm is well worth keeping.

In addition to running the shop, Linda is a knitting celebrity who made the sweaters for the movie, *The Cider House Rules*. One of the film costumers then gave her name to New York City designer, Fiona Walker, designing prototypes for sweaters in her up-and-coming designer fashion line. "I don't think one can own a yarn shop and not do some designing," Linda says. "There never seems to be that very specific pattern someone is looking for."

As a full-service provider, Linda repairs knitted items, even if they are not handknitted, and offers a complete custom knitting service. The staff is prepared to write patterns for beloved worn-out sweaters, or even to knit sweaters from handspun dog hair for people who have had to say good-bye to their furry companions.

11 PLEASANT STREET
NORTHAMPTON, MA 01060
PHONE: (413) 586-4331

Cardigan with Garter-Stitch Trim

Linda Daniels designed this "simple, basic, quick-to-knit, go-everywhere, wear-anytime cardigan" at a customer's request. When the customer was slow to pick up the completed sweater, Linda hung it in the store, and requests for the pattern came in fast and furious. It is easy enough for a beginner and satisfyingly quick for the advanced.

FINISHED SIZE

36 (38, 40, 42)" (91.5 [96.5, 101.5, 106.5] cm) bust/chest circumference. Sweater shown measures 40" and is the longer version.

YARN

Classic Elite Montera (50% llama, 50% wool; 127 yd [117 m]/100 g): #3826 Andes lavender, 7 (7, 8, 9, 10) skeins for short version; 8 (8, 9, 10, 11) skeins for long version.

NEEDLES

Body and Sleeves—Size 10 (6.0 mm). Edging—Size 8 (5.0 mm). Adjust needle sizes if necessary to obtain the correct gauge.

NOTIONS

Stitch holders; tapestry needle; six ¾" (2-cm) buttons for short version, seven ¾" (2-cm) buttons for long version.

GAUGE

16 sts and 24 rows = 4" (10 cm) in stockinette stitch on larger needles.

CARDIGAN WITH GARTER-STITCH TRIM
Linda Daniels

Back

With smaller needles, CO 72 (76, 80, 84) sts. Work in garter st (knit every row) until piece measures 2" (5 cm) from beg, ending with a WS row. Change to larger needles and work St st until piece measures 11 (11, 12, 12)" (28 [28, 30.5, 30.5] cm) from beg for short version; 14 (14, 15, 15)" (35.5 [35.5, 38, 38] cm) from beg for long version, ending with a WS row. *Shape armholes:* BO 5 sts at beg of next 2 rows. Dec 1 st at each end of needle every other row 3 (4, 5, 5) times—56 (58, 60, 64) sts rem. Work even until armholes measure 7 (7½, 8, 8½)" (18 [19, 20.5, 21.5] cm), ending with a WS row. *Shape neck:* (RS) K17 (18, 18, 19), join new yarn and BO center 22 (22, 24, 26) sts, knit to end—17 (18, 18, 19) sts each side. Working each side separately, dec 1 st at neck edge every other row 2 times—15 (16, 16, 17) sts rem each side. Work even until armholes measure 8 (8½, 9, 9)" (20.5 [21.5, 23, 23] cm). Place sts on holders.

Left Front

With smaller needles CO 34 (36, 38, 40) sts. Work garter st until piece measures 2" (5 cm) from beg, ending with a WS row. Change to larger needles and work St st until piece measures same as back to armhole, ending with a WS row. *Shape armhole:* (RS) BO 5 sts at beg of next row, knit to end. Dec 1 st at armhole edge every other row 3 (4, 5, 5) times—26 (27, 28, 30) sts rem. Work even until armhole measures 5½ (6, 6½, 7)" (14 [15, 16.5, 18] cm), ending with a RS row. *Shape neck:* (WS) BO 6 (6, 6, 7) sts at beg of row, work to end. Dec 1 st at neck edge every other row 5 (5, 6, 6) times—15 (16, 16, 17) sts rem. Work even until armhole measures same as back to shoulder. Place sts on holder.

Right Front

Work as for left front, reversing shaping for armhole and neck.

SHORT VERSION

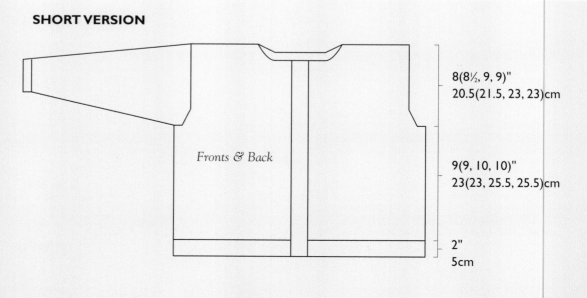

Fronts & Back

8(8½, 9, 9)"
20.5(21.5, 23, 23)cm

9(9, 10, 10)"
23(23, 25.5, 25.5)cm

2"
5cm

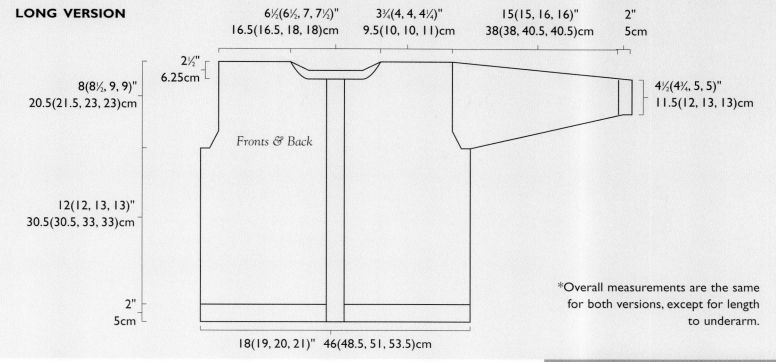

LONG VERSION

6½(6½, 7, 7½)"
16.5(16.5, 18, 18)cm

3¾(4, 4, 4¼)"
9.5(10, 10, 11)cm

15(15, 16, 16)"
38(38, 40.5, 40.5)cm

2"
5cm

2½"
6.25cm

8(8½, 9, 9)"
20.5(21.5, 23, 23)cm

4½(4¾, 5, 5)"
11.5(12, 13, 13)cm

Fronts & Back

12(12, 13, 13)"
30.5(30.5, 33, 33)cm

2"
5cm

18(19, 20, 21)"   46(48.5, 51, 53.5)cm

*Overall measurements are the same
for both versions, except for length
to underarm.

Sleeves

With smaller needles CO 36 (38, 40, 40) sts. Work garter st until piece measures 2" (5 cm) from beg, ending with a WS row. Change to larger needles and work St st until piece measures 4" (10 cm) from beg, ending with a WS row. Inc 1 st each end of needle on next row, then every foll 4 rows 14 (15, 16, 16) times more—66 (70, 74, 74) sts. Work even until piece measures 17 (17, 18, 18)" (43 [43, 46, 46] cm) from beg or desired length to underarm, ending with a WS row. **Shape cap:** BO 5 sts at beg of next 2 rows. Dec 1 st each end of needle every other row 3 (4, 5, 5) times—50 (52, 54, 54) sts rem. BO all sts loosely.

Finishing

Using the three-needle bind-off (see Glossary), join shoulder sts. With yarn threaded on a tapestry needle, sew sleeves into armholes. Sew sleeve and side seams. **Left front band:** With smaller needles, RS facing, and beg at neck edge, pick up and knit 67 (69, 74, 74) sts for short version; 79 (80, 86, 86) sts for long version. Work

garter st for 1½" (3.8 cm). BO all sts loosely. **Right front band:** With smaller needles, RS facing, and beg at lower edge, pick up and knit 67 (69, 74, 74) sts for short version; 79 (80, 86, 86) sts for long version. Knit 3 rows. *Buttonholes:* On next row make 6 buttonholes for short version; 7 buttonholes for long version as foll: *Short version:* K2 (3, 3, 3), *BO 3 sts, k9 (9, 10, 10); rep from *, ending last rep k2 (3, 3, 3). On next row CO 3 sts over each gap. *Long version:* K2 (3, 3, 3), *BO 3 sts, k9 (9, 10, 10); rep from *, ending last rep k2 for all sizes. On next row CO 3 sts over each gap. *For both versions:* Work garter st until band measures 1½" (3.8 cm). BO all sts. **Collar:** With smaller needles and RS facing, pick up and knit 80 (84, 86, 88) sts evenly spaced around neck edge, including front bands. Work garter st for 1½" (3.8 cm). Change to larger needles and cont in garter st for 1½" (3.8 cm) more. BO off all sts loosely. Weave in loose ends. Sew buttons opposite buttonholes. Steam block lightly, if desired.

BUTTONS AND BUTTONHOLES

To preserve the shape of the button band and keep buttons firmly and neatly anchored, back up the front button with a clear, flat button on the inside. Sew through the front button, then through the backup. There's no need for winding around to make a thread shank on the front side; one or two winds on the back side secures both buttons and keeps the placket and sweater looking trim. This method is especially effective working with soft, lofty yarns.

Green Mountain Spinnery

L'ATELIER • When a partnership clicks, there's no limit to what can happen. Consider the history of L'Atelier. Karen Damskey opened Tapestry Sampler, a needlepoint shop, in Manhattan Beach in 1976, and she moved to an expanded location in Redondo Beach under the name L'Atelier only two years later. Partner Leslie Storman helped her develop T. S. Designs, a wholesale line of needlepoint patterns, which soon included knitwear patterns as well. In the late 1980s, Leslie joined Karen in the Redondo Beach store, and "that's when the fun began," they say. They soon expanded to another location in Santa Monica, with each partner managing one of the stores.

Both travel extensively for ideas and sources, and together they collaborate on "Sweater of the Month" offerings which feature three original designs using the most exciting yarns of the moment. And yet, "More than trends and color, L'Atelier has a philosophy of what knitting is about," Karen says. "It's the freedom to express, to create, and to grab a few moments for yourself."

As the craze for knitting has flourished, the two report that their long-standing clients have remained with them, and "they chuckle when they read about this 'new' knitting craze. They've been crazed for the last decade and a half!" The L'Atelier partners enjoy the excitement and challenge of keeping up with it all.

**L'ATELIER
RIVIERA VILLAGE**

1714½ South Catalina Avenue
Redondo Beach, CA 90277
Phone: (310) 540-4440
Orders only: (800) 833-6133

**L'ATELIER
ON MONTANA**

1202A Montana Avenue
Santa Monica, CA 90403
Phone: (310) 394-4665

CABLE-WISE CASHMERE

Cashmere yarn—one of L'Atelier's claims to fame—is featured in this elegant, understated cabled pullover. Of course, it would be handsome in wool or cotton, but the incomparable feel of cashmere takes the design to a different level.

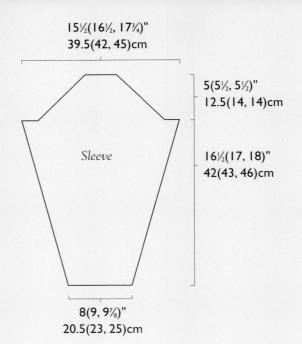

15½ (16½, 17¾)"
39.5 (42, 45)cm

5 (5½, 5½)"
12.5 (14, 14)cm

Sleeve

16½ (17, 18)"
42 (43, 46)cm

8 (9, 9⅞)"
20.5 (23, 25)cm

FINISHED SIZE
38 (42, 44)" (96.5 [106.5, 112] cm)
chest/bust circumference. Sweater shown
measures 38" (96.5 cm).

YARN
Filatura di Crosa (100% cashmere, 153 yd
[140 m]/50 g): #075 gray, 9 (11, 12) balls.

NEEDLES
Body and Sleeves—Size 7 (4.5 mm).
Edging—Size 6 (4 mm). Adjust needle sizes
if necessary to obtain the correct gauge.

NOTIONS
Tapestry needle.

GAUGE
20 sts and 28 rows = 4" (10 cm) in
stockinette stitch on larger needles.

ABBREVIATIONS
2/2RC: Sl 2 sts onto cn and hold in back, k2,
 k2 from cn.
2/2LC: Sl 2 sts onto cn and hold in front, k2,
 k2 from cn.

CABLE-WISE CASHMERE
Karen Damskey and Leslie Storman

Back

With smaller needles, CO 105 (115, 125)
sts. Purl 2 rows. Changer to larger needles
and work as foll:

Row 1: (RS) K13 (18, 23), p4, [k10, p1,
 k10, p4] 3 times, k13 (18, 23).
Row 2: P13 (18, 23), k4, [p10, k1, p10, k4]
 3 times, p13 (18, 23).

Rep Rows 1 and 2 until piece measures 7
(8, 9)" (18 [20.5, 23] cm) from beg, ending
with a WS row. Then work as foll:

Row 1: (RS) K13 (18, 23), p4, *k10, p1,
 k10, p4*, k6, 2/2RC, p1, 2/2LC, k6, p4;
 rep from * to *, k13 (18, 23).
Rows 2, 4, 6, and 8: P13 (18, 23), k4, [p10,
 k1, p10, k4] 3 times, p13 (18, 23).
Row 3: K13 (18, 23), p4, *k10, p1, k10,
 p4*, k4, 2/2RC, k2, p1, k2, 2/2LC, k4,
 p4; rep from * to *, k13 (18, 23).
Row 5: K13 (18, 23), p4, *k10, p1, k10,
 p4*, k2, 2/2RC, k4, p1, k4, 2/2LC, k2,
 p4; rep from * to *, k13 (18, 23).
Row 7: K13 (18, 23), p4, *k10, p1, k10,
 p4*, 2/2RC, k6, p1, k6, 2/2LC, p4; rep
 from * to *, k13 (18, 23).

Rep Rows 1–8 until piece measures 15½
(16½, 17½)" (39.5 [41.5, 44.5] cm) from
beg, ending with a WS row. *Shape armholes:* (RS) BO 5 sts at beg of next 2
rows—95 (105, 115) sts rem. Dec 1 st
each end of needle every other row 11
times, and *at the same time,* when armholes
measure about 2 (1½, 1½)" (5 [3.8, 3.8]
cm), work the 25 sts bet the *s in the same
manner as the center cable for a total of 16
rows, being sure to work the first cable
twist on Row 1 of patt to line up with the
other cable twists. Then work the center
21 sts as k10, p1, k10 for remainder of
length. When armholes measure 8½ (9, 9)"
(21.5 [23, 23] cm), BO all sts.

Front

Work as for back until armholes measure
6" (15 cm). *Shape neck:* Work 28 (31, 34)
sts in patt, join new yarn and BO center 17
(21, 25) sts, work to end. Working each
side separately, at neck edge BO 3 sts
once, then BO 2 sts once, then BO 1 st
every other row 3 times—20 (23, 26) sts

rem each side. Cont even until armholes measure same as back. BO all sts.

Sleeves

With smaller needles, CO 41 (45, 49) sts. Purl 3 rows. Change to larger needles and work cable cuff as foll:

Row 1: (WS) P6 (8, 10), k4, *p10, k1, p10,* k4, p6 (8, 10).

Row 2: K6 (8, 10), p4, *k6, 2/2RC, p1, 2/2LC, k6*, p4, k6.

Cont in patt as est, centering the 21 cable sts (those sts bet *s) and working 8-row cable patt as body for 8 repeats (56 rows), and *at the same time*, work the outer sts in St st while inc 1 st each end of needle every 6 rows 18 (19, 20) times—77 (83, 89) sts. Cont in St st until piece measures 16½ (17,

18)" (41.5 [43, 46] cm) from beg, ending with a WS row. *Shape cap:* BO 5 sts at beg of next 2 rows—67 (73, 79) sts rem. Dec 1 st each end of needle every other row until cap measures 5 (5½, 5½)" (12.5 [14, 14] cm)—35 (37, 43) sts rem. BO 3 sts at beg of next 6 rows—17 (19, 25) sts rem. BO all sts.

Finishing

Lightly steam all pieces. With yarn threaded on a tapestry needle, sew one shoulder seam. *Neckband:* With smaller needles, pick up and knit 78 (82, 86) sts evenly spaced around neck. Purl 2 rows. BO all sts loosely. Sew rem shoulder and neckband seam. Sew sleeves into armholes. Sew side and sleeve seams. Weave in loose ends.

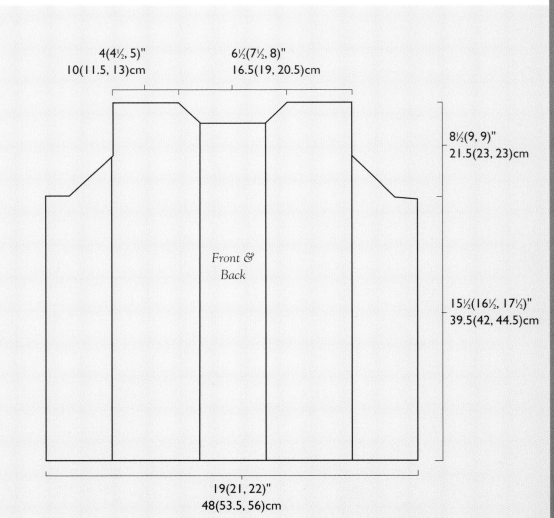

4(4½, 5)"
10(11.5, 13)cm

6½(7½, 8)"
16.5(19, 20.5)cm

8½(9, 9)"
21.5(23, 23)cm

Front &
Back

15½(16½, 17½)"
39.5(42, 44.5)cm

19(21, 22)"
48(53.5, 56)cm

MARJI'S YARNCRAFTS • The path to Marji's Yarncrafts in Granby, Connecticut, passes by a charming pond and through a flower garden. Inside, it's all yarn—everything is covered with yarn, including a couple of antique stoves and many, many baskets. But there's something distinctly unusual about the location: it's in a wing off the back of the 1850s house where Marji LaFreniere lives with her husband and three children.

Marji is the kind of woman who wants to "have it all," and her in-home shop arrangement promotes that—as well as an obliging husband who cooks and does laundry. "This allows me to be full-time mom as well as full-time shopkeeper," she says, which is not without challenges. "There are many days when I have a whole store full of people as well as some catastrophe happening in the house. Things get dicey and are prone to be loud! As people walk in the door, they frequently wonder what's cooking. While they get to enjoy the aroma, I usually don't invite them for dinner."

MARJI'S YARNCRAFTS

381 SALMON BROOK STREET
GRANBY, CT 06035
PHONE: (860) 653-9700

In business since 1988, Marji has found that her merchandising is guided by her own tastes and interests. That means an emphasis on wool and classic yarn and sweater styles. She offers classes in the basics as well as projects—focused workshops—such as the one for her unusual felted tea cozy, featured here.

COTTAGE TEA COZY

Marji LaFreniere designed this felted tea cozy at the suggestion of her teacher and "idea person," Pam Kohan. Her shop has used it as a class theme in which students produce a veritable village of tea cozies, each as unique as its creator. Silk ribbon embroidery can be used as shown to add flowers, butterflies, bees, or whatever the maker fancies. The pattern provided here covers the basics.

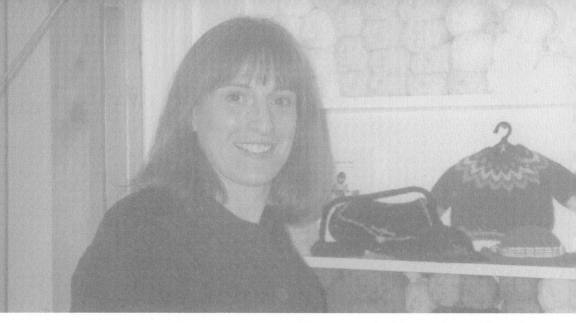

FINISHED SIZE

About 12" (30.5 cm) wide and 8" (20.5 cm) tall, after felting.

YARN

Cascade Yarns Cascade 220 (100% wool; 220 yd [201 m]/100 g): #8407 oyster (MC) and #4011 sparrow (CC), 1 skein each. YLI Silk Ribbon in 4-mm and 7-mm widths in a variety of colors—5 to 7 flower colors and at least 3 leaf colors. Embroidery floss in black, yellow, and green for windows, flower centers, buds, and bumblebees.

NEEDLES

House—Size 10½ (6.5 mm): 24" (60-cm) circular (cir) and set of 4 double-pointed (dpn). Roof, Shutters, and Door—Size 8 (5 mm): set of 4 dpn.

NOTIONS

Markers (m); tapestry needle, size 22 chenille needle.

GAUGE

16 sts and 28 rows = 4" (10 cm) in double seed st on size 8 (5 mm) needles for roof. Gauge for main house before felting is loose, about 3 sts per 1" (2.5 cm), but not critical.

COTTAGE TEA COZY
Marji LaFreniere

House

With MC and larger cir needle, loosely CO 90 sts. Place m and join, being careful not to twist sts. [Knit 1 rnd, purl 1 rnd] 2 times.
Inc rnd: *K9, M1; rep from *—100 sts.
Knit 42 more rnds placing m after 50th st on last rnd. *Shape top:*
Rnd 1: [K1, ssk, knit to 3 sts before m, k2tog, k1] 2 times—96 sts rem.
Rnd 2: Knit.
Rep Rnds 1 and 2 until 52 sts rem—26 sts bet markers. (For a taller cozy, cont dec until 48 sts rem—24 sts bet markers; doing so will require extra MC yarn.) Leave a couple yards of yarn to make a top loop. Break yarn, leaving a tail for grafting or BO all sts and sew top tog. *Top loop:* With MC and dpn, CO 3 sts. Work I-cord (see Glossary) until piece measures 2" (5 cm) from beg. With yarn threaded on a tapestry needle, sew ends of I-cord to center top of house. Weave in loose ends.

Felting

Set washing machine for heavy-duty cycle, low water level, and hot water. Add a few drops of liquid laundry or dishwashing soap to the water. Place the tea cozy inside a lingerie bag and drop into washer. Start wash cycle and allow to agitate. Check progress every 5 minutes until cozy is the desired size. Remove cozy from the washer and check for fit on teapot. Reset the wash cycle if necessary. When desired size is reached, rinse in *cold* water and roll in a towel to remove excess water. Pull and pat into shape if needed, then place on flat surface and allow to air dry. See page 97 for more felting information.

Finishing

Roof: With CC and smaller needle, loosely CO 100 sts. Place m and join, being careful not to twist sts. Work double seed st as foll:
Rnds 1 and 2: *K2, p2; rep from *.
Rnds 3 and 4: *P2, k2; rep from *.
Place m after 50th st to mark halfway point.
Rep Rnds 1–4 and *at the same time*, dec 4 sts every other rnd as foll: [K1, ssk, work as established to 3 sts before m, k2tog, k1] 2 times. Work 4-rnd patt as established

and dec 4 sts every other rnd until piece measures 4" (10 cm) or desired length—place on top of felted tea cozy to check size. BO rem sts. With yarn threaded on tapestry needle, sew upper edges tog, leaving 1½" (3.8 cm) open at center top for I-cord loop.

Door: With CC and smaller needle, loosely CO 9 sts.

Row 1: Knit.

Row 2: Sl 1, k8.

Row 3: Sl 1, [p1, k1] 4 times.

Rep Rows 2 and 3 six more times (15 rows total).

Row 16: Sl 1, ssk, k1, p1, k1, k2tog, k1—7 sts rem.

Row 17: Sl 1, [p2, k1] 2 times.

Row 18: Sl 1, ssk, k1, k2tog, k1—5 sts rem.

Row 19: Sl 1, [p1, k1] 2 times.

Row 20: Sl 1, sl 1, k2tog, psso, k1—3 sts rem.

BO all sts.

Shutters: (Make 4) With CC and smaller needles, loosely CO 4 sts.

Row 1: Sl 1, k3.

Rep Row 1 for desired length. BO all sts. Sew roof, door and shutters to felted cozy. Embellish with embroidery as desired.

The embroidery diagram of the tea cozy is shown here, but sketch your own idea of a cottage garden and enjoy decorating! For more definitive directions on silk ribbon embroidery and very clear pictures, refer to *An Encyclopedia of Ribbon Embroidery Flowers* by the American School of Needlework. Use lazy daisy, straight stitch, French knots, and whatever else you fancy to make flowers and leaves. Let ribbon "rest" on top of the fabric—don't pull it tight or it will disappear. When making French knots, insert sewing needle *next to* where you came up and not into the same hole or your knot will disappear. Don't be too exacting—when you are more relaxed with your embroidery, it looks better and after all, flowers are more beautiful in their imperfection!

tips

JOINING SLEEVES TO SWEATER

If you are familiar with the technique of knitting your shoulders together (three-needle bind-off, see Glossary), try using the same technique for attaching your sleeves on a dropped-shoulder garment. Don't bind off when you are done knitting the sleeves, but finish having just knit a right side row. After you have knit the shoulders together, place the right sides of the armhole and the top of the sleeve together. Knit into the first stitch of the sleeve and into the edge of the garment armhole at the same time, thus knitting them together. Knit another stitch the same way and then bind off the first stitch over the second and continue in this manner until the sleeve is fully attached. Make sure to mark the armhole placement on the sweater so you know where to begin and end, and make sure the center stitch on the sleeve lines up with the shoulder seam. This is not faster than sewing a seam, but it is usually much neater. Your rows will not equal your stitches so you will have to skip a row every so often. I find this doesn't show when you are done. This will also work when you have knit a sleeve in the round from the cuff up. The sleeve is on a circular needle and needs to be kind of shoved inside the body of the inside-out garment. It's a little tricky, but neat.

Marji's Yarncrafts

PATTERNWORKS • It's hard to believe that a dieting bet was the start of one of America's best-known knitting shops/warehouses/catalog companies. Linda Skolnik's payoff to the victorious Nora Galland was a handknitted coat. They couldn't find a pattern that Nora liked, so they designed the coat themselves, and Patternworks was born. Their first offerings were kits using luscious chunky chenille yarn (now back in fashion).

At first Patternworks was more of a hobby, specializing in hard-to-find items for knitters. (Nora went back to the corporate world in 1981, and Linda bought her out.) When Linda's husband Marvin took early retirement from IBM and joined the business in 1986, the mail-order company really started to grow—from the Skolniks' home, to a big second-floor room with a conveyor belt, to a large warehouse where they finally have the space for regular store hours to satisfy their passionate, yarn-hungry customers.

Although mail-order still accounts for eighty percent of the business, Patternworks is a mecca (so named by a regular visitor from Turkey) for knitters from all over the world who come to revel in its vast selection of yarn and accessories. While it may have more of a warehouse feel than the typical yarn shop, it is indeed the "yarn paradise" its catalog proudly proclaims.

PATTERNWORKS

PO Box 1690
36A South Gate Drive
Poughkeepsie, NY 12601
Phone: (845) 462-8000
Orders only: (800) 438-5464
Website: patternworks.com

Everything about this soft Merino baby set was designed to be baby- and parent-friendly. Thanks to handy back buttons, the sweater is easy to put on and take off. And the stockings are carefully shaped to *stay on.*

FINISHED SIZE

17" (43 cm) chest circumference. To fit a newborn baby.

YARN

Karabella Aurora 8 (100% Merino; 98 yd [90 m]/50 g): #1380 seashell pink, 4 balls.

NEEDLES

Sweater and Socks—Size 5 (3.75 mm) and Size 7 (4.5 mm): Straight and set of 4 double-pointed (dpn). Hat—Size 5 (3.75 mm) and Size 7 (4.5 mm): 16" (40-cm) circular (cir). Adjust needle sizes if necessary to obtain the correct gauge.

NOTIONS

Markers (m); tapestry needle; two ½" (1.3-cm) buttons.

GAUGE

20 sts and 30 rows = 4" (10 cm) in stockinette stitch.

BABY'S FIRST LUXURIES
SWEATER, HAT & STAY-ON SOCKS
Linda Skolnik

SWEATER

Body

With smaller needles, CO 102 sts. Knit 9 rows (garter st). Change to larger needles and set up patt as foll: (WS) K5, place marker (pm), p25 for left back, pm, beg with Row 1, work 42 sts according to Cables and Ribs chart for front, pm, p25 for right back, pm, k5. Working the first and last 5 sts in garter st, 25 sts in St st for each back, and 42 sts as charted for front, cont as established for a total of 30 rows—piece should measure about 5" (12.5 cm) from beg. **Divide for armholes:** K30 left back sts and place on holder and place 30 right back sts on another holder. **Front:** Working front sts only, work Rows 1–14 of chart. *Shape neck:* (Row 15 of chart) P17, join new yarn and BO 8 sts, p17. Working each side separately, knit 1 row. Maintaining patt as much as possible, dec 1 st at neck edge every other row 4 times—13 sts rem each side. Work even in patt until piece measures 8½" (21.5 cm) from beg. BO all sts. **Right back:** Place 30 held right back sts onto needle. Rejoin yarn and cont as established until piece measures 1" (2.5 cm) less than right front, ending with a RS row. *Shape neck:* (WS) BO 15 sts, work to end. Work 2 rows even. Dec 1 st at neck edge every other row, 2 times—13 sts rem. BO all sts. **Left back:** Work as for right back, reversing shaping.

Sleeves

With larger dpn, RS facing, and beg at underarm, pick up and knit 36 sts evenly spaced around armhole. Join into a rnd. Knit 1 rnd. On next rnd, dec 2 sts as foll: K1, ssk, knit to last 3 sts, k2tog, k1—34 sts rem. Dec 2 sts in this manner every 5 rnds

4 more times—26 sts rem. Work even until sleeve measures 6" (15 cm). Purl 1 rnd. Knit 1 rnd. Purl 1 rnd. BO all sts.

Finishing

With yarn threaded on a tapestry needle, sew shoulder seams. With smaller needles and RS facing, pick up and knit 21 sts across neck edge of left back, 23 sts around front neck, and 21 sts across neck edge of right back—65 sts. Knit 1 row. Make 2 buttonholes on next row as foll: K2, k2tog, yo, knit to last 4 sts, k2tog, yo, k2. Knit 1 row even. BO all sts loosely. Lap right back over left back and sew on buttons; one on WS of right back, the other on RS of left back to correspond with buttonholes. Weave in loose ends.

HAT

Edge: With smaller cir needle, CO 60 sts. Place marker (pm) and join, being careful not to twist sts. Knit 8 rnds, inc 10 sts evenly spaced on last rnd—70 sts. Change to larger cir needle. Knit 10 rnds.

Body: M1, turn (WS now facing you, this will become the RS), knit to 1 st before the M1 inc, k2tog—70 sts (this eliminates the hole formed from turning). Knit 28 rnds. Work decs as foll, changing to dpn when necessary.

Rnd 1: *K2tog, k5; rep from *—60 sts rem.
Rnd 2 and all even-numbered rnds: Knit.
Rnd 3: *K2tog, k4; rep from *—50 sts rem.
Rnd 5: *K2tog, k3; rep from *—40 sts rem.
Rnd 7: *K2tog, k2; rep from *—30 sts rem.
Rnd 9: *K2tog, k1; rep from *—20 sts rem.
Rnds 11 and 13: *K2 tog; rep from *—5 sts rem after Rnd 13.

LONG-TAIL CAST ON

To gauge where to begin a long-tail cast-on, before making the first stitch, hold the cut end of the yarn snugly against the needle. Wrap yarn loosely around the working needle ten times. Pinch the end, unwrap, and use that length as a single unit of measure for 10 stitches. Fold that length double, triple, or as necessary to reach the number of stitches you want to cast on. Add just a little more for good measure and make your first stitch at that point of the tail.

Countrywool

Knit 3 rnds. Break yarn, leaving a 6" (15-cm) tail. Using a tapestry needle, thread tail through rem sts, pull tight, and fasten off. Weave in loose ends.

STAY-ON SOCKS

With smaller dpn, CO 24 sts. Divide sts evenly onto 3 dpn, with 8 sts on each needle. Place m and join, being careful not to twist sts. Work k2, p2 ribbing for 8 rnds. Change to St st and work 14 rnds. *Dec rnd:* Needle #1: K1, ssk, knit to end; needle #2: Knit; needle #3: Knit to last 3 sts, k2tog, k1—22 sts rem. Knit 1 rnd even. Dec 2 sts in this manner every other rnd 2 more times—18 sts rem. Knit 8 rnds even.
Divide for heel: Remove m. Arrange sts to align heel with leg back as foll: Sl last 4 sts of needle #3 onto empty needle, sl first 4 sts from needle #1 onto same needle (so that there are 8 sts on this needle), and knit these 8 sts. Place rem sts from needles #1 and #3 onto another needle for instep.
Heel flap: Work back and forth on 8 heel sts as foll:
Row 1: (WS) Sl 1, p7.
Row 2: *Sl 1, k1; rep from *.
Rep Rows 1 and 2 until a total of 8 rows have been worked.

Turn heel:
Row 1: P4, p2tog, p1—7 sts rem.
Row 2: Sl 1, k1, ssk, k1—6 sts rem.
Row 3: Sl 1, p2, p2tog—5 sts rem.
Row 4: Sl 1, k2, ssk—4 sts rem.
Gusset: With empty needle, pick up and knit 6 sts along side of heel, pm, k10 held instep sts. With another empty needle, pick up and knit 6 sts along other side of heel—26 sts total. With same needle, k2 heel sts. Sl rem 2 heel sts onto the first needle. Join into a rnd and dec foll:
Rnd 1: Knit.
Rnd 2: Needle #1: Knit to 3 sts before m, k2tog, k1; needle #2: K10; needle #3: K1, ssk, knit to end.
Rep Rnds 1 and 2 two more times—20 sts rem. Knit even for 14 rnds.
Toe:
Rnd 1: Needle #1: Knit to last 3 sts, k2tog, k1; needle #2: K1, ssk, knit to last 3 sts, k2tog, k1; needle #3: K1, ssk, knit to end—16 sts rem.
Rnd 2: Knit.
Rep Rnds 1 and 2 two more times—8 sts rem. Break yarn, leaving a 6" (15-cm) tail. Using a tapestry needle, thread tail through rem sts, pull tight, and fasten off. Weave in loose ends.

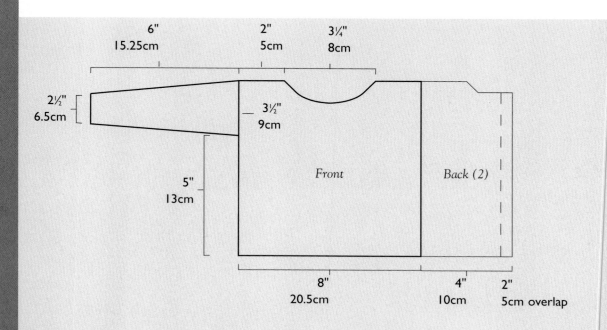

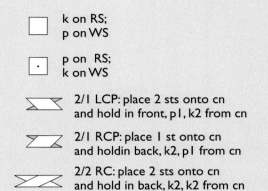

k on RS;
p on WS

p on RS;
k on WS

2/1 LCP: place 2 sts onto cn
and hold in front, p1, k2 from cn

2/1 RCP: place 1 st onto cn
and holdin back, k2, p1 from cn

2/2 RC: place 2 sts onto cn
and hold in back, k2, k2 from cn

Cables and Ribs

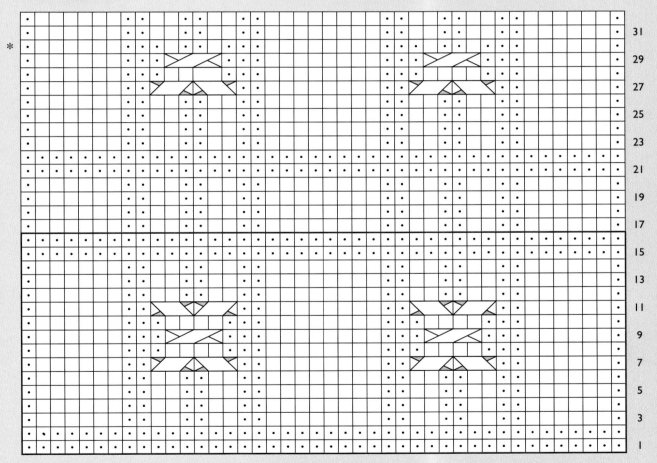

* Note slight change of pattern on WS Row 30. Est patt resumes on Row 31.
Work chart Rows 1-32, separate backs from front, cont front working Rows 1-14. Follow instructions for neckline shaping.

FINE POINTS, INC. • When Sasha Kagan visited Fine Points, she described the place as "funky chaos." Kaffe Fassett remarked that the store's bountiful display of yarns from all over the world made it "indeed a treasure." Fine Points is not only a yarn shop, but the personal palette of its owner and designer, Liz Tekus. Many of the yarns featured in the shop are hand-dyed or one-of-a-kind; Liz hangs on to even the discontinued ones, considering that every single ball of yarn has the potential for creativity. "Wild yarn balls are always on the loose, presenting new surprises at every turn," she says. Her garments often include as many as 150 different kinds of yarn, so this extraordinary stash is necessary for her and a benefit for customers looking for yarns that are a little out of the ordinary.

Fine Points, opened in 1987, is located in historic Little Italy in Cleveland, Ohio, where great art and great food meet. It is within walking distance of University Circle, Cleveland's cultural center and home to Case Western Reserve University, and a variety of museums including the Art Museum.

In 1997 Liz opened a sister shop, Fine Points, Too, a clothing and jewelry store just a few doors down from the knit shop in the old Murray Hill School building. It features one-of-a-kind jewelry and wearable art, including Liz's own knitwear designs.

FINE POINTS, INC.

2026 MURRAY HILL ROAD
CLEVELAND, OH 44106
PHONE: (216)229-6644
WEBSITE: WWW.FINEPOINTS.COM
E-MAIL: LIZ@FINEPOINTS.COM

POINT FIVE
RAGLAN JACKET

This chunky jacket sweater with its big yarn buttons is quick and easy to make and cleverly constructed, yet it makes a bold fashion statement about the person wearing it. As with many of the garments Liz Tekus designs, it features hand-dyed and highly textured yarns.

FINISHED SIZE

53" (134.5 cm) bust/chest circumference, buttoned.

YARN

Colinette Point Five (100% wool; 54 yd [49]/100 g): #55 Toscana, 10 skeins.

NEEDLES

Body—Size 15 (10 mm): 24" (60-cm) circular (cir). Sleeve Ribbing and Collar—Size 10½ (6.5 mm). Waist Ribbing—Size 11 (8 mm). Adjust needle sizes if necessary to obtain the correct gauge.

NOTIONS

Large stitch holders; markers (m); tapestry needle.

GAUGE

9 sts and 12 rows = 4" (10 cm) in stockinette stitch.

POINT FIVE RAGLAN JACKET
Liz Tekus

Note This garment is worked from the neck down. To avoid prominent stripes, work with 2 balls of yarn, alternating between the balls every 2 rows.

Yoke

With largest needle, CO 28 sts.

Row 1: (RS) K2 for right front, place marker (pm), k3 for right sleeve, pm, k18 for back, pm, k3 for left sleeve, pm, k2 for left front.

Row 2: Purl.

Row 3: *K1f&b, knit to 1 st before m, k1f&b, sl m; rep from *, ending last rep k1f&b—38 sts.

Row 4: Purl.

Rep Rows 3 and 4 twice—58 sts; 8 sts for each front, 9 sts for each sleeve, and 24 sts for back. Using the cable method (see Glossary), CO 10 sts at beg of next 2 rows—78 sts. Mark first and last 5 sts of each row and work in garter st for the front bands. Buttonholes are worked at the end of RS rows as foll: Knit to last 5 sts, k2, yo, k2tog, k1. On foll row, knit the yo of the previous row. Work the first buttonhole on the 2nd or 3rd garter ridge after the 10-st inc. Work 3 additional buttonholes spaced 7 garter ridges apart. The final buttonhole is added in the collar. Cont working in patt as established and *at the same time,* inc 1 st each side of each m, excluding the front border markers, every RS row 14 times—190 sts; 32 sts for each front, 37 sts for each sleeve, 52 sts for back. Work even until piece measures about 10" (25.5 cm) from beg, ending with a WS row. Place sts for front, back, and one sleeve on holders.

Sleeves

Working on one set of 37 sleeve sts, CO 2 sts beg of the next 2 rows—41sts. Work in St st, dec 1 st each end of needle every 9 rows 3 times—35 sts rem. Work even for a total of 34 rows, or to desired sleeve length. Dec 7 sts evenly spaced across next row—28 sts rem. Change to size 10½ (6.5 mm) needles and work k1, p1 rib for 10 rows. BO loosely in rib. Rep for other sleeve.

Body

Note: Body is worked back and forth in one piece.

Place held front and back sts onto needle. With RS facing, k32 held left front sts, pick up and knit 4 sts at underarm, k52 held back sts, pick up and knit 4 sts at right underarm, k32 held right front sts—124 sts. Keeping 5 sts at beg and end of each row in garter st, work even as established until piece measures 15½" (39.5 cm), or desired length from beg, and *at the same time,* work a buttonhole every 7th garter ridge. Work 1 row, dec 14 sts evenly spaced—110 sts rem. Change to size 11 (8 mm) needle and work k1, p1 rib for 10 rows, working the fifth buttonhole after 3 ridges. BO all sts loosely in rib.

Collar

With size 10½ (6.5 mm) needles, pick up and knit 57 sts around neck opening. Keeping 5 sts at beg and end of each row in garter st, work rem sts in k1, p1 rib. Work even in patt for 10 rows, adding last buttonhole after 3 garter ridges. BO all sts loosely in rib.

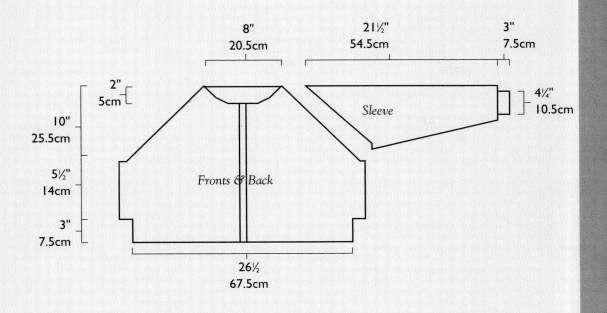

8"
20.5cm

21½"
54.5cm

3"
7.5cm

2"
5cm

10"
25.5cm

5½"
14cm

3"
7.5cm

Sleeve

4¼"
10.5cm

Fronts & Back

26½
67.5cm

Finishing

With yarn threaded on a tapestry needle, sew sleeve seams and weave together any holes around the raglan. **Buttons:** Thread yarn onto a tapestry needle and pull out an 18" (46-cm) length from the ball, but do not cut the yarn. Wind the yarn into a butterfly around your fingers about 5 times (see Glossary). Slide off fingers and thread needle through all the loops to form the button core. With the needle, add shape to the button by taking small sts into and around the core until about 4" (10 cm) of yarn rems. Cut yarn from ball and use ends to attach button to garment. (If you are running low on yarn, you can use a different yarn for the button core.)

tips

BUTTONS AND BUTTONHOLES

For a better-looking horizontal button band, instead of making the buttonholes in the center of the band, move them closer to the body by one or two stitches to prevent the front from gaping open. Space buttonholes evenly, about 2" to 2½" (5 to 6.5 cm) apart, and work the top and bottom buttonholes ½" (1.25 cm) from the edge.

Here's my favorite three-row buttonhole, ideal for horizontal button bands:

Row 1: *Work to desired buttonhole placement, work next two sts tog, yo; rep from * as many times as needed.

Row 2: *Work to buttonhole placement, work into yo in patt as est; repeat from * as many times as needed.

Row 3: *Work to buttonhole placement, work into the hole in patt as est; repeat from * as many times as needed.

Kathy's Kreations

EVA'S NEEDLEWORK

EVA'S NEEDLEWORK • Of course, Eva's Needlework is filled to the brim with wonderful yarn and supplies for knitting, crocheting, and other needlework, but according to owner Eva (Eira) Wiechmann, the shop is really about her customers and their special stories.

For instance, there's Lois, who has survived cancer twice and is convinced she is still alive because she has to knit all the cashmere that she has stashed away. Another, Katie, was eighty-eight years old and "drove a car that was at least the same age." After a stroke prevented her from doing complicated patterning, Eva started a baby blanket program whereby Katie would come in every Saturday for yarn donated by the store. The following Saturday, she would return with the finished garter-stitch blanket and get yarn for the next one. Katie became the store's adopted grandmother and when she passed away, the store adopted her cat, Baby.

Cheery, flower-filled boxes line the windows on the front of the shop, and two tables greet customers as they enter. "It's very unusual if there isn't someone sitting at a table," Eva says. "When people are hanging around the table in the shop, others get to see what they are knitting and they get inspired." The same holds true with Monday night ongoing classes. "When someone sees what another person is doing, it's like an avalanche," Eva says. In fact, when she opened just before Christmas in 1987, the only things in the shop were a table, a Christmas tree, and some afghan yarn. But people came, and the rest is history.

Eva grew up in Finland, learning to knit when she was just four years old. Spending long, cold winters doing needlework has become a lifelong habit, even in sunny southern California. Though she professes to have started the shop to share her love of the needle arts, her husband suspects that Eva opened the yarn shop "just to cover up her addiction to yarns and to have someplace to hide the mountain she has collected!"

EVA'S NEEDLEWORK

1321 E. THOUSAND OAKS BLVD.
THOUSAND OAKS, CA 91362
PHONE: (805) 379-0722
WEBSITE: WWW.EVASNEEDLEWORK.COM
E-MAIL: EVA@EVASNEEDLEWORK.COM

Isabel's Sweater

Eva Wiechmann designed this sweater specifically for her little granddaughter, Isabel, who she reports "has the bluest eyes you have ever seen." Because there were not as many written patterns available in her native Finland, she got used to making up her own. This sweater has been a hit in the shop because it is simple to make, but even more experienced knitters enjoy knitting it. The wave pattern is cleverly made by looping yarn through some of the stitches after the knitting is complete.

123

ISABEL'S SWEATER
Eva (Eira) Wiechmann

FINISHED SIZE
28 (30)" (71 [76] cm) chest circumference.
To fit 2 (4) years. Sweater shown measures
30" (76 cm).

YARN
Berroco Pronto (50% cotton, 50% acrylic;
55 yd [50 m]/50 g): #4411 blue dahlia
(MC), 6 balls; #4400 bleach white (CC),
1 ball.

NEEDLES
Body and Sleeves—Size 10 (6 mm).
Neckband—Size 9 (5.5 mm): 16" (40-cm)
circular (cir). Adjust needle sizes if necessary
to obtain the correct gauge.

NOTIONS
Stitch holders; tapestry needle; marker (m).

GAUGE
12 sts and 21 rows = 4" (10 cm) in seed
stitch on larger needles.

Seed Stitch:
(worked on an even number of sts)
Row 1: (RS) *K1, p1; rep from *.
Row 2: *P1, k1; rep from *.
Repeat Rows 1 and 2 for pattern.

(worked on an odd number of sts)
Row 1: (RS) *K1, p1; rep from *, end k1.
Row 2: K1, *p1, k1; rep from *.
Repeat rows 1 and 2 for pattern.

Back
With CC and larger needles, CO 44 (47)
sts. Change to MC and work seed st until
piece measures 13½ (14½)" (34.5 [37] cm)
from beg, ending with a WS row. **Shape
neck:** Work 12 (13) sts in patt, join new
yarn and BO center 20 (21) sts, work to
end—12 (13) sts each side. Work even for
2 rows. Place sts on holders.

Front
Work same as for back until piece measures 12 (13)" (30.5 [33] cm) from beg,
ending with a WS row. **Shape neck:** Work
16 (17) sts in patt, join new yarn and BO
center 12 (13) sts, work to end—16 (17)
sts each side. Working each side separately, BO 2 sts at neck edge every other row 2
times—12 (13) sts rem each side. Cont

even until piece measures same as back.
Using the three-needle bind-off (see
Glossary), join front to back at shoulders.

Sleeves
Measure 5½ (6)" (14 [15.5] cm) down from
each shoulder on front and back and mark
for sleeve placement. With RS facing and
MC, pick up and knit 38 (40) sts bet
markers. Work seed st for 1" (2.5 cm).
Cont in seed st, dec 1 st each end of needle
every 5 (6) rows 7 times—24 (26) sts rem.
Work even until piece measures 8½ (10)"
(21.5 [25.5] cm) from pick-up row. With
CC, BO all sts in patt.

Finishing
Neckband: With MC, cir needle, RS facing, and beg at right shoulder, pick up and
knit 50 (52) sts evenly spaced around neck
opening. Place m and join. Knit 4 rnds.
With CC, BO all sts. With MC threaded on
a tapestry needle, sew side and sleeve
seams. **Embroidery:** With CC threaded on
a tapestry needle, RS facing, and beg on
the 4th row up from the lower edge, weave
CC into purl stitches diagonally through 3
stitches up, then diagonally 3 stitches
down. Weave in loose ends.

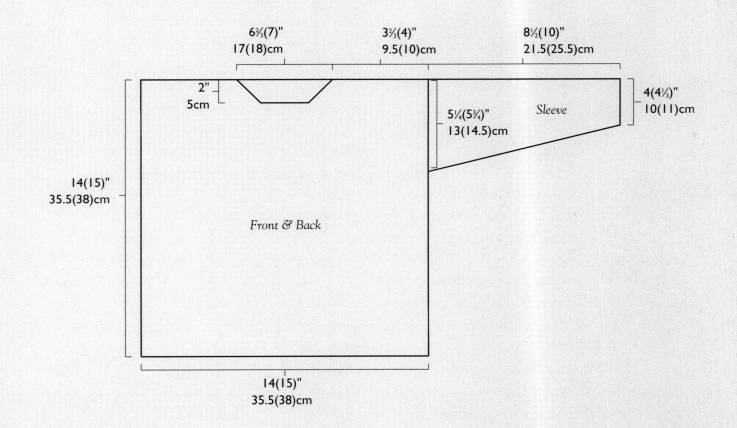

6⅔(7)"
17(18)cm

3⅔(4)"
9.5(10)cm

8½(10)"
21.5(25.5)cm

2"
5cm

4(4⅓)"
10(11)cm

5¼(5¾)"
13(14.5)cm

Sleeve

Front & Back

14(15)"
35.5(38)cm

14(15)"
35.5(38)cm

OVER THE MOON • Chocolate, coffee, and knitting—what more could you want? And you can have it all at Over the Moon Café & Mercantile. Owner Tara Jon Manning designed the shop as a haven for all the things she thinks are wonderful. As you enter, you find a full-service espresso bar featuring great coffee, home-baked pastries, and other gourmet treats. Keep going and you'll pass a discerning collection of books, gifts, jewelry, and cool stuff for babies. Then you come to the magic: natural light, fine yarns, knitting books, and a big table where, more often than not, you'll find other kindred souls. In winter, you can snuggle up to the fireplace and knit; in summer, the outside tables catch a view of the Colorado Rockies. At any season, you'll find Tara's child, Jack, in the store because having him close at hand is a boon to her.

Knitters and non-knitters alike happily coexist at Over the Moon. Children are always welcome—they can play with Jack—and the coffee shop is a comfortable hangout for friends and spouses while knitters do their thing. Reflecting Tara's Irish-American heritage and the subject of her master's thesis, Aran knitting occupies a special place at Over the Moon. But the fisherman knits by no means overshadow what the total shop is about—elegant, colorful yarns and patterns, plus great coffee.

OVER THE MOON CAFÉ & MERCANTILE

MEADOW VIEW VILLAGE
BLDG A, STE D
600 SOUTH AIRPORT ROAD
LONGMONT, CO 80503
PHONE: (303) 485-6778
WEBSITE: WWW.OVER-THE-MOON.NET
E-MAIL: KNITTING@OVER-THE-MOON.NET

CHENILLE JACKET

It's no wonder that this cozy chenille jacket is Tara Jon Manning's most popular pattern. Snuggly and easy to make, it's designed for everyone from infants to the extra-large. It is a wonderful sweater for beginners, yet seasoned knitters will appreciate its versatility and clever construction.

FINISHED SIZE

Child's version: 22 (25, 27, 29)" (56 [63.5, 68.5, 73.5] cm) chest circumference, buttoned (to fit sizes 1 [2, 3, 4] years). Adult version: 42 (46, 48, 50, 52)" (106.5 [117, 122, 127, 132] cm) chest circumference, buttoned. Sweaters shown measure 29" and 46" (73.5 and 117 cm).

YARN

Crystal Palace Cotton Chenille (100% cotton; 98 yd [89 m]/50 g). Child's version: #9628 periwinkle blue, 4 (5, 5, 6) skeins. Adult version: # 5021 dark sage, 10 (11, 13, 13, 14) skeins.

NEEDLES

Size 6 (4.0 mm). Adjust needle size if necessary to obtain the correct gauge.

NOTIONS

Stitch holders; tapestry needle; size H/8 (4.75-mm) crochet hook; spare knitting needle for joining shoulders; four ½" (1.3-cm) buttons for child's version; six ½" (1.3-cm) buttons for adult version.

GAUGE

16 sts and 28 rows = 4" (10 cm) in moss stitch.

NOTES

To make jacket longer, increase length of moss stitch worked. Of course, doing so will affect the amount of yarn required. Chenille yarn, particularly cotton chenille, doesn't stretch like spun and plied yarn. Consider using a larger needle to CO and BO. It is very important to cast on and BO loosely and evenly, and to knit evenly. Achieving an even and exact gauge is very important. An incorrect gauge may affect total yarn requirement.

CHENILLE JACKET
Tara Jon Manning

Stitch

Moss Stitch:
(multiple of 4 sts)
Rows 1 and 2: *K1, p1; rep from *.
Rows 3 and 4: *P1, k1; rep from *.
Rep Rows 1–4 for pattern.

CHILD'S VERSION

Back

Loosely CO 44 (50, 54, 58) sts. Beg with Row 1, work moss st until piece measures 5 (5½, 6, 6½)" (12.5 [14, 15, 16.5] cm) from beg, or 1" (2.5 cm) less than desired length to armholes, ending with Row 4 of patt. *Purl ridge:*
Row 1: (RS) *K1, p1; rep from *.
Rows 2 and 3: Purl.
Rows 4 and 5: Knit.
Row 6: Purl.
Shape armholes: (RS) BO 2 sts at beg of next 2 rows—40 (46, 50, 54) sts rem. Work even in St st until piece measures 11 (12½, 13½, 14½)" (28 [31.5, 34.5, 37] cm) from beg, ending with a RS row. *Shape neck:* (WS) P12 (14, 16, 18), BO center 16 (18, 18, 18) sts, p12 (14, 16, 18). Place 12 (14, 16, 18) sts for each shoulder on holders.

Left Front

Loosely CO 22, (25, 27, 29) sts. Beg with Row 1, work moss st until piece measures 5 (5½, 6, 6½)" (12.5 [14, 15, 16.5] cm) from beg, or 1" (2.5 cm) less than desired length to armhole, ending with Row 4 of patt. Work purl ridge as for back. **Shape**

armhole: (RS) BO 2 sts beg of next row—20 (23, 25, 27) sts rem. Work St st until piece measures 8½ (10, 11, 12)" (21.5 [25.5, 28, 30.5] cm) from beg, ending with a RS row. *Shape neck:* (WS) BO 4 sts at beg of row—16 (19, 21, 23) sts rem. Work 1 row even. Dec 1 st at neck edge every WS row 4 (5, 5, 5) times—12 (14, 16, 18) sts rem. Work even in St st until piece measures same length as back. Place sts on holders.

Right Front

Work as for left front, reversing shaping by binding off for armhole at beg of a WS row and working neck shaping at beg of RS rows, and *at the same time,* work 5 evenly spaced buttonholes along center front edge, working the first ¼" (6 mm) from lower edge and 4 more placed about 2 (2¼, 2½, 2¾)" (5 [5.5, 6.5, 7] cm) apart, ending ¼" (6 mm) before beg of neck decs. Work buttonhole as foll:
Row 1: (RS) Work 2 sts, BO 2 sts, work to end of row in patt.
Row 2: Work in patt, CO 2 sts over BO of previous row, work 2 sts.

Join Shoulders

With WS facing and using the three-needle bind-off (see Glossary), join fronts to back at shoulders for decorative ridge.

Right Sleeve

With RS facing and beg at back edge of armhole, pick up and knit 40 (44, 50, 52) sts. Starting with purl row, beg working in

Child Sizes: 4(4½)" 10(11.5)cm   3(3½, 4, 4½)" 7.5(9, 10, 11.5)cm

Adult Sizes: 7(7½, 8, 8, 9)" 18(19, 20.5, 20.5, 23)cm   6½(7¼, 7½, 8, 8)" 16.5(18.5, 19, 20.5, 20.5)cm

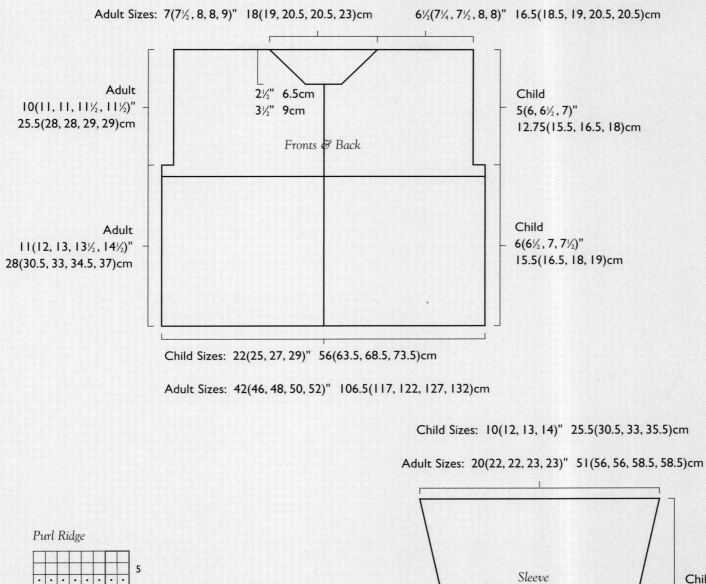

Adult
10(11, 11, 11½, 11½)"
25.5(28, 28, 29, 29)cm

2½" 6.5cm
3½" 9cm

Fronts & Back

Child
5(6, 6½, 7)"
12.75(15.5, 16.5, 18)cm

Adult
11(12, 13, 13½, 14½)"
28(30.5, 33, 34.5, 37)cm

Child
6(6½, 7, 7½)"
15.5(16.5, 18, 19)cm

Child Sizes: 22(25, 27, 29)" 56(63.5, 68.5, 73.5)cm

Adult Sizes: 42(46, 48, 50, 52)" 106.5(117, 122, 127, 132)cm

Purl Ridge

k on RS;
p on WS

· p on RS;
k on WS

pattern repeat

Moss Stitch

Child Sizes: 10(12, 13, 14)" 25.5(30.5, 33, 35.5)cm

Adult Sizes: 20(22, 22, 23, 23)" 51(56, 56, 58.5, 58.5)cm

Sleeve

Child
8½(9½, 10½, 11½)"
21.5(24, 26.5, 29)cm

Adult
17"
43cm

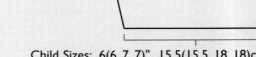

Child Sizes: 6(6, 7, 7)" 15.5(15.5, 18, 18)cm
Adult Sizes: 10(10, 10, 10½, 10½)" 25.5(25.5, 25.5, 26.5, 26.5)cm

CHENILLE

An accurate gauge is the most important factor in successful knitting with chenille yarn. It must be knit tightly and evenly, with gaps between stitches eliminated. In our classes, knitters often end up on needles two to three sizes smaller than those specified in the pattern to achieve the correct gauge. Sometimes a smaller needle than that specified will result in the same gauge but a tighter, woven look. For the Chenille Jacket, I recommend casting on 20 stitches and working the double moss stitch on size 6 needles for a few inches, then progressively work down in needle size until it looks right while maintaining the gauge. If you end up on smaller needles, constantly check your gauge—I find that knitters sometimes hit a "learning curve" with chenille and tighten up mid-project, necessitating a change to a larger needle at that point. Keep an eye on your work, and it won't adversely affect the finished product.

Over the Moon

St st, dec 1 st each end of needle every 4 rows 8 (10, 11, 12) times, and *at the same time*, when sleeve measures 4" (10 cm) from pick-up row, work purl ridge in reverse order (work Rows 6–1), then cont dec in moss st—24 (24, 28, 28) sts rem after all decs. Work even until sleeve measures 8½ (9½, 10½, 11½)" (21.5 [24, 26.5, 29] cm). BO all sts.

Left Sleeve
Work as for right sleeve, but beg at front edge of armhole.

Finishing
Using a matching color yarn such as mercerized cottton or floss threaded on a tapestry needle, sew sleeve and side seams from cuff to lower body edge. Hand- or machine-wash on delicate cycle and lay flat to dry until lightly damp. Place in dryer on *air only* to restore loft. **Edging:** Work 1 row of single crochet (as shown in photo) or blanket stitch (see Glossary) around all edges. Sew buttons to left front opposite buttonholes.

ADULT VERSION

Back
Loosely CO 84, (92, 96, 100, 104) sts. Beg with Row 1, work moss st until piece measures 10 (11, 12, 12½, 13½)" (25.5 [28, 30.5, 31.5, 34.5] cm) from beg, or 1" (2.5 cm) less than desired length to armhole, ending with Row 4 of patt. **Purl ridge:**
Row 1: (RS) *K1, p1, rep from *.
Rows 2 and 3: Purl.
Rows 4 and 5: Knit.
Row 6: Purl.
Shape armholes: BO 2 sts at beg of next 2 rows—80 (88, 92, 96, 100) sts rem. Work even in St st until piece measures 21 (23, 24, 25, 26)" (53.5 [58.5, 61, 63.5, 66] cm) from beg, ending with a RS row. **Shape neck:** (WS) P26 (29, 30, 32, 32), BO center 28 (30, 32, 32, 36) sts, p26 (29, 30,

32, 32). Place 26 (29, 30, 32, 32) sts for each shoulder on holders.

Left Front
Loosely CO 42, (46, 48, 50, 52) sts. Beg with Row 1, work moss st until piece measures 10 (11, 12, 12½, 13½)" (25.5 [28, 30.5, 31.5, 34.5] cm) from beg, or 1" (2.5 cm) less than desired length to armhole, ending with Row 4 of patt. Work purl ridge as for back. **Shape armhole:** (RS) BO 2 sts at beg of next row—40 (44, 46, 48, 50) sts rem. Work St st until piece measures 17½ (19½, 20½, 21½, 22½)" (44.5 [49.5, 52, 54.5, 57] cm) from beg, ending with a RS row. **Shape neck:** (WS) BO 8 (8, 9, 9, 9) sts at beg of row—32 (36, 37, 39, 41) sts rem. Work 1 row even. Dec 1 st at neck edge every WS row 6 (7, 7, 7, 9) times—26 (29, 30, 32, 32) sts rem. Work even in St st until piece measures same length as back. Place sts on holders.

Right Front
Work as for left front, reversing shaping by binding off for armhole at beg of a WS row and working neck shaping at beg of RS rows, and *at the same time,* work 6 evenly spaced buttonholes along center front edge, working the first ¼" (6 mm) from lower edge, and 5 more placed about 3¼ (3¾, 4, 4¼, 4½)" (8.5 [9.5, 10, 11, 11.5] cm) apart, ending about ¼" (6 mm) before beg of neck decs. Work buttonhole as foll:
Row 1: (RS) Work 2 sts, BO 2 sts, work to end of row in patt.
Row 2: Work in patt, CO 2 sts over BO of previous row, work 2 sts.
(*Note:* For larger buttons, BO additional sts as needed to match desired diameter.)

Join Shoulders
With WS facing and using three-needle bind-off (see Glossary), join fronts to back at shoulders.

Right Sleeve
With RS facing and beg at back edge of armhole, pick up and knit 80 (88, 88, 92, 92)

sts. Starting with a purl row, beg working in St st, dec 1 st each end of needle every 4 rows 20 (24, 24, 25, 25) times, and *at the same time,* when sleeve measures 8" (20.5 cm) from pick-up row, work purl ridge in reverse order (work Rows 6–1), then cont in moss st—40 (40, 40, 42, 42) sts rem after all decs. Work even until sleeve measures 17" (43 cm) or desired total length. BO all sts.

Left Sleeve

Work as for right sleeve, but beg at front edge of armhole.

Finishing

Using a matching color yarn such as mercerized cottton or floss threaded on a tapestry needle, sew sleeve and side seams from cuff to lower body edge. Hand- or machine-wash on delicate cycle and lay flat to dry until lightly damp. Place in dryer on *air only* to restore loft. **Edging:** Work 1 row of single crochet (as shown in photo) or blanket stitch (see Glossary) around all edges. Sew buttons to left front opposite buttonholes.

AMAZING THREADS • "How did two guys come to own a fiber arts shop?" is one of the most common questions that Radley Cramer and Michael Murphy are asked. The answer is a bit roundabout: When the two were restoring a Victorian brownstone in New York City, they were flabbergasted by estimates for period window treatments, so they decided to design and sew curtains themselves. They had done all the plastering, electrical and plumbing, floor refinishing, paint stripping, and so forth, so what was a little sewing? What they didn't expect was for those draperies to lead to a passion for all things associated with fiber. It was the early 1990s; Radley was in advertising and Michael in computers, and they felt the glow of the corporate world was growing dim. One of their favorite escapes from the city was Lake Katrine, a hamlet in the Hudson River Valley just minutes away from Kingston and Rhinebeck and near Woodstock. Lots of research, study, and hard work eventually resulted in Amazing Threads, a fiber destination with enticing views of the Catskill Mountains from its doorway.

Step into Amazing Threads and you're surrounded with color and texture. Not only an abundance of yarn and knitted samples, but spinning fibers, looms, buttons, books, sewing machines, finished garments, and racks and racks of colorful sewing thread. In the spaces where you can actually see the walls, they are sponged a soothing blue.

Early on, Radley and Michael were fortunate to find Jacqueline Olsen, a talented knitwear designer who teaches in the shop and creates many of its exclusive designs. These are featured as kits in a lovely catalog, "Knitter's Folio," and on Amazing Threads's internet site. In addition to teaching knitting and featuring knitting experts, the shop presents a well-rounded program that includes sewing, quilting, spinning, weaving, basketry, felting, jewelry-making, papermaking, gourd art, contemporary doll-making, and whatever else its dynamic owners fancy.

AMAZING THREADS

2010 ULSTER AVENUE
PO BOX 758
LAKE KATRINE, NY 12449
PHONE: (845) 336-5322
ORDERS ONLY: (888) SEW.KNIT
WEBSITE: WWW.AMAZINGTHREADS.COM

LACE RIBS PULLOVER

A master of architectural knitting designs, Jacqueline Olsen created Lace Ribs Pullover especially for this book. She loves to perfect the mathematics to make sweaters that fit and flatter. This elegant yet comfortable pullover makes the most of her favorite seamless shaping, which starts at the neck and includes a sleek saddle shoulder. Echoing the sweater's very elastic vertical lace pattern stitch, the neck cast-on is just as elastic and lacy. The sweater employs a lacy bind-off that Jacqueline "unvented" for a shawl class that she teaches.

FINISHED SIZE

44 (56)" (112 [142] cm) bust/chest circumference. Sweater shown measures 44" (112 cm).

YARN

Amazing Threads Private Collection Classic Wool (100% wool; 165 yd [151 m]/100 g): #2002 sage, 7 (10) balls. Small amount of waste yarn.

NEEDLES

Size 8 (5 mm): 24" (60-cm) circular (cir) and set of 5 double-pointed (dpn). You may also choose to use a 16" (40-cm) and 32" (80-cm) cir needle. Adjust needle size if necessary to obtain the correct gauge.

NOTIONS

Markers (m); tapestry needle.

GAUGE

16 sts and 20 rows = 4" (10 cm) in stockinette stitch.

NOTE

Slip all slip stitches purlwise unless instructions specify otherwise.

LACE RIBS PULLOVER

Jacqueline Olsen

Body

Neck: With dpn, CO 2 sts. Turn work, and with a second dpn, *yo, k2tog, turn; rep from * until there is a long strip with 55 yo loops along one side, end last rep k2tog—1 st on right needle. Place the 55 yo loops evenly divided onto 4 dpn and join, being careful not to twist sts—56 sts total; 14 sts each needle.

Rnd 1: *P2, k5; rep from *.

Rnd 2: *P2, k2tog, yo, k1, yo, ssk; rep from *.

Rnds 3 and 4: Rep Rnd 1.

Rep Rnds 1–4 two more times, then work Rnd 1 once (13 rnds total). **Saddle shoulders:** Place marker (pm), work next 9 sts as (M1, p2, k2tog, yo, k1, yo, ssk, p2, M1), pm, place rem 5 sts from this needle onto left needle, place 19 sts from that needle and 19 sts from the needle to the right of the saddle needle onto a piece of waste yarn, sl rem 9 sts (exactly opposite the sts you are working) onto another piece of waste yarn to work later as second saddle. Work back and forth in rows on the current 11 saddle sts as foll:

Rows 1 and 3: (WS) K3, p5, k2, sl 1 pwise with yarn in back (wyb).

Row 2: P3, k5, p2, sl 1 pwise with yarn in front (wyf).

Row 4: P3, k2tog, yo, k1, yo ssk, p2, sl 1 wyf.

Rep Rows 1–4 six more times, then work Rows 1 and 2 once (28 rows total). Break yarn, leaving a 6" (15-cm) tail. Place sts on waste yarn. Place the 9 sts for the second saddle onto a needle and work as for first saddle. **Front yoke:** With RS facing, pick

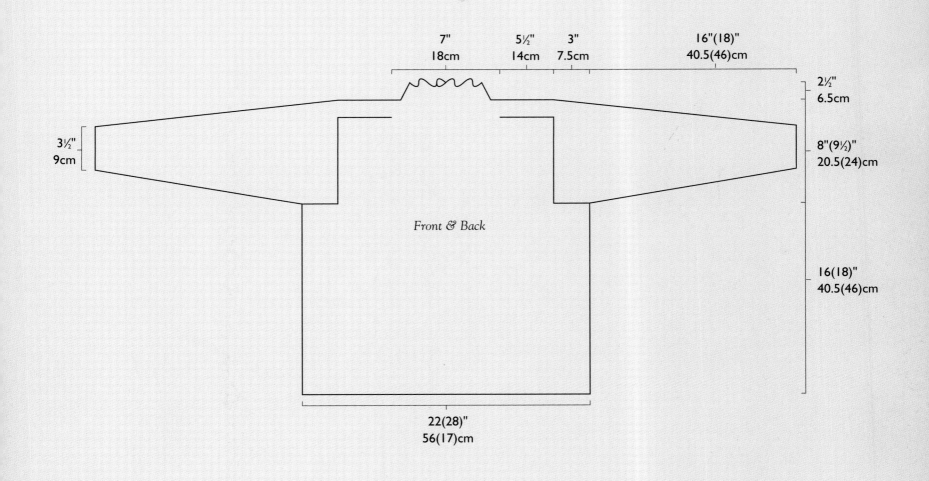

7"
18cm

5½"
14cm

3"
7.5cm

16"(18)"
40.5(46)cm

2½"
6.5cm

3½"
9cm

8"(9½)"
20.5(24)cm

Front & Back

16(18)"
40.5(46)cm

22(28)"
56(17)cm

Buy enough yarn! Dye lots change, yarns are discontinued.

The Yarnery

If you find yourself running out of yarn just inches before completing a project, and the dye lot is no longer available, locate a similar dye lot, rip back a few rows, attach the new dye lot, and work alternate rows of the original dye lot with the new dye lot. In most cases, the eye will blend the color seamlessly and minimize any difference in shade.

Green Mountain Spinnery

up and knit 15 sts along the side of the saddle (pick up from just inside the slipped st selvedge), M1 using the running thread between saddle and neck sts, work 19 neck sts in established patt ([k2tog, yo, k1, yo, ssk, p2] 2 times, k2tog, yo, k1, yo, ssk), M1, pick up and knit 15 sts from the side of second saddle, M1—52 sts. Turn and work as foll:

Row 1: K3, *p5, k2; rep from * 6 more times, M1—53 sts. (*Note:* The M1 is worked only on the first Row 1 to obtain 53 sts; on each subsequent Row 1, omit the M1 at the end of row.)

Row 2: P3, *k5, p2; rep from * 6 more times, sl 1.

Row 3: K3, *p5, k2; rep from * 6 more times, sl 1.

Row 4: P3, *k2tog, yo, k1, yo, ssk, p2; rep from * 6 more times, sl 1.

Work Rows 1–4 a total of 13 (15) times, then work Rows 1–3 once. Break yarn, leaving a 6" (15-cm) tail. Place sts onto waste yarn. **Back yoke:** Work as front yoke, then work 14 (16) entire reps of the 4-row patt worked for front yoke, changing to cir needle on the last row and ending last row as p2tog—52 sts rem; piece should measure about 11¼ (13)" (28.5 [33] cm) from beg of yoke. Do not break yarn. **Extend sides at underarm:** Using a provisional method (see Glossary), CO 47 (61) sts onto same needle as 52 back yoke sts. Place 53 held front yoke sts on empty cir needle and work as foll: P2tog, work Row 4 of patt to last 2 sts, p2tog, provisionally

CO 47 (61) more sts, pm on cir needle in right hand, and join, being careful not to twist sts, work back yoke sts as foll: P2tog, work Rnd 1 of patt to end—196 (224) sts total. Work in the rnd as foll:

Rnds 1, 2, and 3: *P2, k5; rep from *.

Rnd 4: P2, k2tog, yo, k1, yo, ssk, rep from *.

Rep Rnds 1–4 until piece measures 3" (7.5 cm) from provisional CO. Place 196 (224) body sts onto waste yarn.

Sleeves

Note: The sleeve stitches are picked up and worked from the sides of the yoke sections with the lace rib saddle in the center of them. The provisional CO sts of the side extension sts are placed onto the cir needle immediately after the sleeve pick-up. The sleeve sts are worked back and forth like a very large saddle. Each time the body extension sts are reached, a dec is worked, thereby consuming the extension sts and shaping the sleeve. *Pick-up row:* With cir needle, RS facing, and beg at front side edge of yoke, pick up and knit 27 (34) sts along front side edge of yoke (just inside the slipped st selvedge), place 11 saddle sts on needle and work them as foll: (p2tog, p1, k5, p1, p2tog), pick up and knit 27 (34) sts from the back side edge of yoke— 63 (77) sts total. With other tip of cir needle, pick up and knit 47 (61) sts from provisional CO of body extension—110 (138) sts total. Work patt as foll (*Note:* While the patt is the same, the row numbers are changed in order to stay in numerical sequence):

Row 1: (WS) Work the 63 (77) sleeve sts as foll: Sl 1 wyb, *p5, k2; rep from * 8 (10) more times, ending last rep p5, k3tog tbl (1 sleeve st and 2 sts from provisional CO)—63 (77) sleeve sts and 45 (59) provisional CO body extension sts rem.

Row 2: Sl 1 wyf, *k2tog, yo, k1, yo, ssk, p2; rep from * 6 (8) more times, ending last rep p3tog—63 (77) sleeve sts and 43 (57) CO sts rem.

Row 3: Rep Row 1—63 (77) sleeve sts and 41 (55) CO sts rem.

Row 4: Sl 1 wyf, *k5, p2; rep from * 6 (8) more times, ending last rep k5, p3tog—63 (77) sleeve sts and 39 (53) CO sts rem.

Rep Rows 1–4 as established until all but the center 7 sts of side extension have been worked into the decs. Pm at the outer purl st of these 7 sts. From here on, the sleeve is worked in the rnd; make sure that the pattern row of the sleeve continues across the center 7 sts. (*Note:* The patt won't appear continuous with the same patt row of the body because these sts are now "upside down" from how they are worked on the body, and will be offset by half a st—only you will know!). ***Shape sleeve:*** Work in established patt to 1 st before marked purl st, p2tog, work 5 sts in patt, p2tog, work to end—2 sts dec'd. Dec 2 sts in this manner every 4 (3) rnds 21 (28) times—28 sts rem. Work even until sleeve measures 17" (43 cm) or desired length. BO all sts as foll: *Yo, k2tog, place 2 sts from right needle onto the left needle and k2tog, sl st from right needle onto left needle; rep from *.

Lower Body

Place 196 (224) held body sts onto cir needle, rejoin, and cont in established patt until piece measures 16 (18)" (40.5 [46] cm) from underarm, or desired length, ending after completing Rnd 3. BO all sts as for sleeves. Weave in loose ends. Block to measurements.

tips

MY YARN SHOP • Picture a round oak table in a large, bright window facing the Pacific Coast Highway. Picture piles of books and magazines, mounds of colorful yarn, friends gathered together to knit and dream and plan their next projects over a cup of coffee. This is My Yarn Shop, a knitters' oasis on the sparsely populated Oregon coast.

My Yarn Shop is the brainchild of five friends who liked to knit together. They didn't begin in the usual manner by finding a location—they had store fixtures and a huge stash of yarn before they knew where they were going to put it. Happily, a vintage building with just the right feel turned up. The shop even has a huge built-in antique safe. "We have ironclad bragging rights when it comes to where we keep our yarn stash," the owners say.

Because their personal lives got so busy, the original five owners are now three—Liz Keator, Judy Mogan, and Janet Scanlon—and each brings different skills to the enterprise. But best of all, they are delighted to surround themselves with the yarn they love and to share it with others. "We enjoy what we do and suffer no illusions of becoming wealthy. Sharing our love of fibers is wealth beyond measure," they agree.

MY YARN SHOP

264B SOUTH BROADWAY
COOS BAY, OR 97420
PHONE: (541) 266-8230
ORDERS ONLY: (888) 664-9276
WEBSITE: WWW.MYYARNSHOP.COM
E-MAIL: KNITTING@MYYARNSHOP.COM

MY CONSTANT COMPANION

Janet Scanlon designed this bag in response to one of My Yarn Shop's roundtable discussions about the perfect knitting bag. Her sturdy, stylish solution holds a project or two, it's light and easy to carry, it has a practical flat bottom and ingenious draw-string construction. The felted finish is durable and water resistant. The bag is designed with a place for every-thing—and if not, you can add as many pockets as you please.

MY CONSTANT COMPANION
Janet Scanlon

FINISHED SIZE

About 18" (46 cm) wide, 12" (30.5 cm) deep, and 18" (46 cm) high, before felting. About 15" (38 cm) wide, 7½" (19 cm) deep, and 10" (25.5) high, after felting. Note: This bag will shrink to about 60% of the knitted length and 80% of the knitted width.

YARN

Brown Sheep, Nature Spun Worsted (100% wool; 245 yd [224 m]/100 g): #N94 Bev's bear (MC), 6 skeins. Brown Sheep Lamb's Pride Bulky (85% wool, 15% mohair; 125 yd [114 m]/113 g): #M93 dark earth (CC), 1 skein.

NEEDLES

Size 11 (8 mm): 32" (80-cm) circular (cir) and set of 2 double-pointed (dpn). Adjust needle size if necessary to obtain the correct gauge.

NOTIONS

Markers (m); tapestry needle.

GAUGE

About 11 sts = 4" (10 cm) in stockinette stitch.

Base

With cir needle and 2 strands of MC held tog, CO 51 sts. Do not join. Work garter st (knit every row) for 60 rows—30 garter ridges.

Sides

Place marker (pm; use a different color for this marker), pick up and knit 28 sts along left side of base, pm, pick up and knit 51 sts along CO edge, pm, pick up and knit 28 sts along right side of base, pm, k51.
Rnd 1: Knit.
Rnd 2: [Sl 1, k26, sl 1, sl m, k51, sl m] 2 times—158 sts.
Rep Rnds 1 and 2 until piece measures 17" (43 cm) from pick-up rnd. (*Note:* The slipped sts define the corners of the bag.)
I-cord BO: Using the backward loop method (see Glossary), CO 3 sts. *With dpn, k2, k2tog tbl (the third CO st and the first st of bag), return 3 sts to left needle, pull yarn behind these sts, and rep from * 7 more times. *Make slot for strap:* K3, sl next 2 sts pwise to right needle, pass first slipped st over second, sl a third st pwise to right needle, sl second slipped st over third. Return this st to left needle—2 sts have been bound off. Return 3 I-cord sts to left needle. Work 3 rows of I-cord on these 3 sts without binding off any body sts. Resume I-cord BO to 10 sts before m. Make a slot as before. Resume I-cord BO to m. Remove m. **Work I-cord BO for 8 sts. Make slot as before. Cont I-cord BO

To work a mosaic chart, alternate 2 rows CC with 2 rows MC as foll: Work RS rows from right to left using the color indicated by the first st. Knit the sts that are the same color as the first st and slip the other sts pwise with yarn in back. Work WS rows along same row of chart just worked, but work from left to right, using the same color just used and pulling the knit sts of the previous row and slipping the slipped sts pwise with yarn in front.

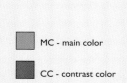

MC - main color

CC - contrast color

Mosaic

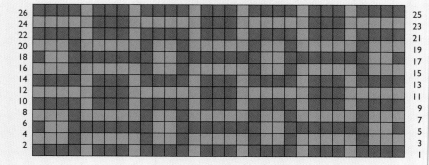

to center front. **Button:** At the center front knit 6" (15 cm) of I-cord without BO any sts. Fold this 6"-length in half and tie into a knot (the button is made). Resume working I-cord BO to 10 sts before m, make slot. Cont working I-cord BO to m. Remove m. Repeat from **, disregarding button instructions, until no bag sts rem, and each side has 2 strap slots. BO rem 3 I-cord sts. With yarn threaded on tapestry needle, sew BO and CO edges of I-cord tog. **Contrast color I-cord:** With cir needle and 1 strand of CC, pick up and knit 158 sts along the top of the I-cord border just made. Using the backward loop method, CO 4 sts. *With dpn, k3, k2tog (last I-cord st with first picked-up st); rep from * until no picked-up sts rem. BO 4 I-cord sts. Sew BO and CO edges of I-cord tog. **Third row of I-cord:** With cir needle and 2 strands of MC, pick up and knit 158 sts along top of previous I-cord edge. Using the backward loop method, CO 3 sts. With dpn, k2, k2tog (last I-cord st with first picked-up st); rep from * to center back panel, opposite the I-cord button. Work 3-st I-cord (see Glossary) for 6" (15 cm) for button loop. Cont with I-cord BO until no picked-up sts rem. BO 3 I-cord sts. Sew BO and CO edges of I-cord tog.

I-Cord Strap

(Make 2) With dpn and 2 strands of MC, CO 4 sts. Work 4-st I-cord (see Glossary) until piece measures 60" (152.5 cm) from beg. BO all sts.

Pocket

With cir needle and 2 strands of MC, CO 31 sts. Do not join. Work St st until piece measures 4" (10 cm) from beg. Join 1 strand of CC and work Rows 1–26 of Mosaic chart. With MC, work 1 row. Using I-cord BO as before, BO all sts. If desired, make additional patterned or plain pockets for inside of bag. Pocket

measures about 7½" by 6½" (19 cm by 16.5 cm) after felting.

Felting

Fill washing machine with hot water on low setting and add a small amount of mild detergent. Add bag, strap, and pocket pieces. Start machine to agitate on normal setting for 5 minutes. Check for degree of felting. Cont to agitate load, stopping to check every 2 minutes to monitor the progress. Felting is complete when the sts are obscured and the pieces have shrunk in size—the amount of time varies from washing machine to washing machine. Turn control to delicate cycle and spin out water. Remove pieces from machine and refill machine with warm water. Replace pieces and agitate on delicate cycle for 1 or 2 minutes, then spin out water. Remove pieces and rinse again by hand in cool water (to harden the felt and firm the fabric). Squeeze out water and roll pieces in towels to remove as much excess water as possible. Set bag on a dry towel and use your hands to pat and stretch into shape (or stretch it over a suitable-sized form). Lay the straps flat or hang to dry. Place pocket(s) on dry towel and pull into shape, making sure that sides and corners are straight and square. Pull and poke the fabric to get the shape you like. Allow pieces to air dry, patting and adjusting, as you feel necessary.

Finishing

Straps: Beg at one side edge, thread one cord in and out through the 8 slits around the bag top, ending at the side edge where you began (see illustration above). Tie the ends in an overhand knot. Beg at the other side, rep with the other cord. **Pocket(s):** If necessary, trim the edges of the pocket(s) to make them straight. With MC and using a blanket stitch (see Glossary), sew pocket(s) in place.

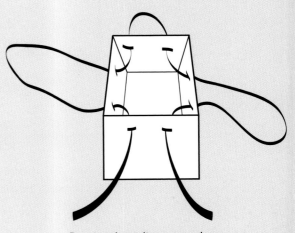

Repeat threading procedure on opposite side using second I-cord.

EWE-NIQUE KNITS • Along with an antique store and a garden shop, Ewe-Nique Knits is one of several businesses in a renovated church building situated at the edge of downtown Royal Oak, a suburb of Detroit. Opened in 1996 by good friends Kathie Gotfredson and Kathy Kamp, the store has a warm, welcoming feeling and an underlying spiritual quality that emanates from the structure's original function. There is nothing hard and modern about this space. Yarns are displayed in natural wooden crates, and sample sweaters hang from dowels, a lattice fence, and an old clothes-drying rack. They look so appealing that customers often buy them right from the displays. A fortuitous antique railroad sign over the counter reads, "Angora"—not the goat, but Angora, Wisconsin.

Both Kathie and Kathy learned to knit when they were Girl Scouts, and continued through college and while raising their families. They met while working at a knit shop and, upon its closing, fulfilled their dream of owning their own shop. With no other staff, it is a very personal enterprise with the two women "doing it all." They share not only the same first name, but the same responsibilities for running the business and teaching its many classes.

A hallmark of the shop is easy and versatile but "ewe-nique" patterns for both adults and children. Their one-of-a-kind designs use lots of color and feature simple pattern stitches and edgings. They don't sell their patterns, but provide them free to customers with their yarn purchases. Individual color choices and special buttons from their large selection make each garment special.

EWE-NIQUE KNITS

515 SOUTH LAFAYETTE
ROYAL OAK, MI 48067
PHONE: (248) 584-3001

SOPHISTICATED BABY JUMPER

Designed by Kathy Kamp, this cotton jumper is multiseasonal. It can be worn alone or layered over a T-shirt or turtleneck. Make this cute and comfy jumper in red with Christmas buttons or Valentine's Day hearts.

If you are making this dress as a gift, include a change of buttons for different occasions.

FINISHED SIZE

15½ (17½, 19)" (39.5 [44, 48.5] cm) yoke circumference. To fit 9 (12, 18) months. Jumper shown measures 15½" (39.5 cm).

YARN

Tahki Cotton Classic II (100% cotton; 74 yd [68 m]/50 g): #2002 black, 5 (6, 7) skeins.

NEEDLES

Body—Size 8 (5.0 mm). Armbands and Neckband—Size 7 (4.5 mm); 16" (40-cm) circular (cir). Adjust needle sizes if necessary to obtain the correct gauge.

NOTIONS

Stitch holders; markers (m); tapestry needle; ten ½–1" (1.3–2.5 cm) assorted black-and-white buttons. Buttons shown are from Durango, Muench, and Knitting Fever.

GAUGE

19 sts and 27 rows = 4" (10 cm) in stockinette stitch on larger needles.

SOPHISTICATED BABY JUMPER
Kathy Kamp

Back:
With larger needles, loosely CO 55 (61, 67) sts. Work p1, k1 ribbing, ending p1, for 3 rows, ending with a WS row. Work in St st until piece measures 9½ (13, 15)" (24 [33, 38] cm) from beg, ending with a WS row. **Shape yoke:** (RS) *K1, k2tog; rep from *, end k1—37 (41, 45) sts rem. Purl 1 row. **Shape armholes:** BO 5 sts at beg of next 2 rows—27 (31, 35) sts rem. Work in St st until armholes measure 3 (4, 4)" (7.5 [10, 10] cm), ending with a WS row. **Shape neck:** K8 (9, 10), place center 11 (13, 15) sts on holder for neck, join new yarn, work to end—8 (9, 10) sts each side of neck. Working each side separately, dec 1 st at neck edge every RS row 2 (3, 3) times— 6 (6, 7) sts rem each side. Work even until armholes measure 6 (7, 7)" (15 [18, 18] cm), ending with a WS row. Place sts on holders.

Front
Work as back.

Finishing
Using the three-needle bind-off (see Glossary), join front to back at shoulders. With yarn threaded on a tapestry needle, sew side seams. **Armbands:** With cir needle and beg at underarm, pick up and knit 60 (68, 68) sts around armhole. Place m and join. Purl 1 rnd. BO all sts knitwise. **Neckband:** With cir needle and beg at right shoulder seam, pick up and knit 14 sts along right back neck, M1 in running strand after last pick up stitch and before held sts, k11 (13, 15) held back neck sts, M1 in running strand between last held st and first pick up st, then pick up and k28 sts to front neck, M1 in running strand before held sts, k11 (13, 15) held front neck sts, M1 in running strand before first pick up st, pick up and knit 14 sts along right front neck—82 (86, 90) sts total. Place m and join. Purl 1 rnd. BO all sts knitwise. Weave in loose ends. Steam block lightly, if desired. Sew 10 buttons evenly spaced across front and back under yoke.

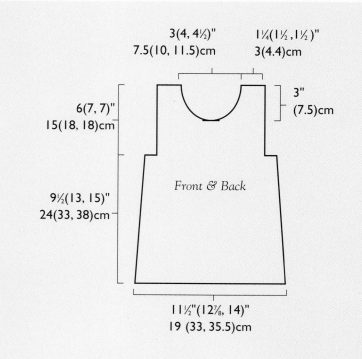

3(4, 4½)"
7.5(10, 11.5)cm

1¼(1½,1½)"
3(4.4)cm

3"
(7.5)cm

6(7, 7)"
15(18, 18)cm

Front & Back

9½(13, 15)"
24(33, 38)cm

11½"(12⅞, 14)"
19 (33, 35.5)cm

TRICOTER •

Tricoter (tree-ko-tay) is French for *to knit*, and it's an apt name for a fashionable yarn shop on Madison Street in Seattle. Here women in business attire shop and knit happily beside moms with babies in strollers. Beautiful fibers line the walls of the store, and inviting round tables in the center encourage all who enter to select some yarn, pull up a chair, and start knitting. Customers have described Tricoter as "an experience rather than a store."

Tricoter's co-owners, Beryl Hiatt and Lindy Phelps, attribute the shop's success to their commitment to helping customers make beautiful sweaters that *really fit.* They also design and knit custom sweaters for non-knitters.

Beryl opened Tricoter in the summer of 1984 as an outgrowth of her lifelong passion for knitting. When a financial analyst asked what made her think she could be successful with so little retail experience, Beryl's response was, "Because I love to entertain and I'm a great hostess." This warm, welcoming style drew an immediate circle of loyal, creative, passionate knitters to the store, many of whom still work there. Since customers also come from countries where knitting is integral to the culture, the shop enjoys an international flair.

When Beryl relocated Tricoter to Madison Park in 1990, she found herself next door to a brand-new coffee shop owned by Lindy Phelps. Their instant friendship soon became a partnership. In addition to running a busy shop, the two have co-authored two books: *Simpy Beautiful Sweaters,* and *Simply Beautiful Sweaters for Men.*

TRICOTER

3121 EAST MADISON
SEATTLE, WA 98112
PHONE: (206) 328-6505
ORDERS ONLY: (877) 554-YARN
WEBSITE: WWW.TRICOTER.COM
E-MAIL: TRICOTER@AOL.COM

TWEEDY CASHMERE PULLOVER

This pullover is typical of sweaters designed by Beryl Hiatt and Lindy Phelps of Tricoter, and it's a favorite in the store. The fiber is luxurious, the pattern is easy to knit, and the resulting pullover projects a wonderfully casual sense of style. A button band and optional suede topstitching are thoughtful finishing touches.

FINISHED SIZE
40 (44, 48)" (101.5 [112, 122] cm) bust/chest circumference. Sweater shown measures 44" (112 cm).

YARN
Filatura di Crosa Tweedy Cashmere (70% virgin wool, 30% cashmere; 126 yd [138m]/50 g): #804 oatmeal (A), 7 (7, 8) skeins, #805 cocoa (B), 3 (3, 4) skeins.

NEEDLES
Body and Sleeves—Size 8 (5.0 mm). Edging—Size 7 (4.5 mm). Adjust needle sizes if necessary to obtain the correct gauge.

NOTIONS
Tapestry needle; five ¾" (2-cm) buttons; suede cord or contrast color yarn for "x" detail at the color transition on body and sleeves (optional).

GAUGE
18 sts and 24 rows = 4" (10 cm) in stockinette stitch on large needles.

TWEEDY CASHMERE PULLOVER
Beryl Hiatt and Lindy Phelps

Note Stitch count includes edge sts for smooth selvedges when sewing together.

Back
With B and larger needles CO 92 (101, 110) sts.
Row 1: (WS) K1, *p3, k3; rep from *, end last rep k4.
Row 2: (RS) K1, *k3, p3; rep from* to last st, k1.
Repeat Rows 1 and 2 until piece measures 6" (15 cm) from beg. Change to A and cont in St st until piece measures 12 (12, 13)" (30.5 [30.5, 33] cm) from beg, ending with a WS row. *Shape armholes:* BO 4 (4, 5) sts at beg of next 2 rows, then BO 3 sts at beg of foll 2 rows, then BO 2 sts at beg of foll 2 rows—74 (83, 90) sts rem. Work 1 row even. Dec 1 st at beg of next 2 (4, 4) rows—72 (79, 86) sts rem. Cont in St st until piece measures 20 (21, 22)" (51 [53.5, 56] cm) from beg, ending with a WS row. *Shape neck and shoulders:* K22 (25, 25), join new yarn and BO center 28 (29, 36) sts, knit to end—22 (25, 25) sts each side. Working each side separately, BO 7 (8, 8) sts at armhole edge once, then BO 7 (8, 8) sts at armhole edge 2 times, and *at the same time,* dec 1 st at neck edge once.

Front
Work as for back until piece measures 6" (15 cm) from beg, ending with a WS row. Change to A and St st, and work as foll: K43 (48, 52), join new yarn and BO center 6 (5, 6) sts, knit to end—43 (48, 52) sts each side. *Right front:* Work even in St st until piece measures 12 (12, 13)" (30.5 [30.5, 33] cm) from beg, ending with a RS row. *Shape armhole:* (WS) At armhole edge, BO 4 (4, 5) sts once, then BO 3 sts once, then BO 2 sts once—5 rows worked; 34 (39, 42) sts rem. Work 1 row even. Dec 1 st at armhole edge every other row 1 (2, 2)

time(s)—33 (37, 40) sts rem. Cont even until piece measures 18 (19, 20)" (48 [48, 51] cm) from beg, ending with a WS row. *Shape neck:* (RS) At neck edge, BO 5 sts once, then BO 3 (3, 4) sts once, then BO 2 (2, 3) sts once—23 (27, 28) sts rem. Work 1 row even. Dec 1 st at neck edge every other row 2 (3, 4) times—21 (24, 24) sts rem. Cont even until piece measures 20 (21, 22)" (51 [53.5, 56] cm) from beg, ending with a RS row. *Shape shoulder:* (WS) At armhole edge, BO 7 (8, 8) sts 3 times—*Left front:* Work as right front, reversing shaping.

Sleeves
With B, CO 32 (38, 38) sts. Work k3, p3 ribbing as for back until piece measures 6" (15 cm) from beg, ending with a WS row and inc 4 sts evenly spaced across last row—36 (42, 42) sts. Change to A and cont in St st, inc 1 st at each end of needle every 3 rows 18 times—72 (78, 78) sts. Work even until piece measures 16 (16½, 17)" (40.5 [42, 43] cm) from beg, ending with a WS row. *Shape cap:* (RS) BO 4 sts at beg of next 2 rows—64 (70, 70) sts rem. BO 2 sts at beg of foll 28 rows—8 (14, 14) sts rem. BO rem sts.

Finishing
With yarn threaded on a tapestry needle, join front to back at shoulders. *Neckband:* With A, smaller needles, RS facing, and beg at right front neck, pick up and knit 18 (18, 20) sts to shoulder seam, 33 (33, 38) sts across back neck to opposite shoulder, and 18 (18, 20) sts from shoulder seam to left front neck—69 (69, 78) sts total. Work k1, p1 ribbing for 1" (2.5 cm). BO all sts loosely. *Buttonband:* With A, smaller needles, and RS facing, pick up and knit 63 (63, 66) sts along left front placket opening. Work k1, p1 ribbing for 1¼ (1, 1¼)" (3

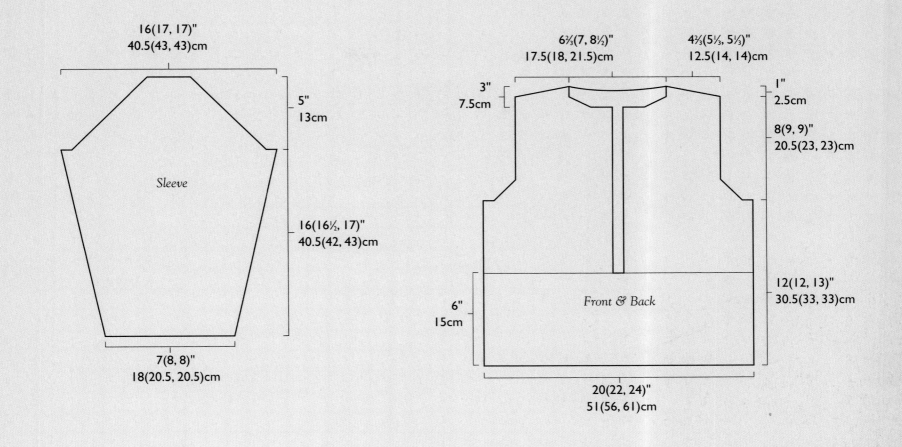

Sleeve

16(17, 17)"
40.5(43, 43)cm

5"
13cm

16(16½, 17)"
40.5(42, 43)cm

7(8, 8)"
18(20.5, 20.5)cm

6⅔(7, 8½)"
17.5(18, 21.5)cm

4⅔(5⅓, 5⅓)"
12.5(14, 14)cm

3"
7.5cm

1"
2.5cm

8(9, 9)"
20.5(23, 23)cm

Front & Back

12(12, 13)"
30.5(33, 33)cm

6"
15cm

20(22, 24)"
51(56, 61)cm

[2.5, 3] cm). BO all sts. **Buttonhole band:** With RS facing, pick up and knit 63 (63, 66) sts along right front placket opening. Working k1, p1 rib to match left side, place five 3-st buttonholes (see instructions at right) along center row of this band (refer to left band to select the exact row in which to make the buttonholes), placing one ¼" (3 cm) below neck edge, one ¼" (3 cm) above lower body edge, and the others evenly spaced in between. Sew buttons to buttonhole band opposite buttonholes. Sew sleeves into armholes. Sew sleeve and side seams.

Optional cross-stitch detail: With suede cord or contrasting yarn threaded on a tapestry needle, work a single row of cross-stitches along the boundary between colors A and B on the body and the sleeves. Secure each cross-stitch as you work by adding a small stitch at the crossing point. Weave in loose ends.

Buttonholes: Work in patt to first buttonhole placement, *BO 3 sts kwise, work in patt to next buttonhole placement; rep from * 5 times total. On next row, cont in patt, CO 3 sts over each gap formed by the BO sts of previous row.

SOPHIE'S YARNS

SOPHIE'S YARNS • Located in a brownstone in Philadelphia's fashionable and historic Rittenhouse Square, Sophie's Yarns was founded in 1995 by Jennifer Carpenter, Suzanne Litke, and Lisa Myers, each of whom had a Great Aunt Sophie. (Two of the Sophies were needle-women; the third preferred canasta.)

Because the three owners have very different tastes, the store stocks yarns of all types. One owner loves natural colors and says things like, "That's a really beautiful shade of white." Another swoons over dramatic hand-dyed yarns. Thus metallic eyelash yarn lives peacefully beside homespun, making for a space filled with color and texture. Sophie's Yarns stocks cashmere and other luxury fibers because the demand for them continues to grow. The owners say, "When people say our shop seems 'warm,' we don't think they're just talking about the emotional environment."

Sophie's Yarns places a strong emphasis on education: Its goal is to create more knitters and to make existing knitters more competent, confident, and independent. "The moments we feel most successful are those when people say, 'I never thought I'd have an interest in [lace, socks, entrelac—just fill in the blank], but when I see this, I want to try it.'" As the only downtown yarn shop in Philadelphia, Sophie's Yarns has a diverse customer base whom it serves with conscientious care.

The walls of the shop are crowded with an ever-changing display of beautiful handknits. Because all three owners are mothers of small children, they have a special interest in wee knits. Surely a visit to the store would have made that canasta-playing Great Aunt Sophie put away her cards.

SOPHIE'S YARNS

2017 LOCUST STREET
PHILADELPHIA, PA 19103
PHONE: (215) 977-YARN
WEBSITE: WWW.SOPHIESYARNS.COM

BOMBER CAP AND MITTENS

Runway fashions and customer
requests inspired Jennifer
Carpenter to design this
young-at-heart cap and mitten
set that appeals greatly to twenty-somethings,
especially in the cold Northeast. Two soft, luxuriously
textured yarns used together create a cozy faux fur
fabric that is warm and silky against the skin.
The set is knitted on fairly big needles and
goes together speedily.

BOMBER CAP AND MITTENS
Jennifer Carpenter

CAP

With shorter cir needle and 1 strand each of Chinchilla and Angora Tweed held tog, CO 60 sts. Place marker (pm) and join, being careful not to twist sts. Work St st until piece measures 5" (12.5 cm) from beg, or desired length. *Shape crown:*
Rnd 1: *K8, k2tog; rep from *—54 sts rem.
Rnds 2 and 4: Knit.
Rnd 3: *K7, k2tog; rep from *—48 sts rem. Cont to dec 6 sts every other rnd in this manner (work 1 less st bet k2togs) until 18 sts rem, changing to dpns when necessary. On next rnd, work k2tog all around—9 sts rem. Cut yarn and thread tail through rem sts, pull tight, and fasten off. Weave in loose ends.
Earflaps: (Both worked the same) Fold cap in half and place a marker in each side at CO edge to indicate center of earflaps. Pick up and knit 11 sts (5 sts on either side of marker plus 1 st at marker). Knit these 11 sts for 5 rows. Dec as foll:

Row 1: (RS) K1, k2tog, knit to last 3 sts, k2tog, k1—9 sts rem.
Row 2: Purl.
Rep Rows 1 and 2 two more times—5 sts rem. On next row, k1, k3tog, k1—3 sts rem. K3tog—1 st rem. **Ribbing:** With longer cir needle, 2 strands of Angora Tweed, and beg at single st rem on needle, pick up and knit 12 more sts along side of earflap (13 sts on needle), pick up and knit 24 sts along one edge of cap, 12 sts along side of other earflap, and the single st rem from that earflap—50 sts total. Work in k2, p2 rib for 3 rows. Work 1 row St st. BO all sts loosely and evenly. Work opposite side of cap in same manner, but pick up 16 sts along each earflap to include edge of finished ribbing. **Make Ties:** With 2 strands of Angora Tweed held tog, pick up and knit 3 sts at base of earflap. Work 3-st I-cord (see Glossary) for 5" (12.5 cm), or desired total length. BO all sts. Tie free end of cord into an

FINISHED SIZE
Hat: 22" (56 cm) circumference; 11½" (29 cm) from crown to tip of ear flap.
Mittens: 8¾" (22 cm) around hand.

YARN
Berroco Chinchilla (100% rayon; 77 yd [70 m]/50 g): #5103 taupe, 3 skeins. Garn Studio Karisma Angora Tweed (70% wool, 30% angora; 165 yd [150 m]/50 g): #6 dark taupe, 2 skeins.

NEEDLES
Size 10½ (6.5 mm): 16" and 24" (40- and 60-cm) circular (cir) and set of 4 double-pointed (dpn). Adjust needle size if necessary to obtain the correct gauge.

NOTIONS
Markers (m); tapestry needle.

GAUGE
11 sts and 14 rows = 4" (10 cm) in stockinette stitch worked in the round.

overhand knot. Make a tassel or pom-pom for the top, if desired.

MITTENS

With 2 strands of Angora Tweed held tog and dpn, CO 28 sts. Place marker (pm) and join, being careful not to twist sts. Work 3 rnds St st. Work 3 rnds of k2, p2 ribbing, dec 4 sts evenly across last rnd — 24 sts rem. Change to one strand each of Chinchilla and Angora Tweed held tog, and work St st for 4½" (11.5 cm). **Thumb opening:** Place first 4 sts onto a holder, knit to end—20 sts rem. On next rnd, CO 4 sts over gap, knit to end—24 sts. Rejoin and cont in St st for 5½" (14 cm), or until piece measures to top of index finger.

Shape top: Divide sts evenly onto 2 needles. Dec 1 st each side of mitten by working k1, k2tog at beg of each needle— 2 sts dec'd. Dec in this manner every rnd until 4 sts rem. Cut yarn, thread tail through rem sts, pull tight, and fasten off. Weave in loose ends. **Thumb:** Join yarn and k4 held sts, pick up and knit 1 st on one side of thumb, 4 sts along CO edge, and 1 st from other side of thumb—10 sts total. Join into a rnd. Work St st until piece measures 2½" (6.5 cm), or to middle of thumbnail. **Shape top:** [K1, k2tog] 3 times, k1—7 sts rem. On next rnd, [k2tog] 3 times, k1—4 sts rem. Cut yarn, thread tail through rem sts, pull tight, and fasten off. Weave in loose ends.

tips

KNITTING FOR KIDS

Instead of worrying that kids will lose a mitten, knit three or four to match—or whatever it takes to keep those little but forgetful hands warm.

Handknitters

Teach a child to knit. You'll be sharing yourself, your time, and something you love. So many of our knitters speak fondly of the relative who took the time to teach them to knit.

Handknitters

BIG SKY STUDIO & GALLERY •

Big Sky Studio & Gallery overlooks a meander-
ing creek; a deck adjacent to the shop
provides knitters with a delightful space to
sit and knit. Flowering plants in pots fill the
space, and the gentle murmur of the water
provides a peaceful background for the quiet
clicking of needles. It's the perfect setting for the
kind of personal creativity that owner Lisa Daniels wants
to encourage in her customers.

Inside the shop, one finds an atmosphere aimed at being adventurous and exciting. "Studio"
is a carefully chosen part of the shop's name. "We want to encourage knitters to follow a
creative and artistic path with their projects, maybe take some chances with color and texture,"
Lisa says. "We give them technical guidance along the way." Yarns are displayed in such a way
that emotional and aesthetic appeal hold sway over brand or fiber type.

The business was originally set up in 1996 as a private design studio for Lisa and her
students. In 1998, public interest prompted her to open the studio three days a week to
other customers. Knitters with high skill and interest levels have the opportunity to join the Studio Group, which gives them access to the space on its "closed" days as well as to design consultation. Lisa splits her time between Big Sky Studio & Gallery and her duties as Creative Director of Muench Yarns International.

BIG SKY STUDIO & GALLERY

961-C MORAGA ROAD
LAFAYETTE, CA 94549
PHONE: (925) 284-1020
WEBSITE: WWW.BIGSKYSTUDIO.COM
E-MAIL: BIGSKYS@PACBELL.NET

OPULENT EVENING SHAWL

Lisa Daniels designed this dramatic shawl to
show off an Italian-made chenille yarn with
extraordinary draping quality. The mitered rows
and light-catching quality of the yarn give the
shawl a three-dimensional look. Lisa credits both
Kaffe Fassett and the Missoni Studios for design
and color inspiration in many of her pieces. This
shawl, like many of her garments, can be thought
of as wearable art. "Be bold, be beautiful, and
enjoy the attention it brings," she says.

OPULENT EVENING SHAWL
Lisa Daniels

FINISHED SIZE

About 87" (221 cm) wide and 20" (51 cm) long, excluding fringe.

YARN

Muench Touch Me (72% viscose, 28% wool; 60 yd [55 m]/50 g): #3600 red, #3620 dark red, #3602 purple, #3635 orange, #3621 teal, #3622 steel, #3639 copper, #3601 burgundy, #3638 lavender, and #3623 rose, 2 balls each; #3632 gold, #3610 olive, #3633 dark green, #3631 pewter, #3618 toast, #3603 dark teal, #3628 dark brown, #3629 eggplant, #3607 black, and #3634 royal, 1 ball each.

NEEDLES

Size 6 (4 mm). Adjust needle size if necessary to obtain the correct gauge.

NOTIONS

Stitch holder; tapestry needle; crochet hook for attaching fringe.

GAUGE

16 sts and 6 rows = 4" (10 cm) in pattern garter stitch.

Notes from the Designer

Touch Me is a very unusual and most unique Italian-made chenille yarn. There really is no substitute for the texture, feel, and light catching three-dimensional quality. It is, however, a more difficult yarn to knit with. I strongly emphasize the necessity to knit tightly to maintain the gauge. Many times the solution in maintaining an even tension is to use a smaller needle size than the size recommended on the yarn band. Be sure to cast on a minimum of 20 stitches and work in garter stitch, alternating two rows each of two colors for a true and realistic sample.

Weave in the ends as you knit as follows: When you join a new color after having cut the old color (so that there are two ends to work with), knit the first two stitches firmly holding the two ends mentioned above. Once the first two stitches have been knitted, grasp both ends, plant your needle ready to work the next stitch, and bring the two ends in front of the working yarn. Then bring the ends down in front of the working yarn as you knit the next stitch. Work the two ends together for about 10 stitches.

Color Groupings and Sequence

There are 6 color groupings centered between the beginning triangles and the crossing of the chevron. Each grouping will use a total of 4 colors over 73 rows. The color stripes will not always end at the same edge of the work. The "Y" color from one section works its way into the next section in most cases.

Stripe series for beginning triangles:

Alternate 2 rows each of first 2 colors. (Do not cut yarns, as working an even numbered repeat you can leave both colors attached at the edge of the work.)

Triangles

(Make 2) The first section is worked alternating red and dark red. With dark red, CO 2 st. Knit 1 row.
Row 1: With red, [k1f&b] 2 times—4 sts.
Row 2: Knit.
Row 3: With dark red, k1f&b, knit to last st, k1f&b—2 sts inc'd.
Row 4: Knit.
Rep Rows 3 and 4 alternating bet red and dark red until there are 70 sts—68 rows worked. Place sts on holder. Work second triangle to match.

Join triangles: Place held sts of first triangle onto front of needle holding second triangle. K1f&b, k68, knit to last st of first triangle, k2tog tbl (last st of first triangle and first st of second triangle) k68, knit to last st of second triangle, k1f&b—141 sts. Knit 1 row.

First Color Group Orange (Y); Red (W); Gold (X); Teal (Z).

First Stripe Series:

Row 1: (RS) With orange (Y), k1f&b, k68, k3tog tbl, k68, k1f&b—141 sts.
Row 2: Knit.
Rep Rows 1 and 2, changing colors and number of rows worked as indicated.
Join red (W) and rep the 2 patt rows. With orange (Y), work the 2 patt rows 2 times—4 rows. Join gold (X) and work 2 rows. With Y, work 4 rows. With X, work 2 rows. Join Y and work 4 rows. Join W and work 2 rows. With Y, work 4 rows. With W, work 2 rows. With Y, work 3 rows—31 rows total.

Second Stripe Series:

With X, work 5 rows. With Z, work 2 rows. With X, work 5 rows. With Y, work 5 rows. With Z, work 2 rows. With Y, work 4 rows. With Z, work 3 rows. With W, work 5 rows. With X, work 2 rows. With W, work 5 rows. With Z, work 2 rows. With X, work 2 rows—42 rows total.

Second Color Group Olive (W); Dark Green (X); Teal (Y); Steel (Y); Pewter (Z).

First Stripe Series:
Note: Teal is (Y) in this section.
Cont in patt as established, work colors as foll: With Y, work 2 rows. With W, work 2 rows. With Y, work 4 rows. With X, work 2 rows. With Y, work 4 rows. With X, work 2 rows. With Y, work 4 rows. With X, work 2 rows. With Y, work 4 rows. With W, work 2 rows. With Y, work 4 rows. With W, work 2 rows. With Y, work 3 rows—31 rows total.

Second Stripe Series:
Note: Steel is Y in this section.
Cont as foll: With X, work 5 rows. With Z, work 2 rows. With X, work 5 rows. With Y, work 5 rows. With Z, work 2 rows. With Y, work 4 rows. With Z, work 3 rows. With W, work 5 rows. With X, work 2 rows. With W, work 5 rows. With Z, work 2 rows. With X, work 2 rows—42 rows total.

Third Color Group Toast (W); Dark Teal (X); Steel (Y); Pewter (Z).
Follow the same row format as the previous color groups, working 31 rows of first stripe series in above colors, then 42 rows of second stripe series.

Fourth Color Group Dark Brown (W); Dark Teal (X); Rose (X); Copper (Y); Steel (Z).

Follow row and color format, using Dark Teal as (X) in first stripe series, and Rose as (X) in second stripe series.

Fifth Color Group Eggplant (W); Rose (X); Burgundy (Y); Black (Z).
Work first and second stripe series in above colors.

Sixth Color Group Royal (W); Black (X); Purple (Y); Lavender (Z).
Work first and second stripe series in above colors.

Begin closing rows: Beg with lavender, alternate 2 rows each of lavender and purple, and *at the same time,* work as foll:
Row 1: K2tog tbl, k67, k3tog tbl, k67, k2tog.
Rows 2 and 4: Knit.
Row 3: K2tog tbl, k65, k3tog tbl, k65, k2tog.
Cont dec 4 sts every other row in this manner 34 times—5 sts rem. Knit 1 row. BO all sts.

Finishing
Weave in loose ends and trim ends. *Fringe:* Using the same 2 colors used at each end, wrap yarn around a piece of cardboard 10" (25.5 cm) wide 2 times—26 pieces of fringe for each end. Use crochet hook to secure fringe to edge of shawl.

tips

BLOCKING AND FINISHING

I base my decisions about fringe on two things: Is there enough remaining yarn, and is the yarn itself pretty as fringe? If the answer to both is "yes," I then decide what length to use. To wrap the yarn for fringe, don't use something too soft—I've used an old magazine, a compact-disc cover, my gauge-checking tool, a notebook, a piece of cardboard. And finally, be generous in your fringing—it just seems to look better.

Big Sky Studio

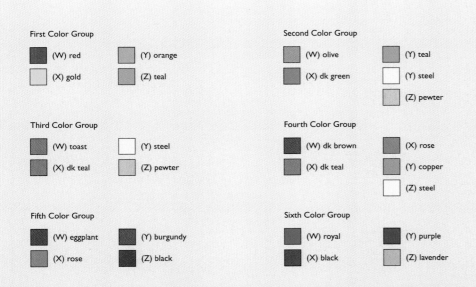

First Color Group

(W) red	(Y) orange
(X) gold	(Z) teal

Second Color Group

(W) olive	(Y) teal
(X) dk green	(Y) steel
	(Z) pewter

Third Color Group

(W) toast	(Y) steel
(X) dk teal	(Z) pewter

Fourth Color Group

(W) dk brown	(X) rose
(X) dk teal	(Y) copper
	(Z) steel

Fifth Color Group

(W) eggplant	(Y) burgundy
(X) rose	(Z) black

Sixth Color Group

(W) royal	(Y) purple
(X) black	(Z) lavender

ABBREVIATIONS

beg	beginning; begin; begins
bet	between
BO	bind off
CC	contrasting color
cm	centimeter(s)
cn	cable needle
CO	cast on
cont	continue
dec(s)	decrease(s); decreasing
dpn	double-pointed needle(s)
foll	following; follows
fwd	forward
g	gram(s)
inc	increase; increasing
k	knit
k1f&b	knit into front and back of same st
k2tog	knit two stitches together
kwise	knitwise
LC	left cross
m(s)	marker(s)
MC	main color
mm	millimeter(s)
M1	make one (increase)
p	purl
p1f&b	purl into front and back of same st
p2tog	purl two stitches together
patt(s)	pattern(s)
pm	place marker
psso	pass slip stitch over
p2sso	pass two slip stitches over
pwise	purlwise
RC	right cross
rem	remain; remaining
rep	repeat; repeating
rev St st	reverse stockinette stitch
rib	ribbing
rnd(s)	round(s)
RS	right side
rev sc	reverse single crochet
sc	single crochet
sk	skip
sl	slip
sl st	slip stitch (sl 1 st pwise unless otherwise indicated)
ssk	slip 1 kwise, slip 1 kwise, k2 sl sts tog tbl
ssp	slip 1 kwise, slip 1 kwise, p2 sl sts tog tbl
st(s)	stitch(es)
St st	stockinette stitch
tbl	through back loop
tog	together
WS	wrong side
wyb	with yarn in back
wyf	with yarn in front
yo	yarn over
*	repeat starting point (i.e., repeat from *)
* *	repeat all instructions between asterisks
( )	alternate measurements and/or instructions
[ ]	instructions that are to be worked as a group a specified number of times

GLOSSARY

Knitting Gauge

To check gauge, cast on 30 to 40 stitches using recommended needle size. Work in pattern stitch until piece measures at least 4" (10 cm) from cast-on edge. Remove swatch from needles or bind off loosely, and lay swatch on flat surface. Place a ruler over swatch and count number of stitches across and number of rows down (including fractions of stitches and rows) in 4" (10 cm). Repeat two or three times on different areas of swatch to confirm measurements. If you have more stitches and rows than called for in instructions, use larger needles; if you have fewer, use smaller needles. Repeat until gauge is correct.

Wraps Per Inch

If you substitute or spin a yarn for a project, you can compare the weight of the yarn to the project yarn by comparing wraps per inch. To do this, wrap your yarn around a ruler for one inch and count the number of wraps. If you have more wraps per inch, your yarn is too thin; fewer wraps per inch, your yarn is too thick.

Reading Charts

Unless otherwise indicated, read charts from the bottom up. On right-side rows, read charts from right to left. On wrong-side rows, read charts from left to right. When knitting in the round, read charts from right to left for all rows.

Long-Tail (Continental) Cast-On

Leaving a long tail (about ½" to 1" [1.3 to 2.5 cm] for each stitch to be cast on), make a slip knot and place on right needle. Place thumb and index finger of left hand between the yarn ends so that the working yarn is around index finger and the tail end is around thumb. Secure the ends with your other fingers and hold your palm upwards, making a V of yarn (Figure 1). Bring needle up through loop on thumb (Figure 2), grab first strand around index finger with needle, and go back down through loop on thumb (Figure 3). Drop loop off thumb and, placing thumb back in V configuration, tighten resulting stitch on needle (Figure 4).

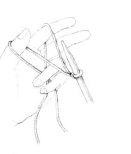

Figure 1   *Figure 2*

Figure 3   *Figure 4*

Knitted Cast-On

Place slip-knot on left needle if there are no established stitches. *With right needle, knit into the first stitch (or slip-knot) on left needle (Figure 1) and place new stitch onto left needle (Figure 2). Repeat from *, always knitting into the last stitch made.

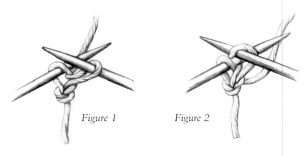

Figure 1   *Figure 2*

Cable Cast-On

Begin with a slip-knot and one knitted cast-on stitch if there are no established stitches. Insert right needle between first two stitches on left needle (Figure 1). Wrap yarn as if to knit. Draw yarn through to complete stitch (Figure 2) and slip this new stitch to left needle as shown (Figure 3).

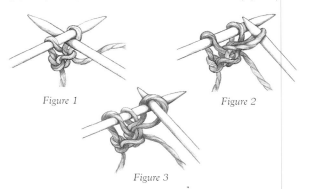

Figure 1   *Figure 2*

Figure 3

Backward Loop Cast-On

*Loop working yarn and place it on needle backward so that it doesn't unwind. Repeat from *.

Invisible (Provisional) Cast On

Place a loose slipknot of working yarn on needle. Hold waste yarn next to slipknot and wind working yarn under waste yarn, over needle, and in front of and then behind waste yarn for desired number of stitches. When you're ready to work in the opposite direction, remove waste yarn and pick up loops.

Crochet Chain (Provisional) Cast-On

Make a crochet chain 4 stitches longer than the number of stitches you need to cast on. Pick up and knit stitches through back loops of the crochet chain. Pull out the crochet chain to expose live stitches when you're ready to knit in the opposite direction.

SSK Decrease

This is a left-slanting decrease.

Slip two stitches knitwise.

Insert the point of the left needle into the front of the two slipped stitches and knit them together through the back loop with the right needle.

Make 1 (M1) Increase

Unless otherwise specified, use M1L. *Make 1 left (M1L):* With left needle tip, lift the strand between last knitted stitch and first stitch on left needle, from front to back (Figure 1). Knit the lifted loop through back (Figure 2). Makes a left slant. *Make 1 right (M1R):* With left needle tip, lift the strand between last knitted stitch and first stitch on left needle, from back to front (Figure 3). Knit lifted loop through the front (Figure 4). Makes a right slant.

Figure 1

Figure 2

Figure 3

Figure 4

I-Cord

With dpn, CO desired number of sts. *Without turning the needle, slide sts to other end of needle, pull yarn around back, and knit the sts as usual; rep from * for desired length.

Applied I-Cord

As I-cord is knitted, attach it to the garment as follows: With garment RS facing and using a separate ball of yarn and cir needle, pick up the desired number of sts along the garment edge. Slide these sts down the needle so that the first picked-up st is near the opposite needle point. With dpn, CO desired number of I-cord sts. Knit across the I-cord to the last st, then knit the last st tog with the first picked-up st on the garment, and pull the yarn behind the cord (pull the yarn in front of the cord for reverse I-cord). Knit to the last I-cord st, then knit the last I-cord st tog with the next picked-up st. Cont in this manner until all picked-up sts have been used.

Note: When working attached I-cord, as in all picked-up edge finishes, do not pick up every st. Work the edging for about 2" (5 cm), then lay the piece flat to make sure that the cord lies flat along the edge—if not pull out the necessary sts and rework, picking up more or fewer sts along the garment edge, as needed.

Invisible Seam

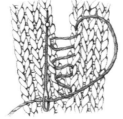

Working from the right side of the garment, place the pieces to be seamed on a flat surface, right sides up. Begin at the lower edge and work upward, row by row. Insert a threaded tapestry needle under two horizontal bars between the first and second stitches in from the edge on one side of the seam, and then under two corresponding bars on the opposite side. Continue alternating from side to side, pulling the yarn in the direction of the seam, not outward toward your body, to prevent the bars from stretching to the front. When the seam is complete, weave the tail end down through the seam allowance for 2" (5 cm).

Three-Needle Bind-Off

Place stitches to be joined onto two separate needles. Hold them with right sides of knitting facing together. *Insert a third needle into first stitch on each of the other two needles and knit them together as one stitch. Knit next stitch on each needle the same way. Pass first stitch over second stitch. Repeat from * until one stitch remains on third needle. Cut yarn and pull tail through last stitch.

Crochet Chain (ch)

Make a slipknot on hook. Yarn over hook and draw it through loop of the slipknot. Repeat, drawing yarn through the last loop formed.

I-Cord Bind-Off

This method forms an I-cord band along the bind-off edge. It's attractive along necklines and pocket tops. With right side facing and using the knitted method, cast on 3 stitches (for cord) onto the end of the needle holding stitches to be bound off (Figure 1), *k2, k2tog through back loops (the last cord stitch with the first stitch to be bound off; Figure 2), slip these 3 stitches back to left needle (Figure 3), and pull yarn firmly from back. Repeat from * until 3 stitches remain. Bind off remaining stitches using the standard method.

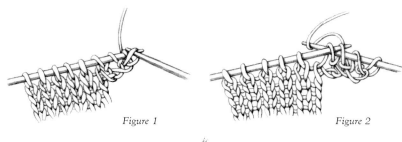

Figure 1

Figure 2

Figure 3

Single Crochet (sc)

Figure 1

Figure 2

Insert the hook into a stitch, yarn over hook and draw a loop through stitch, yarn over hook (Figure 1) and draw it through both loops on hook (Figure 2).

Half-double Crochet

Take yarn over the hook, insert the hook into a stitch, yarn over the hook and draw a loop through the stitch (3 loops on hook), yarn over the hook and draw it through all the loops on the hook.

Kitchener Stitch

Step 1: Bring threaded needle through front stitch as if to purl and leave stitch on needle.

Step 2: Bring threaded needle through back stitch as if to knit and leave stitch on needle.

Step 3: Bring threaded needle through the same front stitch as if to knit and slip this stitch off needle. Bring threaded needle through next front stitch as if to purl and leave stitch on needle.

Step 4: Bring threaded needle through first back stitch as if to purl (as illustrated), slip that stitch off, bring needle through next back stitch as if to knit, leave this stitch on needle.

Repeat Steps 3 and 4 until no stitches remain on needles.

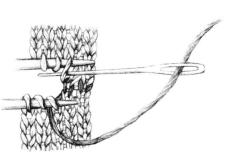

Double Crochet

Figure 1

Figure 2

Yarn over the hook, insert the hook into a stitch, yarn over the hook (Figure 1) and draw a loop through the stitch (3 loops on hook), yarn over the hook and draw it through 2 loops, yarn over the hook and draw it through the remaining 2 loops (Figure 2).

Duplicate Stitch

Horizontal: Bring threaded needle out from back to front at the base of the V of the knitted stitch you want to cover. *Working right to left, pass needle in and out under the stitch in the row above it and back into the base of the same stitch. Bring needle back out at the base of the V of the next stitch to the left. Repeat from *.

Vertical: Beginning at lowest point, work as for horizontal duplicate stitch, ending by bringing the needle back out at the base of the stitch directly above the stitch just worked.

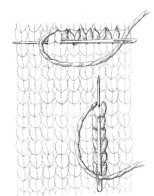

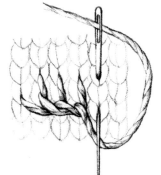

Blanket Stitch

Bring threaded needle out from back to front at the center of a knitted stitch. *Insert needle at center of next stitch to the right and two rows up, and out at the center of the stitch two rows below. Repeat from *.

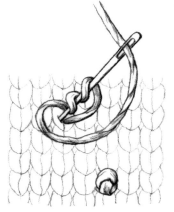

French Knot

Bring needle out of knitted background from back to front, wrap yarn around needle one to three times, and use thumb to hold in place while pulling needle through wraps into background a short distance from where it came out.

Cross-Stitch

*Bring threaded needle out from back to front at lower left edge of the knitted stitch you want to cover. Working left to right, insert the needle at the upper right edge of the same stitch and bring it back out at the lower left edge of the adjacent stitch, directly below and in line with the insertion point. Repeat from * to form one half of the cross. Then work from right to left in the same manner to work the other half of the cross.

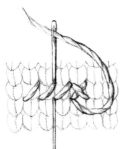

Tassels

Loop yarn around a stiff piece of cardboard that is the desired tassel length. Tie one end of the loops with a piece of yarn—this will be used to attach the tassel to the knitted piece. Slip the loops off the cardboard and tie another piece of yarn several times around the loops near the top. Secure the end of this yarn through the loops and down to the bottom of the tassel. Cut the lower ends to the desired length.

Making a Butterfly

For the intarsia portions of the yoke patterning, use yarn butterflies. Make a butterfly by placing a tail of yarn in the palm of your left hand, end down towards the wrist, clasp it with your last three fingers while holding your thumb and index finger out straight. With your right hand, wrap the yarn around your thumb and index finger in a figure-eight pattern. When the butterfly is the size you want, remove your fingers, hold the bundle in the middle, and wrap yarn firmly around the center several times. Cut the yarn, leaving a short tail. Twist a loop in the tail, wrap the yarn once around the bundle in the opposite direction, put the end through the loop, and pull it tight. The yarn will pull easily from the center of the butterfly beginning with the tail that was in the palm of your hand.

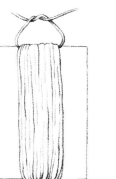

DIRECTORY OF YARN SHOPS

ALABAMA

Memory Hagler Knitting, Etc., 712 Chestnut St., Birmingham, AL 35216; (205) 822-7875

Yarn Expressions, 7914 S. Memorial Pkwy., Huntsville, AL 35802; (256) 881-0260

ALASKA

Knitting Frenzy, 4240 Old Seward Hwy. Ste. 18, Anchorage, AK 99503; (907) 563-2717

INUA Wool Shop, 202 Henderson Rd., Fairbanks, AK 99709; (907) 479-5830

Black Sheep, 222 N. Binkley, Soldotna, AK 99669; (907) 262-5817

ARIZONA

Bonnie's Yarn Crafts, 201 Easy St., Carefree, AZ 85377; (480) 595-7229

Sally Knits, 6823 N. 58th Ave., Glendale, AZ 85301-3220; (623) 934-8367

Fiber Factory, 150 W. Main St., Mesa, AZ 85201; (480) 969-4346

Phoenix Knit and Needlepoint Co., 5044 N. 7th St., Phoenix, AZ 85014; (602) 230-8104

Fiber Shop, 208 N. McCormick, Prescott, AZ 86301; (520) 445-2185

Red Rock Knit & Needlepoint Shop, 3100 W. Hwy. 89A, Sedona, AZ 86336; (520) 204-1505

Berry'd Treasure, Inc., 3250 N. Campbell Ave. #110, Tucson, AZ 85719; (520) 320-1172

Purls, 7862 N. Oracle Rd., Tucson, AZ 85704; (520) 797-8118

Purls, 7810 E. Speedway Blvd., Tucson, AZ 85710; (520) 296-6363

ARKANSAS

Yarn Mart Inc., 5717 Kavanaugh Blvd., Little Rock, AK 72207; (501) 666-6505

CALIFORNIA

Newton's Yarn Country, 2020 E. Howell Ave. Ste. H, Anaheim, CA 92806; (714) 634-9116

Velona Needlecraft, 5753-D Santa Ana Canyon Rd., Anaheim Hills, CA 92807; (714) 974-1570

Auburn Needlework Co., 1039 High St. Ste. #15, Auburn, CA 95603; (530) 888-0202

Fabrications, 826 Lincoln Way, Auburn, CA 95603; (530) 887-0600

Classy Knits and Yarns, 1833 F St., Bakersfield, CA 93301; (661) 325-7226

Forget-Me-Knot Needle Arts, 17828 Bellflower Blvd., Bellflower, CA 90706; (562) 866-8208

Stitches in Time, 17411 Woodruff Ave., Bellflower, CA 90706; (562) 804-9341

Fibretech, 248 Harbor Blvd., Belmont, CA 94002; (650) 610-0554

Lacis, 2982 Adeline St., Berkeley, CA 94703; (510) 843-7290

Nettie's Needlecraft, 9742 Wilshire Blvd., Beverly Hills, CA 90212; (323) 272-7700

Calistoga Yarns, 1458 Lincoln Ave., Calistoga, CA 94515; (707) 942-5108

Ball & Skein & More, 4070 Burton Dr. Ste. #1, Cambria, CA 93428; (805) 927-3280

Rug & Yarn Hut, 350 E. Campbell Ave., Campbell, CA 95008; (408) 354-9316

The Yarn Place, 625 Capitola Ave., Capitola, CA 95010; (831) 476-6480

Knitting by the Sea, 5th Ave. near Junipero, PO Box Y-1, Carmel, CA 93921; (831) 624-3189

A Time When Needlework Supplies, 4615 Manzanita Ave., Carmichael, CA 95608; (916) 481-YARN

Treasure Hunt, 919 Maple St., Carpenteria, CA 93013; (805) 684-3360

Bishop Yarns and Knitting Machines, 21820 Devonshire St., Chatsworth, CA 91311-2905; (818) 407-1069

Happy Hooker Yarn Center, 21619 Devonshire, Chatsworth, CA 91311; (818) 709-3995

The Yarn Basket, 2015 Palm Ave., Chico, CA 95926; (530) 345-2187

Piecemakers, 1720 Adams Ave., Costa Mesa, CA 92626; (714) 641-3112

Filati Yarns, 125-F Railroad Ave., Danville, CA 94526; (925) 820-6614

In Sheep's Clothing, 219 E St. Ste. D, Davis, CA 95616; (530) 759-9276

Skein Lane, 7512 Fairmont Ave., El Cerrito, CA 94530; (510) 525-1828

Black Sheep, 1060 S. Coast Hwy. 101, Encinitas, CA 92024; (760) 436-9973

Common Threads, 466 S. Coast Hwy. 101, Encinitas, CA 92043; (760) 436-6119

Value Craft, 342 W. El Norte Pkwy., Escondido, CA 92026; (760) 747-9222

Boll Weaver, 2748 E. St., Eureka, CA 95501; (707) 443-8145

Rivian Lande Designs, 6461 Rainbow Heights Rd., Fallbrook, CA 92029; (760) 723-8670

Navarro River Knits, 301 N. Main St. Ste. G, Fort Bragg, CA 95437; (707) 964-9665

Show and Tell Studio at Nyles Boulevard Antique Center, 37825 Nyles Blvd., Fremont, CA 94536; (510) 742-1624

Ancient Pathways, 1294 N. Wishon, Fresno, CA 93704; (559) 264-1874

KSR Designs, 528 N. Yale Ave., Fullerton, CA 92831-2738; (714) 526-4934

Sylvia's Flowers and Lace, 332 E. Amerige Ave. #3, Fullerton, CA 92832; (714) 449-1306

Let's Knit Yarn Shop, 16126 S. Western Ave., Gardena, CA 90247; (310) 327-4514

Lights Creek Studios, 6120 Diamond Mtn. Rd., Greensville, CA 95947; (916) 284-7077

The Lazy Daisy, 2127 E. Florida Ave., Hemet, CA 92544; (909) 658-8134

Sharon Wovens, 16865 Lyons Valley Rd., Jamul, CA 91935; (619) 468-3701

Knitting in La Jolla, 7863 Girard Ave., La Jolla, CA 92037; (858) 456-4687

Marie Aubes, 7736 Fay Ave., La Jolla, CA 92037; (858) 459-1552

Needlepoint of La Jolla, 7710 Fay Ave., La Jolla, CA 92037; (858) 456-4687

Betsy's Knit n' Stitch, 1042 Brown Ave., Lafayette, CA 94549-3902; (707) 748-1294

Big Sky Studio, 961-C Moraga Rd., Lafayette, CA 94549; (925) 284-1020

Strands & Stitches, 1516 S. Coast Hwy., Laguna Beach, CA 92651; (949) 497-5648

Knit Nut, 4144 Paramount Blvd., Lakewood, CA 90712; (562) 420-9009

Uncommon Threads, 293 State St., Los Altos, CA 94022; (650) 941-1815

Myra Burg, 6180 W. Jefferson #Y, Los Angeles, CA 90016; (310) 399-5040

Passap Home Knitting Machines, 10294 Cresta Dr., Los Angeles, CA 90064-3431; (310) 838-8688

Pearl Art and Craft, 1250 S. La Cienega Blvd., Los Angeles, CA 90035; (310) 854-4900

Wright's Handicraft, 2735 Pecho Valley Rd., PO Box 6232, Los Osos, CA 93412-6000; (805) 528-5648

Yarn Collection, 234 Strawberry Village, Mill Valley, CA 94941; (415) 383-9276

Fran's Closet, 5550 Etiwanda Ave., Mira Lom, CA 91752; (909) 360-0581

Phebie's Needleart Corner, 5436 Arrow Hwy. #C, Montclair, CA 91763; (909) 985-3778

Knitting Basket, 2054 Mountain Blvd., Oakland, CA 94611; (510) 339-6295

Monarch Knitting & Quilts, 529 Central Ave. Ste. 3, Pacific Grove, CA 93950; (831) 647-9276

Rumpelstiltskin Yarn Shop, 620 Petaluma Blvd. N 2C, Petaluma, CA 94952; (707) 762-9406

Lofty Lou's, 585 Main St., Placerville, CA 95667; (530) 642-2270

Antique Yarn Shop, 12939 Pomerado Rd., Poway, CA 92064; (858) 748-4586

The WoolRoom, 211 Lawrence St., PO Box 353, Quincy, CA 95971; (530) 283-0648

Powell Sheep Company, 1826 Keyes Rd., Ramona, CA 92065; (760) 789-1758

Jane Palmer Knits, 6024 Paseo Delicias, PO Box 2254, Rancho Sante Fe, CA 92067; (858) 756-1634

The Enchanted Unicorn, 415 Tennessee Ste. E & F, Redlands, CA 92373; (909) 792-2046

L'Atelier, 1714½ S. Catalina Ave., Redondo Beach, CA 90277; (800) 833-6133

Amazing Yarns, 2559 Woodland Pl., Emerald Hills, CA 94062; (650) 306-9218

Black Sheep Spindles and Shuttle, 8920 Limonite Ave. Unit 187, Riverside, CA 92509-5067; (909) 360-0725

Cozy Corner, 5225 Canyon Crest Dr. Ste. 17C, Riverside, CA 92507; (909) 684-3831

Knit'n Stitch, 6730 Brockton, Riverside, CA 92506; (909) 684-7632

Elf Hand Knitwerks, 75 Executive Ave. #5, Rohnert Park, CA 94928;

(707) 584-8635

Concepts in Yarn and Needlepoint, 627 Silver Spur Rd. #202, Rolling Hills Estates, CA 90274; (310) 265-6694

Rumpelstiltskin, 1021 R St., Sacramento, CA 95814; (916) 442-9225

The Needlecraft Cottage, 870 Grand Ave., San Diego, CA 92109; (858) 272-8185

The Needleworks, 1400 Camino De La Reina, San Diego, CA 92108; (619) 295-8505

Artfibers, 124 Sutter, 2nd floor, San Francisco, CA 94104; (888) 326-1112

Atelier Yarns, 1945 Divisadero, San Francisco, CA 94115; (415) 771-1550

Greenwich Yarn, 2073 Greenwich St., San Francisco, CA 94123; (415) 567-2535

Creative Accents, 109 Pelton Center Way, San Leandro, CA 94577; (510) 351-5760

Machine Knitting Emporium, 900 Doolittle Ste. 3A, San Leandro, CA 94577; (510) 562-9872

Spin-Knit, 570 Higuera St. #11, San Luis Obispo, CA 93401; (805) 594-0267

Vanessa's Needlepoint Shoppe, 204A 2nd Ave., San Mateo, CA 94401; (650) 343-7745

Dharma Trading Co., 1604 4th St., San Rafael, CA 94915; (415) 456-1211

Ursula's Yarn Boutique, 2441 N. Tustin Ave. Ste. D, Santa Ana, CA 92705; (714) 834-1908

BB's Knits, 3030 State St., Santa Barbara, CA 93105; (805) 569-0531

In Stitches, 5 E. Figueroa St., Santa Barbara, CA 93101; (805) 962-9343

Santa Barbara Knitting Studio, 440 Alan Rd., Santa Barbara, CA 93109; (805) 563-4987

The Golden Fleece, 303 Potrero St. Ste. 29-101, Santa Cruz, CA 95060; (831) 426-1425; www.goldenfleece.com

Nimble Needles, 1522 Marilyn Way, Santa Maria, CA 93454; (805) 925-3865

L'Atelier, 1202A Montana Ave., Santa Monica, CA 90403; (310) 394-4665

Wild Fiber, 1453-E 14th St., Santa Monica, CA 90404; (310) 458-2748, www.wildfiber.com

Three Geese, 17135 Bodega Hwy., Bodega, CA 94922; (707) 829-0931

Knot Garden, 4526 Saugus Ave., Sherman Oaks, CA 91403; (818) 986-6642

Needle World, 4321 Woodman Ave., Sherman Oaks, CA 91423; (818) 784-2442

The Yarn Shop, PO Box 171, Sky Forest, CA 92385; (909) 336-0080

Village Spinning & Weaving, 425 Alisal Rd., Solvang, CA 93463; (805) 686-1192

The Wool Tree, 3119 Harrison Ave., South Lake Tahoe, CA 96150; (530) 542-3947

Cottage Yarn, 607 W. Orange Ave., South San Francisco, CA 94080; (650) 873-7371

La Knitterie Parisienne, 12642 Ventura Blvd., Studio City, CA 91604-2414; (818) 766-1515

The Ultimate Point, 3186 Dona Marta Dr., Studio City, CA 91604; (818) 763-3355

Eva's Needlework, 1321 E. Thousand Oaks Blvd., Thousand Oaks, CA 91362; (805) 379-0722

Silver Threads, 1050 Fourth St., Santa Rosa, CA 95404; (707) 578-7052

Needles and Niceties, 1655 N. Mountain Ave. Ste. 116, Upland, CA 91784; (909) 985-6264

A-Major Knitwork, 6746 Balboa Blvd., Van Nuys, CA 91406-5532; (818) 787-2569

Braidbox Kniting Studio, 14567 Big Basin Way, Saratoga, CA 95070

The Weaver's Cottage, 15559 W. Sierra Hwy., Canyon Country, CA 91351; (888) 251-5033

COLORADO

Aurora Yarn Supply, 1730 S. Abilene St., Aurora, CO 80012; (303) 755-7276

Shuttles, Spindles & Skeins, 635 S. Broadway Unit #F, Boulder, CO 80303; (303) 494-1071

Green Valley Weavers Supply, 1805 N. Weber, Colorado Springs, CO 80907; (719) 448-9963 R

Red Needle West, 708 S. Tejon St., Colorado Springs, CO 80903; (719) 633-8008

The Unique, 1708 W. Colorado Ave., Colorado Springs, CO 80904; (719) 473-9406

Knit 4-U Yarn Shop, 745 Yampa Ave., Craig, CO 81625; (970) 824-7851

Ewenique Yarns, 290 Fillmore St., Denver, CO 80206; (303) 377-6336

Strawberry Tree, 2200 S. Monaco Pkwy., Denver, CO 80222; (303) 759-4244

Gossamer Threads & More, 575 E. 4th Ave., Durango, CO 81301; (970) 247-2822

On the Fringe, 835 Main #222, Durango, CO 81301; (970) 247-7833

Switzer-Land Alpacas, 1236 Glacier View, Estes Park, CO 80517; (970) 586-4624

Lambspun of Colorado, 1101 E. Lincoln Ave., Ft. Collins, CO 80524; (970) 484-1998

Mountain Valley Textiles, 209 8th St., Glenwood Springs, CO 81601; (970) 928-0774

The Needle Cottage, 803 White Ave., Grand Junction, CO 81501; (970) 245-2884

Recycled Lamb, 2010 Youngfield, Lakewood, CO 80215; (303) 234-9337

Showers of Flowers Yarn Shop, 6900 W. Colfax Ave., Lakewood, CO 80215; (800) 825-2569

Over the Moon Café & Mercantile, 600 S. Airport Rd., Longmont, CO 80503; (303) 485-6778; www.over-the-moon.net; knitting@over-the-moon.net

Alpine Knits & Gifts, Inc., 106 Second St., Monument, CO 80132; (719) 488-0550

Edelweiss Needlework Chalet, 362 Pagosa St., Pagosa Springs, CO 81147; (970) 264-3233; edelweiss@pagosa.net

Hearts Song, 311 1/2 S. Union Ave., Pueblo, CO 81003; (719) 545-2297

Bead Song/Salida Fibers, 107 F St., Salida, CO 81201; (719) 530-0110

Fiber Space, 113 N. 2nd St., Sterling, CO 80751; (970) 521-9041

CONNECTICUT

The Wool Connection, E. Main St., Avon, CT 06001; (860) 678-1710

Crocker Hill Farm, Rte. 87, Franklin, CT 06254; (860) 642-7088

Marji's Yarncrafts, 381 Salmon Brook St., Granby, CT 06035; (860) 653-9700

Finally Woolies, 78 N. Moodus Rd., Moodus, CT 06469; (860) 873-1111

Needleworks, 10 E. Cedar St., Newington, CT 06111; (860) 665-0277

Country Knits, Inc., 32 Stewart Rd., Pawcatuck, CT 06379; (860) 599-5755

The Wool Works at Mrs. Bridge's Pantry, 136 Main St., Putnam, CT 06260; (860) 963-7040

Selma's Yarn & Needleworks, Heritage Inn Arcade, Southbury, CT 06488; (203) 264-4838

Needle Arts Gallery, 116 1/2 Grove St., Vernon, CT 06066; (860) 871-1817

Country Yarns, 327 N. Colony Rd., Wallingford, CT 06492; (203) 269-6662

Fetheridge Designs, 4 Green Hill Rd., PO Box 504, Washington Depot, CT 06794; (860) 868-1933

Dagmar's Yarn Shop, 106 Boston Post Rd., Waterford, CT 06385; (860) 442-8364

Lamb's Quarters, 81 Stonebridge Rd., Wilton, CT 06897; (203) 762-8909

The Yarn Barn, 24 Selden St., Woodbridge, CT 06525; (203) 389-5117

DELAWARE

The Knitty Gritty, 240 Rehoboth Ave., Rehoboth Beach, DE 19971; (302) 226-0500

FLORIDA

The Giving Tree, 248 Giralda Ave., Coral Gables, FL 33134; (305) 445-3967

Yarn and Needlepoint Center, 15200 Jog Rd., Delray Beach, FL 33446; (561) 498-1456

The Classy Needle, 316C Centre St., Fernandina Beach, FL 32034; (877) 877-3170

Idle Hours Needle Art, 8595 College Pkwy., Fort Myers, FL 33919; (941) 481-1947

Your Knit Parade, 1400 Colonial Blvd., Royal Palm Square, Fort Myers, FL 33907; (941) 274-0242; www.knitparade.com

Yarnworks, 4113 NW 13th St., Gainsville, FL 32609-1808; (352) 337-9965; www.yarnworks.com

Art Needle 'n Canvas, 800 E. Hallandale Beach Blvd., Hallandale, FL 33009; (954) 458-7515

Knits by Pearl and Bridgette, 6663 Lake Worth Rd., Lake Worth, FL 33467; (561) 641-2553

Doodle Dee, 275 Magnolia St., Merritt Island, FL 32953; (321) 454-4466

Elegant Stitches, 8841 SW 132nd St., Miami, FL 33176; (305) 232-4005; www.elegant-stitches.com

Golden Hand Knit Shop, 5841 SW 73rd St., Miami, FL 33143-5209; (305) 665-2492

Golden Knitting Gallery, 873 105th Ave. N., Naples, FL 34108; (941) 514-4099

Knitting With Nancy, 5087 Timiami Trail E., Naples, FL 34113; (941) 793-8141

Uncommon Threads, 31962 U.S. 19 N., Palm Harbor, FL 34684; (727) 784-6778

Cross Stitchers Three, 801 S. University Dr. #C123, Plantation, FL 33324; (954) 476-3788

Knit Nook, 2249 Bee Ridge Rd., Sarasota, FL 34239; (941) 922-4233

Spinning Wheel, 2083 Siesta Dr., Sarasota, FL 34239; (941) 953-7980

E. T. Yarns, 5300 E. Silver Springs Blvd., Silver Springs, FL 34488; (352) 236-3000

Stuart Stitchery & Yarns, 214 SW Ocean Blvd., Stuart, FL 34994-2944; (561) 283-8089

Jean's Designer Yarn, 8541 W. Mcnab Rd., Tamarac, FL 33321; (954) 722-2753

Valerie Hill Designs, 2614 W. Watrous Ave., Tampa, FL 33629; (813) 251-2825

Sip and Knit, 421 W. Fairbanks Ave., Winter Park, FL 32789; (407) 622-5648

GEORGIA

Needlenook, 2165 Briarcliff Rd., Atlanta, GA 30329; (404) 325-0068

Strings & Strands Inc., 4632 Wieuca Rd., Atlanta, GA 30342; (404) 252-9662

In Stitches, 3124 Washington Rd., Augusta, GA 30907; (706) 868-9276

Yarn Barn, 4719 Ball Ground Hwy., Canton, GA 30114; (770) 479-5083

Pat's Sewing Porch, 46 Timberlake Dr., Cleveland, GA 30528; (706) 892-8400

Davis-Reagan House, Spinning Shop, Dahlonega, GA 30533; (706) 864-8924

Nana's Knitting Bag at Canterbury's, 1015 Peachtree Pkwy. N., Peachtree City, GA 30269; (770) 486-7444

Cast-On Cottage, 1003 Canton St., Roswell, GA 30075; (770) 998-3483

Twiggs of Savannah, 241 Abercorn St., Savannah, GA 31401; (912) 447-5225

HAWAII

Isle Knit, 1270 Queen Emma St., Honolulu, HI 96813; (808) 533-0853

IDAHO

Knit Wits, 8850 Fairview, Boise, ID 83704; (208) 376-0040

Gini Knits, 7225 Main, PO Box 854, Bonners Ferry, ID 83805; (208) 267-5921

House of Needlecraft, 1314 N. Fourth St., Coeur D'Alene, ID 83814; (208) 667-2822

Knit-Wit, 1603 3rd St., Coeur D'Alene, ID 83814; (208) 667-4634

Village Knits and Crafts, 507 W. Main, Grangeville, ID 83530; (208) 983-2948

Isabel's Needlepoint, Inc., 351 Leadville Ave. N., Ketchum, ID 83340; (208) 725-0408

Keep Me in Stitches, 136 E. Lake St., McCall, ID 83638; (208) 634-2906

Haneke Wool Fashions, 630 N. Blackcat Rd., Meridian, ID 83642; (800) 523-WOOL

The Fiber House, 55 E. State Ave., Meridian, ID 83642; (208) 884-1200

The Needle Nook, 175 S. Main, Moscow, ID 83843; (208) 882-2033

Florence's Attic, 1131 Wilson, Pocatello, ID 83201; (208) 237-4963

ILLINOIS

Gene Ann's, 117 E. Station St., Barrington, IL 60010; (847) 842-9321

Fancy That, 10 S 760 Jackson St., Burr Ridge, IL 60521; (630) 655-1022

Londa's Sewing Etc., Inc, 404 S. Duncan, Champaign, IL 61821; (217) 352-2378; www.londas-sewing.com

Knitters Niche, 3206 N. Southport, Chicago, IL 60657; (773) 472-YARN

Making Memories, 2256 Lincoln Park W. C-3, Chicago, IL 60614-3814; (773) 477-4712

Textile Arts Centre, 916 W. Diversey Pkwy, Chicago, IL 60614; (773) 929-5655

Windfall Wool Co., 946 N. 2nd St., Chillicothe, IL 61523; (309) 274-8191

Sunflower Samplings, 89 N. Williams, Crystal Lake, IL 60014; (815) 455-2919

Mosaic Yarn Studio, Ltd., 1585 Ellinwood St. Unit 2, Des Plaines, IL 60016; (847) 390-1013

Great Yarn Loft Co., 120 N. York Rd. Ste. 220, Elmhurst, IL 60126-2806; (630) 833-7423

Have Ewe Any Wool, 120 N. York Rd. Ste. 220, Elmhurst, IL 60126; (630) 941-9276

Close Knit, Inc., 622 Grove St., Evanston, IL 60201; (847) 328-6760

Euro Needlecraft Studio, 1047 Waukegan Rd., Glenview, IL 60025-3034; (847) 724-0346

Village Knit Whiz, 1802 Glenview Rd., Glenview, IL 60025; (847) 998-9772

Magic Needle, 463 Roger Williams Ave., Highland Park, IL 60035; (847) 432-9897

Perfect Touch, 1059 Taylor St., Joliet, IL 60435; (815) 727-2744

The Keweenaw Shepherd, 202 E. Westminster Rd., Lake Forest, IL 60045-1840; (847) 295-9524

Claire's Needleworks, 129 S. Kickapoo St., Lincoln, IL 62656; (217) 732-8811

The Fold, 3316 Millstream Rd., Marengo, IL 60152; (815) 568-5320

Country Lace and Wood Creations, 111 W. Main St., PO Box 559, Maroa, IL 61756; (217) 794-5048; ixsttch2@locomp.net

Jefferson Stitches, 232 S. Washington, Naperville, IL 60540; (630) 983-6310

Knitting Etc., 9980 W. 151st St., Orland Park, IL 60462; (708) 349-7941

Basket of Stitches, 11 N. Bothwell, Palatine, IL 60067; (847) 991-5515

Skeins and Shuttles, 4707 N. Prospect Rd., Peoria Heights, IL 61614; (309) 686-1446

The Fine Line, 6 N. 158 Crane Rd., St. Charles, IL 60175; (630) 584-9443

Craftique/Never Enough Knitting, 119-121 N. Main, Wheaton, IL 60187; (630) 752-9192

Caroline's, 542 Chestnut Ave., Winnetka, IL 60093; (847) 441-0400

INDIANA

Yarns Unlimited, 129 Fountain Square Mall, Bloomington, IN 47404; (812) 334-2464

Wanda's Yarn and Cross Stitch, 533 E. Main St. #B, Brownsburg, IN 46112; (317) 852-7230

Cass St. Depot, 1004 Cass St., Fort Wayne, IN 46808; (219) 420-2277

Golden Thimble, 6418 Carrolton Ave., Indianapolis, IN 46220; (317) 257-2626

Knit 2 Together, 3089 N. High School Rd., Indianapolis, IN 46224; (317) 293-9502

Ding-A-Ling, 519 Main St., Lafayette, IN 47901; (765) 742-8552

Sheep St. Fibers, Inc., 125 W. Washington St., Morgantown, IN 46160; (812) 597-5648

Weave Haus, 527 Church, New Harmony, IN 47631; (812) 682-3750

Heckaman's Quilts and Yarns, 63028 U.S. 31 S., South Bend, IN 46614; (219) 291-3918

Sheeps Clothing Knitting Supply, 60 Jefferson, Valparaiso, IN 46383; (219) 462-4300

IOWA

Rose Tree Fiber Shop, 2814 West St., Ames, IA 50014; (515) 292-7076

Cottage Creations, at the Farm on Deer Creek, Carpenter, IA 50426-0070; (515) 324-1280

Vanberia, 217 W. Water St., Decorah, IA 52101; (319) 382-4892

Knitting Shoppe, 2141 Muscatine Ave., Iowa City, IA 52240; (319) 337-4920

Creative Corner, Inc., 332 5th St., West Des Moines, IA 50265; (515) 255-7262

KANSAS

Yarn Barn of Kansas and Victorian Video, 930 Massachusetts St., Lawrence, KS 66044; (785) 842-4333

Laura May's Cottage, 518 E. Lincoln, Lindsborg, KS 67456; (785) 227-3948

Locke's Stitchery, Inc., 5919 Woodson, Mission, KS 66202; (913) 236-5310

Knit Wit, 1815 S. Ridgeview, Olathe, KS 66062; (913) 780-KNIT

Heritage Hut, 2427 E. Douglas, Wichita, KS 67211; (316) 682-4082

K.N.I.T.S. Etcetera, 956 S. Oliver, Wichita, KS 67218; (316) 652-0073

KENTUCKY

Crafty Hands, 9985 Scottsville Rd., Alvaton, KY 42122; (270) 846-4865

Knit One-Purl Once, Inc., 153 Patchen Dr. #3B, Lexington, KY 40517; (606) 268-0894

LSH Creations, 1584 Wellesley Dr., Lexington, KY 40513; (859) 231-0258

Carma Needlecraft, 718 Lyndon Ln., Louisville, KY 40222; (502) 425-4170

Handknitters, Ltd., 11726 Main St., Louisville, KY 40243; (502) 254-9276

LOUISIANA

Bette Bornside Co., 2733 Dauphine St., New Orleans, LA 70117; (504) 945-4069

Persian Cat, 8211 Hampson St., New Orleans, LA 70118; (504) 864-1908

Quarter Stitch, 630 Chartres St., New Orleans, LA 70130; (504) 522-4451

MAINE

Wooly Works, 24 Sanford Rd., Alfred, ME 04002; (207) 324-9425

Halcyon Yarn, 12 School St., Bath, ME 04530; (207) 442-7909

Blue Hill Yarn Shop, Rte. 172, Blue Hill, ME 04614; (207) 374-5631

Willow's End, 25 Townsend Ave., Boothbay Harbor, ME 04538; (800) 242-9276

Yankee Yarns, 149 Maine St. 6A, Tontine Mall, Brunswick, ME 04011; (207) 729-4223

Stitchery Square, 11 Elm St., Camden, ME 04843; (207) 236-9773

The Stitching Mantis, 535 Shore Rd., Cape Elizabeth, ME 04107; (207) 767-5076

Pine Tree Yarns, Main St., PO Box 506, Damariscotta, ME 04543; (207) 563-8909

Grace Robinson & Company, 475 U.S. Rte. One Ste. One, Freeport, ME 04032; (207) 865-6110

Water St. Yarn, 184 Water St., Hallowell, ME 04347; (207) 622-5500

Bartlettyarns, Inc., 20 Water St., Harmony, ME 04942; (207) 683-2251

Spin-A-Yarn, 144 Wells Rd., Kennebunk, ME 04043; (207) 967-4377

Farmhouse Yarns, 421 Sound Dr., Mt. Desert, ME 04660; (207) 276-4282

Artemis, 179 High St., S. Portland, ME 04106; (207) 741-2509

Central Yarn Shop, 53 Oak St., Portland, ME 04101; (207) 775-0852

Yarngoods Center, Downtown Shopping Center, Waterville, ME 04901; (207) 872-2118

MARYLAND

Misty Mountain Fiber Workshop, 1330 Cape St. Claire Rd., Annapolis, MD 21401; (410) 349-9695; mmfiber@aol.com

The Yarn Garden of Annapolis, 2302 Forest Dr. Ste. 1, Annapolis, MD 21401-3849; (800) 738-9276

Woolworks, Inc., 6305 Falls Rd., Baltimore, MD 21209; (410) 337-9030

The Needlework Attic, 4706 Bethesda Ave., Bethesda, MD 20814; (301) 652-8688, (800) 654-6654

Yarns International, Westwood Center II, 5110 Ridgefield Rd. Ste. 200, Bethesda, MD 20816; (301) 913-2980

Woolstock Knit Shop & Fiber Fantasy, 4848 Butler Rd., Glyndon, MD 21071; (410) 517-1020

Cloverhill Yarn Shop, 75 Mellor Ave., Katonsville, MD 21228; (410) 788-7262

Fran's Knitting Boutique, 651 Main St., Patuxent Place, Laurel, MD 20707; (301) 725-4264

Stitches Etc. Inc., 3451 Sweet Air Rd., Manor Center, Phoenix, MD 21131; (410) 667-9522

G St. Fabrics, 11854 Rockville Pike, Rockville, MD 20852; (301) 231-8998

Designed Fibers, 8600 Foundry St. Ste. 217A, Savage, MD 20763; (301) 483-9510

Fashionably Yours, 2201 Parallel Ln., Silver Spring, MD 20904; (301) 236-4750

MASSACHUSETTS

The Creative Needle, Carriage Shops at 233 N. Pleasant St., Amherst, MA 01002; (413) 549-6106

Knit Witts, 56 Allen Rd., Brookfield, MA 01506; (508) 867-9449; www.knitwitts.com

Mind's Eye Yarns, Porter Square, 22 White St., Cambridge, MA 02140; (617) 354-7253; www.channel1.com

The Knittin' Kitten, 93 Blanchard Rd., Cambridge, MA 02138; (617) 491-4670

Woolcott and Co., 61 JFK St., Cambridge, MA 02138; (617) 547-2837

Textile Traditions, 165 Front St., Chicopee, MA 01013; (413) 557-1505

Needle Arts of Concord, 88 Commonwealth Ave., Concord, MA 01742; (978) 371-0424

Creative Handcrafts, 79 Elm St., Danvers, MA 01923; (978) 774-7770

Ladybug Knitting Shop, 612 Rte. 6A Main St., Dennis, MA 02638; (508) 385-2662

Fabric Place, 136 Howard St., Framingham, MA 01702; (508) 872-4888

Wonderful Things, 232 Stockbridge Rd., Great Barrington, MA 01230; (413) 528-2473

Bare Hill Studios (Fiber Loft), 9 Massachusetts Ave. Rte. 11, Harvard, MA 01451; (978) 456-8669

Adventures in Knitting, 557 Main St., Harwich Port, MA 02646; (508) 432-3700

Tregellys Fibers, 15 Dodge Branch Rd., Hawley, MA 01339; (413) 625-9492

The Heather Shop, 1061 Main St., Holden, MA 01520; (508) 829-4005

Colorful Stitches, 48 Main St., Lenox MA 01240; (413) 637-8206

Wild and Woolly Studio, 7A Meriam St., Lexington, MA 02420; (781) 861-7717; wwooly@aol.com

World in Stitches, 298 Great Rd., Littleton, MA 01460; (978) 486-8330

Hub Mill Store, 300A Jackson St., Lowell, MA 01852; (978) 937-0320

Stahly's Stitchery, 665 State Rd., PO Box 2195, Manomet, MA 02345; (508) 224-7077

The Yarn Shoppe, 270-272 N. Main St., Mansfield, MA 02048; (508) 339-8361

Snow Goose Yarn Shop, 10 Bassett St., Milton, MA 02186; (617) 698-1190

Creative Warehouse, 220 Reservoir St., Needham, MA 02494; (781) 444-9341

Knits and Pieces, 8 Hale St., Newton, MA 02464; (617) 969-8879

Northampton Wools, 11 Pleasant St., Northampton, MA 01060; (413) 586-4331

Country Village Yarn, 158 Main St. Rte. 113, Pepperell, MA 01463; (978) 433-3131

Knitting Treasures, 65 Main St., Plymouth, MA 02360; (508) 747-2500

Arbella Yarns, Inc., Pickering Wharf, Salem, MA 01970; (978) 745-1978

Interlaken School of Art, 13 Willard Hill Rd., Stockbridge, MA 01262; (413) 298-5252

Heath Hen Yarn & Quilt Shop, Tisbury Market Place Beach Rd., PO Box 4429, Vineyard Haven, MA 02568; (508) 693-6730

Dee's Nimble Needles, 21 West St., Walpole, MA 02081; (508) 668-8499

Bags Full of Yarn Shop, 38 South St., Westborough, MA 01581; (508) 366-6688

In Stitches/The Threaded Needle, 454 Boston Post Rd., Weston, MA 02493; (781) 891-4402

The Yarnbarn, 602 Route 6A, East Sandwich, MA 02537; (508) 888-2195

MICHIGAN

Marr Haven Wool Farm, 772-39th St., Allegan, MI 49010; (800) 653-8810

Rosza Handworks, 610 Third St., Ann Arbor, MI 48103; (734) 769-1657

The Quiltery, 1540 E. Columbia Ave., Battle Creek, MI 49014; (616) 965-2116

Ivelise Yarn Shop, 159 E. Napier, Benton Harbor, MI 49022; (616) 925-0451

The Yarn Market, PO Box 87, Beulah, MI 49617; (231) 882-4640

Knitting Room, 251 Merrill, Birmingham, MI 48009; (248) 540-3623

Right off the Sheep, 357 S. Woodward, Birmingham, MI 48009-2063; (248) 646-7595

Rochelle Imber's Knit Knit Knit, 6369-B Orchard Lake Rd., West Bloomfield, MI 48322; (248) 855-2114; www.knitknitknit.com

Aspects of Wool, 11955 E. Lovejoy Rd., Byron, MI 48418; (810) 266-6563

Basketful of Yarn, 5 S. Main, Clarkston, MI 48346; (248) 620-2491

Hillside Farm & The Sheep Shed, 8351 Big Lake Rd., Clarkston, MI 48346-1003; (810) 625-1181

Elaine's Yarn, 219 E. Flint St., Davison, MI 48423; (810) 653-9010

Old Mill Yarn, 109 E. Elizabeth, PO Box 7, Eaton Rapids, MI 48827; (517) 663-2711

Yarn Works, 1100 Ludington St. #103, Escanaba, MI 49829; (906) 428-4092

The Yarn Tree, 26312 Gibraltar Rd., Flat Rock, MI 48134; (734) 782-2015

Rapunzel's Yarn, 664 S. Main, Frankenmuth, MI 48734; (517) 652-0453

Stitches Yarn & Needlework Center, 4485 Plainfield NE Ste. 205, Grand Rapids, MI 49525; (616) 363-6631

Parrot's Perch, 207 Michigan Ave., Grayling, MI 49738; (517) 348-2743

The Wool and the Floss, 397 Fisher Rd., Grossepointe, MI 48230; (313) 882-9110

Lady Peddler, 142 E. State St., Hastings, MI 49058; (616) 948-9644; ladyp@mvcc.com

The Spinning Loft, 2400 Faussett Rd., Howell, MI 48843; (517) 546-5280

Whippletree Yarn, 3500 Chicago Dr., Hudsonville, MI 49426; (616) 669-4487

Dropped Stitch, 109 W. Washington, Jackson, MI 49201; (517) 768-8280

Athena Bookshop, 300 S. Kalamazoo, Kalamazoo, MI 49007; (616) 342-4297

Crafty Lady, Crosswinds Corners, 15401 Hall Rd., Macomb, MI 48044; (810) 566-8008

Knit-n-Purl, 1010 W. Washington, Marquette, MI 49855; (906) 225-0914

Windsong Yarn and Needlearts, 149 W. Michigan Ave., Marshall, MI 49068; (616) 789-1210

The Elegant Ewe, 501 First St., Menominee, MI 49858; (906) 863-2296

The Granny Square, 1001 E. Carpenter St., Midland, MI 48640; (517) 832-2899

Strawberry Patch, 116 W. Exchange, Owosso, MI 48867; (517) 723-1478

Knit-Cetera, 10 S. Washington St., Oxford, MI 48371; (248) 628-5590

Calico Crafts, 1691 U.S. 131 S., Petoskey, MI 49770; (231) 347-1511

Bellairs Fiber Farm (Formerly Hillside Farms), 3770 E. Territorial Rd., Pleasant Lake, MI 49272; (517) 589-0443

Old Village Yarn Shop, 42307 E. Ann Arbor Rd., Plymouth, MI 48170; (734) 451-0580

Mary Maxim Inc., 2001 Holland Ave., Port Huron, MI 48060; (810) 987-2000; www.marymaxim.com

A-Kay's Craft Corner, 6016 Lover's Ln., Portage, MI 49002; (616) 321-8832

Stitching Memories, 1808 W. Milham Rd., Portage, MI 49024; (616) 552-9276

Ewe-Nique Knits, 515 S. Lafayette, Royal Oak, MI 48067; (248) 584-3001

It's Stitching Time, 150 E. Main Ave., Seeland, MI 49464; (616) 772-5525

Yarns And, 25511 Southfield Rd. Ste. 104, Southfield, MI 48075-1830; (248) 647-2400

Yarn Oasis, 26108 W. U.S. 12, Sturgis, MI 49091; (616) 659-7474

Tawas Bay Yarn Co., 402 W. Lake St., Tawas City, MI 48763; (517) 362-4463

Lost Art Yarn & Needlepoint Shoppe, 123 E. Front St., Traverse City, MI 49684; (231) 941-1263

Yarn Quest, 819 S. Garfield, Traverse City, MI 49686; (231) 929-4277

Forma, 111 E. Northfield Church Rd., Whitmore Lake, MI 48189; (734) 761-1102

Threadbender Yarn Shop, 2767 44th St. SW, Wyoming, MI 49509; (616) 531-6641

The Yarn Shop, Sleeping Bear Dunes National Lakeshore, Glen Arbor, MI 49636

MINNESOTA

Zandy's Yarns Etc., 13710 Nicollet Ave., Burnsville, MN 55337; (612) 890-3087

Yarn Harbor, 103 Mt. Royal Shopping Circle, Duluth, MN 55803; (218) 724-6432

Sisu Designs Weaving and Yarn Shop, 31 W. Chapman St., Ely, MN 55731; (218) 365-6613; SisuDesigns@email.com; http://SisuDesigns.theshoppe.com/index.html

River Ridge Wool 'n Weavers, 12428 Cty. Rd. 26, Hutchinson, MN 55350; (320) 587-9622

Playing With Yarn, 276 Scenic Dr., Knife River, MN 55609; (218) 391-0516

Creative Fibers, 5416 Penn Ave. S., Minneapolis, MN 55419; (612) 927-8307

Depth of Field, Inc., 405 Cedar Ave., Minneapolis, MN 55454; (612) 339-6061; www.depthoffieldyarn.com

Linden Hills Yarns, 2720 W. 43rd St., Minneapolis, MN 55410; (612) 929-1255

Needlework Unlimited, 3006 W. 50th St., Minneapolis, MN 55410; (612) 925-2454

Skeins, 11309 Hwy. 7, Minnetonka, MN 55305; (612) 939-4166

Pieces of String, 810 22nd Ave. S., Moorhead, MN 56560; (218) 233-6670

Nadel Kunst Ltd., 212 N. Minnesota St., New Ulm, MN 56073; (507) 354-8708

Bonnie's Spinning Wheel, 16-21st Ave. S., St. Cloud, MN 56301; (320) 253-2426

The Yarnery, 840 Grand Ave., St. Paul, MN 55105; (651) 222-5793

Three Kittens Yarn Shoppe, 805 Sibley Memorial Hwy., St. Paul, MN 55118; (800) 489-4969

Mary Lue's Knitting World, 101 W. Broadway, St. Peter, MN 56082; (507) 931-3702

Woodward's, 1425 S. 12th Ave., Thunderbird Mall, Virginia, MN 55792; (218) 741-1744

A Sheepy Yarn Shoppe, 2185 3rd St., White Bear Lake, MN 55110; (651) 426-5463

MISSISSIPPI

No listings

MISSOURI

Carol Leigh's Hillcreek Fiber Studio, 7001 S. Hillcreek Rd., Columbia, MO 65203; (573) 874-2233; www.hillcreekfiberstudio.com

Nancy Almond Interiors, 3415 Augusta Dr., Columbia, MO 65203-0987; (573) 442-9046

Weaving Department, 180 Dunn Rd., Florissant, MO 63031; (314) 921-7800

Ileen's Needle Nook, 4106 W. Ely Rd., Hannibal, MO 63401; (573) 221-9456; www.ileen.com

The Niddy Noddy, 205 Center St.., Hannibal, MO 63401; (573) 248-8040; www.niddynoddy.com

Knitcraft, Inc., 500 N. Dodgion, Independence, MO 64050; (816) 461-1217

Pennie's Place, 10414 Manchester Rd., Kirkwood, MO 63122; (314) 821-1728

Wray & Company, 117 E. Cherry St., Nevada, MO 64772; (417) 667-8028

Uniquely Yours, 1019 Kings Hwy. Ste. 5, Rolla, MO 65401; (573) 364-2070

Thread Peddler, 2012 S. Stewart, Springfield, MO 65804; (800) 482-3584

Exquisitely Angora, 1222 Mackay Pl., St. Louis, MO 63104; (314) 771-6302

Hearthstone Knits, 11429 Concord Village Ave., St. Louis, MO 63123; (314) 849-9276

Artistic Needles, 119 N. Kingshighway, St. Charles, MO 63301; (636) 946-0046

MONTANA

The Yarn Shop, 17 W. Olive St., Bozeman, MT 59715; (406) 585-8335

The Yarn Center, 110 Pinckney, Hamilton, MT 59840; (406) 363-1400

Joseph's Coat, 115 S. 3rd W., Missoula, MT 59801; (406) 549-1419

Knit Wit Yarn Shop, 800 Kensington Ave. #108, Missoula, MT 59801; (406) 543-9368

Mountain Colors, 4072 Eastside Hwy., Stevensville, MT 59870; (406) 777-3377

Old MacDonald's Craft Barn, 128 Skyline Dr. NE, Great Falls, MT 59404; (406) 454-2077

Wild West Wools, 3920 Ste. B, Stevensville, MT 59870; (406) 777-4114

NEBRASKA

The Plum Nelly, 1360 W. Prairie Lake Rd., Hastings, NE 68901; (402) 463-6262

Personal Threads Boutique, 8025 W. Dodge Rd., Omaha, NE 68114; (800) 306-7733

NEVADA

Wooly Wonders, 2320 Apaloosa Rd., Henderson, NV 89015; (702) 564-7113

Strands of Silk, 1801 E. Tropicana Ste. 19, Las Vegas, NV 89119; (702) 736-7626

NEW HAMPSHIRE

Wool Room at Meadow Brook Farm, 218 Pleasant St., Antrim, NH 03440; (603) 588-6637

The Designery, 43 Maple St., PO Box 308, Center Sandwich, NH 03227; (603) 284-6915

The Elegant Ewe, 71 S. Main St., Concord, NH 03301; (603) 226-0066

Knitting Nook, 358 South Rd., Sullivan, NH 03445; (603) 357-0516

Charlotte's Web, 137 Epping Rd., Exeter, NH 03833; (603) 778-1417

The Fiber Studio, 9 Foster Hill Rd., PO Box 637, Henniker, NH 03242; (603) 428-7830

Yarn Shop & Fibers, 549 Main St., Laconia, NH 03246; (603) 528-1221; yarnshop@cyberportal.net

The Designery, 375 Daniel Webster Hwy., Meredith, NH 03253; (603) 279-9865

Hodge Podge Handicrafts, 59 Belknap Ave., Newport, NH 03773; (603) 863-1470

The Yarn Basket, 18 Ladd St., Portsmouth, NH 03801; (603) 431-9301

Grand View Country Store, U.S. Rte. 2, Randolph, NH 03570; (603) 466-5715

The Knitting Knook, 358 South Rd., Sullivan, NH 03445; (603) 357-0516

NEW JERSEY

Village Stitchery & Gift Shoppe, 37 S. Main, Allentown, NJ 08501; (609) 259-2339

Needles and Things, 1108 Main St., Belmar, NJ 07719; (732) 681-6363

Fiber Arts Studio & Yarn, 311 Rte. 9S., Cape May Court House, NJ 08210; (609) 465-8484

Sophisticated Stitchery, 22 N. Whittier St., Carteret, NJ 07008; (732) 969-0408

The Stitching Bee, 240A Main St., Chatham, NJ 07928; (973) 635-6691; www.stitchingbee.com

Aunt Jean's Handiworks, 38 Center St., Clinton, NJ 08809; (908) 713-0101

Knitting Gallery, The Courtyard, Rte. 34 N., Colts Neck, NJ 07722; (732) 294-9276; www.knittinggallery.com

Knitter's Workshop, Inc., 345 N Ave., Garwood, NJ 07027; (908) 789-1333

Auntie Knits, Inc., 212 Rock Rd., Glen Rock, NJ 07452; (201) 447-1331

Simply Knit, 23 Church St., Lambertville, NJ 08530; (609) 397-7101

The Millstone Workshop, 1393 Main St., Millstone, NJ 08876; (908) 874-3649

Astrid, 51 Church St., Montclair, NJ 07042; (973) 746-2626

Elly's Knits 'n Rest, 16 Church St., Montclair, NJ 07042; (973) 744-1034

The Needleworks Barn, 123 E. Main St., Moorestown, NJ 08057; (856) 235-7640

Accents on Knits, 36 Speedwell Ave., Morristown, NJ 07960; (973) 829-9944

The Spinnery, 1367 Hwy. 202 N., Neshanic Station, NJ 08853; (908) 369-3260

Fabric Land, 855 Rte. 22, North Plainfield, NJ 07060; (908) 755-4700

Knitting Niche, 1330 Asbury Ave., Ocean City, NJ 08226; (609) 399-5111

Glenmarle Woolworks, 330 Cold Soil Rd., Princeton, NJ 08540; (609) 921-3022

Brenda's Gifts, 16A Bridge St., Stockton, NJ 08559; (609) 397-8448

Barbara's Bits 'n Pieces, 33 Bryant Rd., Waretown, NJ 08758; (609) 693-7125

NEW MEXICO

B's Yarns and Needlearts, 6001 San Mateo Blvd. NE #E-4, Albuquerque, NM 87109; (505) 881-8373

Village Wools, Inc., 3801 -C San Mateo NE, Albuquerque, NM 87110; (505) 883-2919

Tierra Wools, 91 Main St., PO Box 229, Los Ojos, NM 87551; (888) 709-0979

Fiesta Yarns, 206 Frontage Rd., Rio Rancho, NM 87124; (505) 892-5008

McBride's Yarn & Needlework, 65 W. Marcy St., Santa Fe, NM 87501; (505) 983-4830

Needle's Eye, 927 Paseo De Peralta, Santa Fe, NM 87501; (505) 982-0706

Santa Fe School of Weaving, Miriams Well, Santa Fe, NM 87501; (505) 982-6312

La Lana Wools, 136 Paseo Norte, Taos, NM 87571; (505) 758-9631

Rio Grande Weavers Supply, 216 B N. Pueblo Rd., Taos, NM 87571; (505) 758-0433

The Yarn Shop, 120B Bent St., Taos, NM 87571; (505) 758-9341

Weaving Southwest, 216-B Pueblo Norte, Taos, NM 87571

NEW YORK

Knitworks/Weaveworks, 174 Park Ave., Amityville, NY 11701; (631) 264-1304

Woodside Weavers, 4946 Consaul Rd., Amsterdam, NY 12010; (518) 399-7991; kbcurtis@pop.net

Knit Pick, 2000 Grand Ave., Baldwin, NY 11510; (516) 623-8400

Spin a Yarn, 9 Mitchell Ave., Binghamton, NY 13903; (607) 722-3318

The Woolroom, 172 Joe's Hill Rd., Brewster, NY 10509; (914) 279-7627; www.woolroom.com

Barkow Yarn Shop, 2978 Nostrand Ave., Brooklyn, NY 11229; (718) 253-3369

Sew Brooklyn, 228 7th Ave., Brooklyn, NY 11215; (718) 499-7383

Stitch 'n Stitch, 1320 Coney Island Ave., Brooklyn, NY 11230; (718) 692-0110

Warm Ewe, 31 Main St., Chatham, NY 12037; (518) 392-2929

Happiknits Yarn Boutique, Inc., 6333 Jericho Turnpike, Commack, NY 11725; (516) 462-5558

Highland Springs Farm, Peakes Brook Rd., Delhi, NY 13753; (607) 746-3316

The Woolly Lamb, 712 Main St., East Aurora, NY 14052; (716) 655-1911

Knitlove, 42 Gingerbread Ln., East Hampton, NY 11937; (516) 329-0700

Knitting Knook, 1777 Grand Central Ave., Elmira Hts., NY 14903; (607) 735-5668

Garden City Stitches, 725 Franklin Ave., Garden City, NY 11530; (516) 739-5648

The Open Door to Stitchery, 87A Middle Neck Rd., Great Neck, NY 11021; (516) 487-9442

General Bailey Homestead Farm, 340 Spier Falls Rd., Greenfield Center, NY 12833-2005; (518) 893-2015

Needle Works, 99 Main St., Greenwich, NY 12834; (518) 692-8980

Goldman's Yarn Stores, 391 N. Central Ave., Hartsdale, NY 10530-1811; (914) 761-1222

Countrywool, 59 Spring Rd., Hudson, NY 12534; (518) 828-4554

Knit Wit Kreations, 265 Main St., Hudson Falls, NY 12839; (518) 747-4010

Granny's Yarn Shoppe, 465 Main St., Islip, NY 11751; (631) 581-9236

Homespun, 314 E. State St., Ithaca, NY 14850; (607) 277-0954

Knitting Machines, Etc., 903 Mitchell St., Ithaca, NY 14850; (607) 277-1164

Amazing Threads, 2010 Ulster Ave., PO Box 758, Lake Katrine, NY 12449; (914) 336-5322

The Little Store, 56 Gnarled Hollow Rd., Long Island, NY 11733; (631) 689-8172

Sheep & Wool Shop, 4849 Cory Corners, Marion, NY 14505; (315) 926-5765

Downtown Yarns, 45 Avenue A, New York, NY 10009-7324; (212) 995-5991

Erdal Yarns, Ltd., 303 Fifth Ave. Ste. 1101, New York, NY 10016; (212) 725-0162

Gotta Knit, 498 6th Ave., New York, NY 10011; (212) 989-3030

Knits Incredible, 971 -A Lexington Ave., New York, NY 10021; (212) 717-0477

School Products, 1201 Broadway 3rd Floor, New York, NY 10001; (212) 679-3516

Stitches East, 55 E. 52nd St., New York, NY 10022; (212) 421-0112

The Woolgathering, 318 E. 84th St., New York, NY 10028; (212) 734-4747

Wallis Mayers Needlework Inc., 30 E. 68th St., New York, NY 10021; (212) 861-5318

The Yarn Co, 2274 Broadway, New York, NY 10024; (212) 787-7878

The Yarn Connection, 218 Madison Ave., New York, NY 10016; (212) 684-5099

Embraceable Ewe, 213 Main St., Hamburg, NY 14075; (716) 667-2957

Rosemary Olmsted, Handweaver, 48 Haynes Rd., Plattsburgh, NY 12901; (518) 561-6166

Knitting Cove, 206 E. Main St., Port Jefferson, NY 11777; (516) 473-2121

Knitting Place Inc., 191 Main St. #4, Port Washington, NY 11050; (516) 944-9276

Patternworks, 36A South Gate Dr., PO Box 1690, Poughkeepsie, NY 12601; (845) 462-8000

Yarn with Susan, 2325 Lower Mountain Rd., Ransomville, NY 14131; (716) 754-7183

Knit 'n Purl Ltd ., 2900 Monroe Ave., Rochester, NY 14618; (716) 248-8339

The Village Yarn Shop, 200 Midtown Plaza, Rochester, NY 14604; (716) 454-6064

Inn Stitches Yarn Shop, 139 Purchase St., Rye, NY 10580; (914) 925-6786

Lonesome Landing, 172 Lake Flower Ave., Saranac Lake, NY 12983; (518) 891-4555

Knitting Machines, 41 Primrose Ave., Scarsdale, NY 10583; (914) 472-8475

Ye Olde Yarn & Gift Shoppe, 1604 Union St., Schenectady, NY 12309; (518) 393-2695

Elegant Needles, 5 Jordan St., Skaneateles, NY 13152; (315) 685-9276

The Yarn Bin, 51 Fennell St., Skaneateles, NY 13152; (315) 685-5070

Wild and Wooly, 18 New Dorp Ln., Staten Island, NY 10306; (718) 987-7000; wwooly@aol.com

Lantern, 232 Rockaway Ave., Valley Stream, NY 11580; (516) 825-5004

Liberty Ridge, 6175 Greenway Lowell Rd., Verona, NY 13478; (315) 337-7217

Knit Knacks, 1875 Wantagh Ave., Wantagh, NY 11793; (516) 785-2282

Fiber Design Studio, 10 Wisner Trail, Warwick, NY 10990; (914) 987-7975

Smiley's Yarns, 92-06 Jamaica Ave., Woodhaven, NY 11421; (718) 849-9873

Rita's Knit One Purl Two, 264 Woodridge Mountaindale Rd., Woodridge, NY 12789; (914) 434-9300

NORTH CAROLINA

Earth Guild, 33 Haywood St., Asheville, NC 28801; (828) 255-7818

Naked Sheep Yarn Shop, 102 Sutton Ave., Black Mountain, NC 28711; (828) 669-0600

Settawig Gallery, 10952 Old Hwy. 64 W., Brasstown, NC 28902; (828) 837-3450

Shuttles Needles & Hooks, 214 E. Chatham St., Cary, NC 27511; (919) 469-9328

Knit a Bit, Village Plaza Mall, Chapel Hill, NC 27514; (919) 929-6562

The Knit Wits, 1037 Providence Rd., Charlotte, NC 28207; (704) 377-1984

The Needlecraft Center, PO Box 1652, Davidson, NC 28036; (704) 892-8988

The Yarn Corner, 64 Front St., Dillsboro, NC 28725; (828) 586-3420

Fiberspace, 770 Ninth St., Durham, NC 27705; (919) 286-3400

Yearning For Yarn, 106 E. King St., Edenton, NC 27932; (252) 482-2977

Hunters Needlecraft and Knit Shop, 705 Milner Dr., Greensboro, NC 27410; (336) 299-5904

Stitch Point, 1614C W. Friendly Ave., Greensboro, NC 27403; (336) 272-2032

Yarns Etc., 231 S. Elm St., Greensboro, NC 27401; (800) 335-5011

Swedish Yarn Imports, 126-A Wade Street, PO Box 2069, Jamestown, NC 27282

Bovidae Farm, 1186 Jarvis Branch Rd., Mars Hill, NC 28754; (828) 689-9931; bovidae@madison.main.nc.us

Weaver's Webb, 602 Pollock St., New Bern, NC 28562; (252) 514-2681

Great Yarns, 1208 Ridge Rd., Raleigh, NC 27607; (919) 832-3599

Norsk Fjord Fiber, 49 U.S. Hwy. 64 West, Sapphire, NC 28774; (828) 884-2195

Angelwing Needleworks, 108 E. Moore St., Southport, NC 28461; (910) 454-9163

Knit One Smock Too, Inc., 3905 A Country Club Rd., Winston-Salem, NC 27104; (336) 765-9099

NORTH DAKOTA

Yarn Renaissance, 1226 S. University Dr., Fargo, ND 58103; (701) 280-1478

Sage Junction Yarns, 3355 Country Rd. 139, Mandan, ND 58554; (701) 663-2720

OHIO

Edie's Knit Shop, Inc., 215 W. Garfield Rd., Aurora, OH 44202; (330) 562-7226

The Knit Shop, 214 S. Chillicothe Rd., Aurora, OH 44202; (330) 562-7226

Fiberworks, 3102 Maginn Dr., Beavercreek, OH 45434; (937) 426-5522

Fiber Naturell, 9424 Shelly Ln., Cincinnati, OH 45242; (513) 793-4940

One More Stitch, 2030 Madison Rd., Cincinnati, OH 45208; (513) 533-1170

Peach Mountain Studio, 7010 Miami Ave., Cincinnati, OH 45243; (513) 271-3191

Wizard Weavers, 2701 Observatory Ave., Cincinnati, OH 45208; (513) 871-5750

Fine Points, Inc., 2026 Murray Hill Rd., Cleveland, OH 44106; (216) 229-6644

Susan Yarns, 2132 S. Taylor Rd., Cleveland Hgts., OH 44118; (216) 321-2687

Little House, 1927 N. Main St., Clyde, OH 43410; (419) 547-9210

Nan Fisher Designs, 992 Medinah Terrace, Columbus, OH 43235; (614) 459-5837

The Yarn Shop, 1156 Kenny Centre, Columbus, OH 43220; (614) 457-7836

Wolfe Fiber Arts, 1188 W. 5th Ave., Columbus, OH 43212; (614) 487-9980

Stitch, Piece 'n Purl, 2018 State Rd., Cuyahoga Falls, OH 44223; (330) 928-9097

The Yarn Basket, 1994 Turnbull Rd., Dayton, OH 45432; (937) 427-2726

The Fifth Stitch, 300 Clinton St., Defiance, OH 43512-2629; (419) 782-0991

Yarn Dome, 418 S. Broadway, Greenville, OH 45331; (937) 548-2242

Sheep in a Heep Knit Shoppe, 17008 Madison Ave., Lakewood, OH 44107; (216) 228-4477

Bright Meadow Farms, 210 Creston Rd., Mansfield, OH 44906; (419) 529-9338

Eileen's Knit and Sew Center, 2789 Medina Rd., Medina, OH 44256; (330) 722-2798

Needle Point, 7312 Center St., Mentor, OH 44060; (440) 255-5575

Craftsman Hill Fibers, 15 N. Main St., PO Box 166, Mount Vernon, OH 43050; (740) 392-7724

Artistic Yarns & Threads, 1142 S. Main St., North Canton, OH 44720; (330) 494-8838

Knit-Wit Knits, 645 E. State St., Salem, OH 44460; (330) 337-5648

Sally Houk Exclusives, 50 Grand Blvd., Shelby, OH 44875; (419) 347-7969

Martha's Yarn House, 1002 Bechtle Ave., Springfiled, OH 45504; (937) 322-6102

Honey Rock Enterprises, 10363 Loches Rd. NE, Saint Louislie, OH 43071; (740) 745-2832

Village Crafts, 62 E. Cherry St., Sunbury, OH 43074; (740) 965-3476; www.villagecrafts.com

Sally's Shop, 141 College St., Wadsworth, OH 44281; (330) 334-1996; sallyshop@compuserve.com

Yarn Palette, 100 W. Main St., Wilmington, OH 45177-2239; (937) 382-3455

OKLAHOMA

Sara's Shoppe, 1969 Marie Dr., Durant, OK 74701; (405) 924-0217

Ewe and Me Needlework Shop, 2120 Hwy. 59 N., Grove, OK 74345-0046; (918) 786-3588

Sealed With a Kiss, 2022 W. Noble, Guthrie, OK 73044; (405) 282-8649; www.swakknit.com

OREGON

The Web*Sters, 11 N. Main St., Ashland, OR 97520; (541) 482-9801

The Wool Company, 990 2nd St. SE, Bandon, OR 97411; (541) 347-3912

Mill End Store, 4955 SW Western Ave., Beaverton, OR 97005; (503) 646-3000

P T Yarn, 16006 Hwy. 101 S., Brookings, OR 97415; (541) 469-6286

Damascus Pioneer Craft School, 14711 SE Anderson Rd., Clackamas, OR 97015; (503) 658-2704

My Yarn Shop, 264 Broadway, Coos Bay, OR 97420; (541) 266-8230

Fiber Nooks & Crannys, 351 NW Jackson Ave #2, Corvallis, OR 97330; (541) 754-8637

Northwest Peddlers, 2101 Bailey Hill Rd., Eugene, OR 97405; (541) 465-9003

Soft Horizons Fibre, 412 E. 13th Ave., Eugene, OR 97401; (541) 343-0651

The Knit Shop, 2821 Oak, Eugene, OR 97405; (541) 434-0430

Mimi's Yarn Shop, 125 W. California St., Jacksonville, OR 97530; (800) 303-1320

Molehill Farm, 16722 SW Boones Ferry Rd., Lake Oswego, OR 97035; (503) 697-9554

Robin and Russ Handweaver, 533 N. Adams St., McMinnville, OR 97128; (503) 472-5760

Mill End Store, 9701 SE McLoughlin Blvd., Milwaukie, OR 97222; (503) 786-1234

By the Bay Creations, 1887 Union Ave., North Bend, OR 97459; (541) 756-7978

Northwest Wools, Inc., 3524 SW Troy St., Portland, OR 97219; (503) 244-5024

Yarn Garden, 1413 SE Hawthorne Blvd., Portland, OR 97214; (503) 239-7950

Trudy's Afghans & Yarn Supply, 1225 W. Harvard Ave., Roseburg, OR 97470; (541) 957-0629

Artistic Needles, Inc., 1545 Hawthorne Ave. NE, Salem, OR 97301; (503) 589-1485

Mission Mill Museum, 1313 Mill St. SE, Salem, OR 97301; (503) 585-7012

Windsor Farms Rabbitry, 4151 Mountain View Rd., Silverton, OR 97381; (503) 873-3128; http://members.aol.com/angoralady/index.htm

Ewe to You, 305 Long Valley Rd., Sutherlin, OR 97479; (541) 459-5739

Heriloom Creations, 10005 Hughey Ln., Tilamook, OR 97141; (503) 842-2982

Yarn For All Seasons, 722A W. Hwy. 20, Toledo, OR 97391; (541) 336-4884

Nitting Niche, 217 E. Columbia River Hwy., Troutdale, OR 97060; (503) 232-1193

Wool 'n Wares Yarn Shop, 21540 Willamette Dr., West Linn, OR 97068; (503) 657-7470, woolywiley@aol.com

Woodland Woolworks, 262 S. Maple St., Yamhill, OR 97148; (800) 547-3725

PENNSYLVANIA

Tucker Yarn Co. Inc., 950 Hamilton St., Allentown, PA 18101; (610) 434-1846

Tangled Yarns, 519 Main St., Bethlehem, PA 18018; (610) 867-0318

Irene's Needleworks, 429 Washington Ave., Bridgeville, PA 15017; (412) 221-8130

Ashford Knitting Studio, 301 Greason Rd., Carlisle, PA 17013; (717) 249-7447

The Knitters Underground, 308 S. Pennsylvania Ave., Centre Hall, PA 16828; (814) 364-1433; www.knitters-underground.com

A Garden of Yarn, Olde Ridge Village #10, Chadds Ford, PA 19317; (610) 459-5599

The Mannings Handweaving School & Supply Center, 1132 Green Ridge Rd., East Berlin, PA 17316; (717) 624-2223

Stephanie's Yarn and Needlepoint, 910 Township Line Rd., Elkins Park, PA 19027; (215) 635-2132

Needle Art Studio, 356 Main St., Emmaus, PA 18049; (610) 967-5633

The Yarnsmith, 2020 Swamp Pike, Gilbertsville, PA 19525-0374; (610) 323-1553

Busy Body's, 385 Lancaster Ave., Haverford, PA 19041; (610) 649-9477

Victoria's House of Needleart, 314 Allegheny St., Hollidaysburg, PA 16648; (814) 696-0331

Country Spun Studio, 18 S. 7th St., Indiana, PA 15701; (724) 465-PURL

Wool Gathering, 131 E. State St., Kennett Square, PA 19348; (610) 444-8236

Knitnit Needlecrafts, 713 Olde Hickory Rd., Lancaster, PA 17601; (717) 569-3951

Oh Susanna, 2204 Marietta Ave., Lancaster, PA 17603; (717) 393-5146

Exclusively Yarns, Dreshor Arcade, Landsdale, PA 19446; (215) 368-9644

Lamb's Wool, 32 E. Blaine St., Landsdale, PA 19446; (215) 361-9899; www.thelambswool.com

Needle Nest, 34 Round Hill Rd., Levittown, PA 19056; (215) 946-9260

Kathy's Kreations, 141 E. Main St., Ligonier, PA 15658; (724) 238-9320; www.kathys-kreations.com

Otter Creek Store, 106 S. Diamond St., Mercer, PA 16137; (724) 662-2830

Mary Koons, 408 Chestnut St., Mifflinburg, PA 17844; (570) 966-0341

Bonnie Knits, 4042 Monroeville Blvd., Monroeville, PA 15146; (412) 856-7033

Kraemer Yarn Shop, 240 S. Main St., Nazareth, PA 18064; (610) 759-1294

Tonidale Yarn & Needlecraft, 1050 Montour Church Rd., Oakdale, PA 15071; (412) 788-8850

Sophie's Yarns, 2017 Locust St., Philadelphia, PA 19103; (215) 977-9276

The Tangled Web, 7900 Germantown Ave., Philadelphia, PA 19118; (215) 242-1271

The Knitting Studio, 141 Nutt Rd. Rte. 23, Phoenixville, PA 19460; (610) 933-2561

Needle World, 208 Olive St., Sayre, PA 18840; (570) 888-4111

Yarns Unlimited, 435 Beaver St., Sewickley, PA 15143; (412) 741-8894

Town Stationery, 43 W. King St., Shippensburg, PA 17257; (717) 532-8779

The Colonial Yarn Shop, 7 Front St., Shiremanstown, PA 17011; (717) 763-8016

Knit Wit Shop, 1 Byron St., Smethport, PA 16749; (814) 887-9942

Knitting Basket, 540 Second St. Pike, Southampton, PA 18966; (215) 355-2666

Yarn Shop on the Farm, 1235 Red Run Rd., Stevens, PA 17578; (717) 336-5860

Bucks Country Knitting Machines, 2858 Old Lincoln Hwy., Trevose, PA 19053; (215) 639-5251

RHODE ISLAND

The Picket Fence, 71 Maple Ave., Barrington, RI 02806; (401) 245-0484

Knitting Needles, 626 Thames St., Newport, RI 02840; (401) 841-5648

And the Beadz Go On, 1 W. Main, Wickford, RI 02852; (401) 268-3899

Textile Fiber Arts Studio, 64 Paris Irons Rd., North Scituate, RI 02857; (401) 568-7837

Wayland Yarn Shoppe, 112 Raleigh Ave., Pawtucket, RI 02860; (401) 726-4696

Sakonnet Purls, 3988 Main Rd., Tiverton, RI 02878; (888) 624-9902

Never Enough Yarn, 603 Clinton St., Woonsocket, RI 02895; (401) 766-3992

SOUTH CAROLINA

Hook 'n Needle, 28 Diamond Ln., Columbia, SC 29210; (803) 772-1335

Needle Niche, 518 W. Palmetto St., Florence, SC 29501; (843) 678-9373

The NeedleTree, Inc., 3 Cateechee Ave., Greenville, SC 29605-2904; (864) 235-6060

The Elegant Stitch, PO Box 809, Pawleys Island, SC 29585; (843) 237-1600

KJ Yarn Nook, 875 Albright Rd. Ste. 109, Rock Hill, SC 29730; (803) 325-1890

SOUTH DAKOTA

Cindy's Yarn Garden, 201 Main St., Rapid City, SD 57701; (605) 341-5210

TENNESSEE

Genuine Purl, 140 N. Market St., Chattanooga, TN 37405; (800) 862-2890

Unique Yarns & Crafts, 2824 Scenic Dr., Clarksville, TN 37043-5312;
(931) 358-0830

Cumberland Yarn Shop, 51 Birchwood Ln. #11, Crossville, TN 38555;
(931) 707-1026

The Needlecraft Inc., 201 Colonial Heights Rd., Kingsport, TN 37663;
(423) 239-5791

Knit 'n Purl, 9222 Kingston Pike, Knoxville, TN 37922; (423) 690-9983

Angel Hair Yarn Co., 4121 Hillsboro Pike #205, Nashville, TN 37215;
(615) 269-8833; www.angelhairyarn.com

Eva R. Works in Yarn, 39-E Tennessee Ave., Oak Ridge, TN 37830;
(615) 483-7492

Terri's Yarns & Crafts, 927 Dolly Parton Pkwy., Sevierville, TN 37862;
(423) 453-7756

Foothills Fiberworks, 7325 E. Lamar Alexander Pkwy., Townsend, TN 37882;
(423) 448-1114

Yarn to Go, 2889 Poplar Ave., Memphis, TN 38111; (901) 454-4118;
yarn_to_go_2889@msn.com

TEXAS

Stitch 'n Knit, 3323 Bell Ste. I, Amarillo, TX 79106; (806) 355-8811

Yarn Heaven, 1292 W. Arkansas Ln., Arlington, TX 76013; (817) 226-9276

European Knits, 3431 Northhills Dr. #116, Austin, TX 78731;
(512) 345-0727

Hill Country Weavers, 1701 S. Congress, Austin, TX 78704; (512) 707-7396

Keep You in Stitches, 3663 Bee Caves Rd. #4B, Austin, TX 78746;
(512) 306-9763

Heritage Arts, 807 W. Henderson, Cleburne, TX 76031; (817) 517-5800

Desert Designs, 4950 Beltline Rd. #180, Dallas, TX 75240;
(972) 392-9276

Yarn and Stitches, 206 Spanish Village, Dallas, TX 75248; (972) 239-9665

Stonehill Spinning, Ltd., 104A E. Ufer, Fredericksburg, TX 78624;
(830) 990-8952

Pandora's Closet, 2610 Lee St., Greenville, TX 75401; (800) 544-3957

Turrentine's Needlecraft, 5266 Beechnut St., Houston, TX 77096;
(713) 661-9411; nanknit@swbell.net

Upstairs Studio, 304 W. Main, Laporte, TX 77571; (281) 470-0108

Stitches n' Stuff, PO Box 483516 E Loop 281, Longview, TX 75606;
(903) 753-3829

Country Cottons and Wools, 502 Fannin St., Millsap, TX 76066;
(940) 682-2290

The Woolie Ewe, 1301 Custer Rd. #238, Plano, TX 75075; (972) 424-3163

Yarn Barn of San Antonio, 4300 McCullough, San Antonio, TX 78212;
(210) 826-3679

UTAH

Needlepoint Joint, 241 Historic 25 St., Ogden, UT 84401; (801) 394-4355

Heindeselman's, 176 W. Center St., Provo, UT 84601-4418; (801) 373-5193

The Wool Cabin, 2020 E. 3300 S., Salt Lake City, UT 84109;
(801) 466-1811

Wooly West, 1417 S. 1100 E., Salt Lake City, UT 84105; (801) 487-9378

Heindselman's Too Knit & Needlework, 50 E. Tabernacle St., Saint George,
UT 84770-3450; (435) 652-4694

VERMONT

Not Just Yarn, 20 Technology Dr., Brattleboro, VT 05301; (802) 257-1145

Naked Sheep, 1785 Monument Ave., Bennington, VT 05201;
(802) 442-4340

Mary Booth Yarn Shop, 69 Main St., Essex Junction, VT 05452;
(802) 878-5847

Greensboro Wool, RR 1 Box 1240, Greensboro, VT 05841; (802) 533-7746

Miller Sports, 106 Main St., Montpelier, VT 05602; (802) 223-5281

Ellen's ½ Pint Farm, 85 Tucker Hill Rd., Norwich, VT 05055;
(802) 649-5420

Northern Nights Yarn Shop, Corner of Elm and Main St., Norwich, VT
05055; (802) 649-2000

Green Mountain Spinnery, 7 Brickyard Ln., Putney, VT 05346;
(802) 387-4528

Mostly Merinos/Joie De Vivre Farm, Rt. 2 Box 232, Putney, VT 05346;
(802) 869-2388

Lamb's Yarn Shop, 38 Kendall Ave., Rutland VT, 05701; (802) 775-5992

Wool Away! Fiber Arts, 10 Eastern Ave. Ste. 3, St. Johnsbury VT 05819;
(802) 748-5767

Northeast Fiber Arts Center, 7531 Williston Rd., Williston VT 05495;
(802) 288-8081

The Good Shepherd, RFD Box 192, Old Cheney Rd., Windham, VT 05359;
(802) 874-4182

Whipple Tree Yarn Shop, 7 Central St., Woodstock, VT 05091;
(802) 457-1325

Virginia

For listings, see www.interweave.com

WASHINGTON

Ana-Cross Stitch, 713 Commercial Ave., Anacortes, WA 98221;
(360) 299-9010

Churchmouse Yarns & Teas, 9964 NE Lafayette, Bainbridge Island, WA
98110; (206) 780-2686

Parkside Wool Company, Inc., 17 102nd Ave. NE, Bellevue, WA 98004;
(425) 455-2138

The Columbine Yarn, 24207 39th Ave. SE, Bothell, WA 98021;
(425) 806-8129; www.columbineyarn.com

Knot Just Yarn, 500 E. Fairhaven, Burlington, WA 98233; (360) 755-7086

Paradise Fibers, 70 Parvin Road, Colfax, WA 99111; (888) 320-SPIN

E Z Knit, 165 N. Main, Colville, WA 99114; (509) 684-2644

Island Knits and Notions, PO Box 741, Friday Harbor, WA 98250;
(360) 378-9658

Yarns Galore, Inc., 660 NW Gilman Blvd. #C4, Issaquah, WA 98027;
(800) 391-9276

Kirkland Yarn & Stitchery, 12071 124th Ave. NE, Kirkland, WA 98034;
(425) 821-2132

Jennings Yarn Shop, 104 S. 1st St., La Conner, WA 98257; (360) 466-3177

Enchanted Needle, Lopez Village, Lopez Island, WA 98261; (360) 468-2777

Spinsters Cottage, 1702 Third St., Marysville, WA 98270; (360) 651-8639

Hellen's Needlework, 320 First St., Mount Vernon, WA 98273;
(360) 336-3024

Tapestry Rose, 1024 Bay Ave., Ocean Park, WA 98640; (360) 665-5385

Canvas Works, 317 N. Capital Way, Olympia, WA 98501; (360) 352-4481

Amanda's Art-Yarns & Fiber, 18846-E Front St. NE, Poulsbo, WA 98370;
(360) 779-3666

The Wild & Woolly Yarn Co., 19020 Front St., Poulsbo, WA 98370;
(360) 779-3222

Paradise Fibers, NW 115 State St. Ste. 112B, Pullman, WA 99163;
(509) 338-0827

Ritzy Things, 16132 NE 87th St., Redmond, WA 98052; (425) 883-2442;
ritzy@ritzythings.com

Knittery, 601 S. Grady Way #C, Renton, WA 98055; (425) 228-4694

Nancy's Knits, 17174 116th Ave. SE, Renton, WA 98058; (425) 255-7392

Custom Twist Woolen Mill, 2650 Salk Ave. Ste. 101, Richland, WA 99352;
(509) 371-9403

Perk's Sewing, Yarn & Quilting Center, 621 Parkway, Richland, WA 99352;
(509) 943-1149

Sheep's Clothing, 1515 A Wright Ave., Richland, WA 99352;
(877) 422-9276

Acorn St. Yarn Shop, 2818 NE 55th St., Seattle, WA 98105; (206) 525-1726

Tricoter, 3121 E. Madison, Seattle, WA 98112-4262; (206) 328-6505

The Weaving Works, 4717 Brooklyn Ave. NE, Seattle, WA 98105;
(206) 524-1221

Yarn Gallery, 5633 California Ave. SW, Seattle, WA 98136; (206) 935-2010

Banana Belt Yarns, 228 W. Bell St., Sequim, WA 98382; (360) 683-5852

Fancy Image Yarn, SE 591 Arcadia Rd., Shelton, WA 98584; (360) 426-5875

Linda's Knit 'n Stitch, 9361 Bayshore Dr., Silverdale, WA 98383;
(360) 698-7556

The Fiber Attic, 1009 1st Ste. #201, Snohomish, WA 98290;
(360) 563-0330

Allinda Knitting Boutique, 321 W. Indiana, Spokane, WA 99205;
(509) 328-4670

Lamb's Ear Farm, 18312 40th Ave. E., Tacoma, WA 98446; (253) 875-3629

Chicken House Weavery, Rte. 4 Box 311, Walla Walla, WA 99362;
(509) 525-3339

It's a Crewel World, 982 E St., Washougal, WA 98671; (360) 835-9649;
(800) 676-2302

Annemarie's Yarn, 206 Yelm Ave., Yelm, WA 98597; (360) 458-8325

Cascade Yarns Distributor of Fine Yarns, PO Box 58168, Tukwila, WA
98138-1168

Spin-A-Yarn, 523 Main St., Edmonds, WA 98020

Washington, D.C.

For listings, see www.interweave.com

WISCONSIN

Appleton Yarn Shop, 630 W. Wisconsin Ave., Appleton, WI 54911;
(920) 731-2221

Jane's Knitting Hutch, 132 E. Wisconsin Ave., Appleton, WI 54911;
(920) 954-9001

Susan's Fiber Shop, N. 250 Hwy. A, Columbus, WI 53925; (920) 623-4237

Granite Creek Farm, 642 27th Ave., Cumberland, WI 54829;
(715) 822-8766

Needles 'n Pins Yarn Shop, W9034 County Trunk A, Delavan, WI 53115;
(608) 883-9922

Studio S Fiber Arts, W8903 County Rd. A, Delavan, WI 53115;
(608) 883-2123

Hooks 'n Needles, 211 E. Wall St., Eagle River, WI 54521; (715) 479-7287

Nordic Accents/Scandinavain Imports, 81 S. Lake St., Elkhart Lake, WI
53020; (920) 876-2520

The Yarn House, 940 N. Elm Grove Rd., Elm Grove, WI 53122;
(262) 786-5660

Grafton Yarn Store, 1300 14th Ave., Grafton, WI 53024; (414) 377-0344

Stone Fox Fibre Works, 1544 East River Rd., Grafton, WI 53024;
(414) 375-2779

Lakeside Fibers, 402 W. Lakeside St., Madison, WI 53715; (608) 257-2999

The Knitting Tree, 2614 Monroe St., Madison, WI 53711; (608) 238-0121

Weaving Workshop, 920 E. Johnson St., Madison, WI 53703;
(608) 255-1066

Joslyn's Fiber Farm, 5738 East Klug Rd., Milton, WI 53563; (608) 868-4070

French Knots, 8585 N. Port Washington Rd., Milwaukee, WI 53217;
(414) 351-2414

Ruhama's Yarn & Fabrics, 420 E. Silver Spring Dr., Milwaukee, WI 53217;
(414) 332-2660

Yarns By Design, 247 E. Wisconsin Ave., Neenah, WI 54956;
(888) 559-2767

Books & Company, 1039 Summit Ave., Oconomowoc, WI 53066;
(414) 567-0106

Needleworks of Racine, 702 High St., Racine, WI 53402; (262) 634-4762;
(877) 894-8838

Sutter's Gold 'n Fleece, 9094 County Rd. O, Saint Germain, WI 54558;
(715) 479-7634

Easy Stitchin' Needleart, 326 Country Walk Ln., Sister Bay, WI 54234;
(920) 854-2840

Leisure Time Craft, 106 E. Clark St., Spencer, WI 54479; (715) 659-5518

Northwind Book & Fiber, 212 Walnut St., Spooner, WI 54801;
(715) 635-6811

Prairie Junction Needlework, 227 E. Main St., Sun Prairie, WI 53590;
(608) 837-8909

Sievers School of Fiber Arts, Jackson Harbor Rd., Washington Island, WI
54246; (920) 847-2264

Genesee Woolen Mill, S40 W28178 Hwy. 59, Waukesha, WI 53189;
(262) 521-2121

Edgewood Arts, 109 N. Main St., Waupaca, WI 54981; (715) 258-0909

Black Purl, 300 3rd St., Wausau, WI 54403; (715) 842-4102

Cairns & Cairns, 141 Swenson Rd., Woodruff, WI 54568; (715) 356-4190

West Virginia

For listings, see www.interweave.com

WYOMING

Ewe Count, 823 Randall Ave., Cheyenne, WY 82001; (307) 638-1148

Iron Kettle Yarn Emporium, 1531 Beck Ave., Cody, WY 82414;
(307) 587-5660

Mountain Magic, 913 Main, Evanston, WY 82930; (307) 789-1460

The Yarn Farm, 316 Home Stretch, Evanston, WY 82930; (307) 789-8044

Knit on Pearl, 107 E. Pearl, Jackson, WY 83001; (307) 733-5648

Grethe's Knit 'n Needle, 433 Parks, Lander, WY 82520; (307) 332-5389

SUPPLIER LIST

Amazing Threads
2020 Ulster Ave.
Lake Katrine, NY 12449
(845) 336-5322

Berroco
PO Box 367
14 Elmdale Rd.
Uxbridge, MA 01569
(800) 343-4948

Brown Sheep Co.
100662 Cty. Rd. 16
Mitchell, NE 69357
(308) 635-2198

Cascade Yarns
PO Box 58168
Tukwila, WA 98138
(206) 574-0440

Classic Elite Yarns
300A Jackson St.
Lowell, MA 01852-2180
(978) 453-2837

Crystal Palace Yarns
2320 Bissell Ave.
Richmond, CA 94804
(510) 237-9988

Euro Yarns
35 Debevoise Ave.
Roosevelt, NY 11575
(800) 645-3457

Euroflax, Inc.
PO Box 241
Rye, NY 10580
(914) 967-9342

Filatura di Crosa
c/o Tahki Yarns
Stacy Charles
1059 Manhattan Ave.
Brooklyn, NY 11222
(800) 338-YARN (Tahki Yarns)
(800) 962-8002 (Filatura di Crosa)

Green Mountain Spinnery
PO Box 568
Putney, VT 05346
(802) 387-4528

Haneke Wool Fashions
630 N. Blackcat Rd.
Meridan, ID 83642
(208) 888-3128

Karabella Yarns
1201 Broadway
New York, NY 10001
(212) 684-2665

La Lana Wools
136 Paseo Norte
Taos, NM 87571
(505) 758-9631

Lorna's Laces
PO Box 795
Somerset, CA 95684
(530) 626-4514

Marks & Kattens Peluche
c/o Swedish Yarn Imports
PO Box 2069
Jamestown, NC 27282
(800) 331-KNIT

Mountain Colors Yarn
PO Box 156
Corvallis, MT 59828
(406) 777-3377

Muench Yarns
285 Bel Marin Keys Blvd. Unit J
Novato, CA 94945
(415) 883-6375

Pine Tree Yarn
PO Box 506
Damariscotta, ME 04543
(207) 549-7104

Plymouth Yarn Co.
PO Box 28
Bristol, PA 19007
(215) 788-0459

Tahki Yarns
Stacy Charles
1059 Manhattan Ave.
Brooklyn, NY 11222
(800) 338-YARN

The Drop Spindle
417 E. Central
Santa Maria, CA 93454
(805) 922-1295

Yarns International
5110 Ridgefield Rd. at River Rd.
Bethesda, MD 20816
(301) 913-2980

Index

Gauge Chart

Have yarn, don't know what to make?
Look for the projects below that will fit your gauge.

6½ sts and 9 rows = 4"	Rumpelstiltskin's Toddler Jacket, 72
6 sts and 9 rows = 4"	Fog Chaser Jacket, 82
7½ sts and 12 rows = 4"	Quick Knit Rug, 42
8 sts and 12 rows = 4"	Outer Banks Throw, 4
9 sts and 12 rows = 4"	Point Five Raglan Jacket, 120
10 sts and 14 rows = 4"	Bette's Poncho, 20
11 sts = 4"	My Constant Companion, 140
11 sts and 14 rows = 4"	Bomber Cap and Mittens, 152
12 sts and 21 rows = 4"	Isabel's Sweater, 124
14½ sts and 21 rows = 4"	Sonoma Spring Cantata, 50
14 sts = 4"	Meadow Flowers Shawl, 24
14 sts and 21 rows = 4"	Farmhouse Rug, 42
14 sts and 24 rows = 4"	Magic Friends, 86
15 sts and 20 rows = 4"	Ladders of Elegance, 46
16 sts = 4"	Felted Fish, 96
16 sts and 20 rows = 4"	Lace Ribs Pullover, 134
16 sts and 24 rows = 4"	Cardigan With Garter Stitch Trim, 102
16 sts and 28 rows = 4"	Chenille Jacket, 128
16 sts and 28 rows = 4"	Cottage Tea Cozy, 110
16 sts and 6 rows = 4"	Opulent Evening Shawl, 156
17 sts and 25 rows = 4"	Angora Furred Teddy Hood, 66
18 sts and 22 rows = 4"	Penelope's Pillow, 62
18 sts and 23 rows = 4"	Age of Aquarius Trio, 12
18 sts and 24 rows = 4"	Tweedy Cashmere Pullover, 148
19 sts and 27 rows = 4"	Sophisticated Baby Jumper, 144
20 sts and 22 rows = 4"	Celtic Cardigan, 90
20 sts and 28 rows = 4"	Cable-Wise Cashmere, 106
20 sts and 30 rows = 4"	Baby's First Luxuries, 114
21 sts and 32 rows = 4"	Garter Ridge Washcloth, 77
21 sts and 36 rows = 4"	Tile Stitch Washcloth, 79
22 sts and 34 rows = 4"	Lacy Vine Washcloth, 77
23 sts and 38 rows = 4"	Basket Weave Washcloth, 76
23 sts and 40 rows = 4"	Seed Stitch Stripe Washcloth, 79
24 sts and 28 rounds = 4"	Graduated Ribbed Top, 7
24 sts and 32 rows = 4"	Marie Louise's Lace Sweater, 28
26 sts and 32 rows = 4"	Horseshoe Lace Washcloth, 77
26 sts and 42 rows = 4"	Dragon Scales Washcloth, 76
28 sts and 30 rows = 4"	Feather and Fan Washcloth, 77
32 sts and 32 rows = 4"	River Run Pullover, 36
32 sts and 40 rows = 4"	Heavenly Camisole and Scarf, 58

Rainforests

Lucy Bowman

Designed by Samantha Meredith

Illustrated by Natalie Hinrichson

Reading consultant: Alison Kelly, Roehampton University
Rainforest consultant: Dr. Julia Jones, Bangor University

Contents

In the rainforest

Tropical rainforests are thick, leafy jungles. They grow in warm places where it rains a lot.

Many different plants, animals and people live in them.

Towering trees

Plants and trees need sunlight to grow.

The branches of the tallest trees are spread out so that their leaves get plenty of sunlight. This layer is called the canopy.

Some of the biggest trees in rainforests are over 1,000 years old.

Less sunlight reaches this layer. It is called the understorey. The plants here have big leaves to catch as much light as they can.

The forest floor is dark, so there aren't many plants.

Canopy climbers

The canopy layer is full of life. Some of the animals that live there never go down to the forest floor.

Sloths have long, sharp claws that help them hang from branches. They move very slowly and spend most of their lives asleep.

Howler monkeys gather in groups at the tops of the trees.

They hang from their tails, and pick fruit and leaves to eat.

They howl loudly to warn other monkeys to keep away.

Aye-ayes have long middle fingers that they use to pull bugs out of branches.

In the understorey

Beneath the canopy, the trees are covered with different kinds of plants.

Hummingbirds use their long beaks to feed from orchids.

The roots of these plants soak up water from the air.

Some plants fill up with water. Frogs sometimes lay their eggs in them.

Woody vines, called lianas, grow up trees to get closer to the sunlight.

These leaves have pointed 'drip tips', so that water runs off them quickly.

On the ground

Millions of bugs live beneath the trees, on plants and on the forest floor.

Leafcutter ants bite leaves into small pieces.

The ants carry the pieces to their nest, then chew them into a pulp.

The pulp rots, and a fungus grows on it. The ants eat the fungus.

Gladiator
spiders weave
sticky nets
to drop onto
their prey.

This Brazilian
wandering
spider has
caught a bug and
bitten it with its
poisonous fangs.

Getting about

Many animals travel through the rainforest without touching the ground.

Flying frogs have long legs and wide, webbed feet.

They jump from a branch, then glide through the air to another tree.

Gliding snakes can leap from tree to tree. They steer in the air by wiggling their bodies.

12

A baby spider monkey clings to its mother's tummy. The mother uses her arms and tail to swing through the trees.

A flying squirrel sits on a tree branch.

It leaps into the air...

...then stretches out its arms and legs, and glides to another branch.

13

Big beasts

Some large rainforest animals hunt other animals for food.

This jaguar is prowling around on the forest floor, looking for prey such as deer and pigs.

An anaconda quietly slithers up to a tapir by a river.

It wraps itself around the tapir and squeezes tightly.

Gorillas are huge, powerful animals, but they just like to eat plants.

The anaconda opens its jaws and slowly swallows the tapir.

After its huge meal, the snake doesn't eat for several months.

After dark

Some animals sleep during the day and only come out at night.

A red-eyed tree frog wakes up to feed. It catches insects with its long tongue.

An owl hears the frog moving and swoops down from a tree to catch it.

The frog shows its bright body and eyes to surprise the owl, then escapes.

16

Tarsiers have huge eyes so they can see when there isn't much light.

They catch insects with their long fingers, then eat them.

With so many creatures, rainforests can be very noisy at night.

Smelly plants

Rainforest plants can attract insects with their smell.

Rafflesia flowers can be as big as truck wheels. They smell like rotting meat to attract flies. The flies spread the flower's pollen.

A fly is attracted to a pitcher plant by its strong smell.

The fly lands on the waxy edge of the leaf. It slips inside into a special liquid.

The fly's body dissolves until it is liquid too. It is now food for the plant.

Some water lilies trap beetles when they close their petals at night. The beetles get covered in pollen and then escape.

Beaky birds

Rainforest birds have beaks in many shapes and sizes. They are good for different things.

This macaw has a strong beak that can pierce fruit and crack nut shells.

Harpy eagles are so big they can grab monkeys out of trees. They eat them with their sharp, hooked beaks.

Toucans have long
beaks. They can
pick berries that
are hard for other
birds to reach.

Rainforest rivers

Many rainforests have large rivers running through them. The most famous is the Amazon, in South America.

Lots of animals live and hunt in the Amazon.

Capybaras have large front teeth for nibbling long grass.

Scarlet ibises use their long beaks to find food in the mud.

Caimans hunt with only their eyes and noses above water.

Piranhas have sharp teeth that they use to tear animal flesh.

Rich rainforests

Rainforest plants can provide food and other useful things.

The seeds in cocoa pods are used to make a paste called cocoa butter.

Cocoa butter is used to make candles...

soap...

and chocolate.

Bananas were first found in rainforests.

This bud will unfold, and the flowers inside will turn into bananas.

Some people chew the leaves of the Kawakawa plant to cure toothache.

Tropical tribes

Groups of people, called tribes, have lived in rainforests for thousands of years.

The people in this photo built their home with wood and reeds from the rainforest.

They live near a river, so the house is on stilts in case the river floods.

People search in rainforests for fruit that they can eat, such as mangoes.

Men hunt animals to eat, using spears, bows and arrows, and blow pipes.

Boats carry people and goods quickly through the rainforest.

27

Ruining rainforests

Rainforests could be lost forever because so many trees are being cut down.

People use the wood to make things such as paper and furniture.

The land is also cleared so that farmers can grow crops and keep cows.

When rainforests are destroyed, animals like these orang-utans lose their homes.

If an animal dies out forever, it becomes extinct.

Bali tigers lost their rainforest home, and are now extinct.

Glossary of rainforest words

Here are some of the words in this book you might not know. This page tells you what they mean.

 tropical - hot, rainy weather. Rainforests grow in tropical places.

 canopy - a thick layer of leaves and branches at the top of tall trees.

 understorey - the part of a rainforest between the canopy and the ground.

 liana - a woody vine that grows up a tree towards the sunlight.

 drip tips - pointed tips on leaves that help water to run off them.

 pollen - a powder that plants use to make seeds.

 extinct - when animals and plants die out and there are no more left.

Websites to visit

You can visit exciting websites to find out more about rainforests.

To visit these websites, go to the Usborne Quicklinks Website at **www.usborne.com/quicklinks** Read the internet safety guidelines, and then type the keywords "**beginners rainforests**".

The websites are regularly reviewed and the links in Usborne Quicklinks are updated. However, Usborne Publishing is not responsible, and does not accept liability, for the content or availability of any website other than its own. We recommend that children are supervised while on the internet.

Chameleons change colour to show what kind of mood they are in.

Index

Acknowledgements

Photographic manipulation by John Russell

Photo credits
The publishers are grateful to the following for permission to reproduce material:
© **Ingo Arndt/Minden Pictures/FLPA** 18; © **Cn Boon/Alamy** 25; © **Jean Paul Ferrero/ardea.com** 29;
© **Michael Fogden/Oxford Scientific** 12; © **David Haring/DUPC/Photolibrary** 17;
© **Steve Kaufman/Corbis** 20; © **Frans Lanting/Corbis** Cover; © **Buddy Mays/Corbis** 6-7;
© **Gavin Parsons/ardea.com** 2-3; © **Ken Preston-Mafham/Premaphotos** 10-11;
© **Anup Shah/naturepl.com** Cover; © **Shattil & Rozinski/Naturepl** 14-15; © **Kevin Schafer/Alamy** 31;
© **Paul A. Souders/Corbis** 1; © **Steve Vidler/Photolibrary** 22; © **Staffan Widstrand/naturepl** 21;
© **Alison Wright/Robert Harding** 27.

Every effort has been made to trace and acknowledge ownership of copyright. If any rights have
been omitted, the publishers offer to rectify this in any subsequent editions following notification.